T0294198

FORGOTTEN
FOOTBALL
CLUBS

Philip O'Rourke

FORGOTTEN FOOTBALL CLUBS

Fifty Teams Across the World, Gone but Never Forgotten

First published by Pitch Publishing, 2023

Pitch Publishing
9 Donnington Park,
85 Birdham Road,
Chichester,
West Sussex,
PO20 7AJ
www.pitchpublishing.co.uk
info@pitchpublishing.co.uk

A CIP catalogue record is available for this book
from the British Library.

ISBN 978 1 80150 178 1

Typesetting and origination by Pitch Publishing
Printed and bound in Great Britain by TJ Books, Padstow

Contents

Introduction

NOSTALGIA IS a strong thing and is something that a lot of people turn to when they want to feel happy again. Going back to a certain moment in time when nothing else mattered, and just that happy feeling was felt, is something that most football fans can experience. But for some, nostalgia is the only way they can see or feel what it is like to support their football club, as they can't just go to a game at the weekend or create new memories, because their club no longer exists. Of course, they can go and support another football club and maybe it might even be a 'phoenix club' but it will never be the original. It just isn't the same.

In every country across the world there is a 'Forgotten Club'. No country is safe from the perils of mismanagement or financial difficulties when it comes to its football clubs. Sure, look at some of today's modern football giants. FC Barcelona for example, one of the finest institutions of football in the world, and they are hundreds of millions of euros in debt. Will they survive? I hope they do.

But othershave not been so lucky. Clubs like Accrington Stanley, Wimbledon FC, Parma, Rangers FC, Chievo Verona and many other high-profile names have become defunct over the years, with the ones I have just mentioned being the more recent and famous of those. Some clubs have been lucky and have had a loyal fan base that brought them back to life in what is known as a 'phoenix club', where, although they have technically dissolved or 'died', they have been resurrected and follow on from the original entity of the club the fans once adored and followed.

In writing this book about 'Forgotten Clubs', I have interviewed so many people, who are so passionate and knowledgeable about the game, and I try to cover as much of the world as possible. Most of the clubs that feature are from Europe, with clubs coming from the Republic of Ireland, England, Spain, Italy, Germany, Luxembourg, Albania, the Netherlands, Belgium, Sweden, Norway, Finland and many others, while I have also visited South America five times, and Central America, North America, Asia, Africa and Australia as well. Nowhere in the world is safe from seeing its football clubs becoming defunct. I have estimated that in the current 195 countries in the world, there are over 5,000 clubs that could be considered a 'Forgotten Club'. Unfortunately, I couldn't cover all of them, and so I give you just *Forgotten Football Clubs, 50 Clubs: Teams Across the World., Gone But Never Forgotten.*

1.

Sporting Fingal FC
(Republic of Ireland)

SPORTING FINGAL FC were founded in 2007, a project that was funded partly by the Fingal County Council and property developer Gerry Gannon. The idea was to bring League of Ireland football to the area of Fingal, which had no football club to represent it, despite being the third most populated area in Ireland. The club's colours were black and green, with the away strip white and green. They were granted permission to play at Morton Stadium, a venue that had been used previously by current League of Ireland club Shamrock Rovers and former League of Ireland club and now defunct, Dublin City. Liam Buckley was appointed manager and director of football.

The proposed plan was to create a community club and to use the schoolboy teams in the area to produce talent, giving the players a pathway to play League of Ireland football. The club were not expected to play in the League of Ireland in their first year and had applied to play in the A Championship, a league just below the First Division, with mostly amateur clubs competing in it. However, Kilkenny City folded and became another casualty of Irish football, and they vacated the space for Sporting Fingal FC to fill in the First Division.

And so, the club prepared for their debut season, signing players such as former Bohemians and St Patrick's Athletic striker, Robbie Doyle, Peter Hynes and local former Universit College Dubline (UCD) player Conan Byrne.

Not much was expected of the new club and their League of Ireland debut came at Flancare Park, the home of Longford Town, who had just been relegated the previous season. Only nine Sporting Fingal fans had travelled to the game (I know this because I was one of them) and they witnessed their side take a surprising lead when Hynes's 35-yard shot lobbed the goalkeeper. (It still remains one of the best goals I have seen at a live game.) But that would be all the nine fans would be cheering about, as Longford Town justified their tag as favourites and ran out 5-1 winners.

That wasn't to be the way things went for the rest of the season, as Sporting Fingal ended up finishing fourth out of the ten clubs. They had Doyle's goals to thank for their success as he finished up as the league's top marksman on 16 goals that season. Dundalk were promoted as champions, one point clear of Sporting Fingal's local rivals Shelbourne, a rivalry that most Shelbourne fans dismissed, stating that Sporting Fingal were nothing more than a franchise, even nicknaming them 'Sporting Franchise'. Sporting got the better of Shelbourne that season, winning one (2-1 at home) and drawing the other three games (1-1, 1-1 and 0-0).

It was during the second season that Sporting Fingal put their name in the history books of Irish football. Once again, expectations had been realistic and a play-off spot was the target, even with the challenge being made a little harder with the expansion of the First Division from ten clubs to 12. It was a four-horse race as to who would win the First Division title and automatic promotion. There was no surprise that UCD, who had been relegated the season before, were the favourites, along with Shelbourne who had been flirting with promotion back to the highest level for a few seasons. Waterford United were the other contenders, alongside Sporting Fingal. The Students of UCD pipped Shelbourne to the title by just one point, with Sporting Fingal beating Waterford to third spot, ensuring that they would get the chance to gain promotion via the play-offs.

The first game was a one-off fixture against local rivals Shelbourne, at Tolka Park, Shelbourne's home ground. They were given home advantage as they had finished second that season. The game itself drew in an attendance of 1,632 and was played on 10 November 2009. Sporting Fingal took a 2-0 advantage into the half-time break with goals from Libyan international Eamon Zayed (39th minute) and Shaun Williams (41st minute), a player who has gone on to play for MK Dons, Millwall and Portsmouth, as well as earning three caps for the Republic of Ireland national team. Shelbourne hit back in the second half and pulled one back from the penalty spot. Shelbourne's top goalscorer that season, McAllister converted the spot kick in the 72nd minute. It should have given Shelbourne the momentum, but Anto Flood saw red in the 73rd minute to make their task of equalising that little bit harder. Fingal held on to beat their rivals and book their place in the promotion/relegation decider against the side who finished bottom of the Premier Division that season. That side was Bray Wanderers.

The final was made into a two-legged affair, with Sporting Fingal getting home advantage in the first leg. On 13 November the First Division side won the match 2-0 in front of a crowd of 740 at Morton Stadium. Goals from Stephen Paisley (51st minute) and Conan Byrne (67th minute) ensured they had a healthy advantage going into the second leg at the Carlisle Ground in Bray three days later. This time Fingal took the lead in the second half, when Zayed scored in the 59th minute. With Fingal 3-0 up on aggregate, the contest looked to be all but over, but Bray came back fighting and Flood scored in the 83rd minute to give the Seagulls a glimmer of hope. Sporting Fingal's defence held out, and it looked to be a matter of time before the final whistle would be blown and they would be confirmed as a Premier Division side for the 2010 season.

Bray, however, kept going and in the 91st minute, Chris O' Connor scored to put them in front on the night and make it 3-2 on aggregate. But in their desperation to get that third goal, Bray were left open at the back, which Sporting Fingal exploited and in the 92nd minute Robert Bayley scored to level the game 2-2 on the night and make it 4-2 on aggregate for Fingal, which meant the North Dublin side were promoted to the Premier Division in only their second season as a club. To add icing to the cake Conan Byrne finished as top goalscorer that year with 21 goals.

The 89th edition of the FAI Cup ended with one of Ireland's newest clubs lifting the famous trophy. Sporting Fingal's cup run started in the third round in an away tie against Cork side, Blarney United FC. Sporting ran out 2-0 winners to advance into the fourth round, where they played fellow First Division club Athlone Town. They took on the midland club at Morton Stadium. Once again, Fingal didn't find many problems and won the game, 4-1. The win set up a huge quarter-final tie against Shamrock Rovers, a game that nobody gave Sporting Fingal any hope in. But as they did in their league campaign, Fingal defied the odds and took Shamrock Rovers to a replay, after drawing the first game 2-2 at Morton Stadium. The replay was another tight affair and the two clubs couldn't be separated within the 90 minutes, meaning the tie went to extra time. Unbelievably, Sporting Fingal scored the winner and knocked out one of the giants of Irish football.

At this point, many thought Sporting Fingal's name was on the trophy; however, they still had to navigate their way past Premier Division side Bray Wanderers in the semi-final. The game was played at Morton Stadium on 25 October 2009 and those who attended were given goals straight away. Fingal took an early lead with Eamon Zayed scoring in the fourth minute and he doubled the advantage seven minutes later. Alan Kirby sent the home fans into raptures as he made it 3-0 on the day in just the 22nd minute. Sporting Fingal went into the break in complete control and had one foot in the final. The second half was a much cagier affair, with Fingal just looking to keep their three-goal advantage. Bray huffed and puffed but only broke the deadlock in the 74th minute through Gary McCabe. It didn't give the visitors much time to reduce the deficit and in the end Sporting Fingal punished them as they took more risks. Robert Bayley all but ended the tie in the 82nd minute when he made it 4-1. Bray did reply once more through John Mulroy, but it proved to be no more than a consolation. Bray also ended the game with ten men, when Chris Deans was shown a red card in injury time.

Their first-half dominance was enough to put Sporting Fingal into their first FAI Cup Final, in only their second season in existence. Not only was the famous trophy on the line, but qualification forthe following season's Europa League would be granted to the winner of the cup. The club that stood in their way was Premier Division Sligo Rovers.

The west of Ireland club were overwhelming favourites to lift the cup at Tallaght Stadium on 22 November. The game was played in poor weather conditions and both sides found it difficult to create chances. It remained 0-0 at the break, with the First Division team holding their own. But in the 57th minute it seemed as though the game would be going according to script as Sligo took the lead through Eoin Doyle. It would have been easy for Sporting Fingal to play out a heroic defeat, but they decided to go for it, and their courage was rewarded in the 85th minute when they were awarded a penalty. Colm James put the spot kick away which set up a frantic final five minutes. Both clubs went for it but it was the underdogs who snatched it late on when Gary O'Neil scored in the 90th minute to send the Fingal fans mental. The game was attended by 8,105, with most of them being Sligo Rovers fans, who returned to the west of Ireland empty-handed as Sporting Fingal won the game and the cup.

Along with promotion to the Premier Division that season and winning their first bit of silverware as a club, Fingal now had the Europa League to look forward to. Things could not have looked better for Ireland's newest club. However, their demise came even quicker than their success.

Halfway through the 2010 season, Sporting Fingal were to play a Europa League tie against Portuguese Primeira Liga side, Maritimo. On 15 July the club travelled to the Estadio de Madeira to make their European debut. It was a game that nobody expected the Irish club to win, but as usual Sporting Fingal surprised everyone. With the new signing of experienced striker and Republic of Ireland international Glen Crowe, Fingal felt confident, and it showed. The away side took a surprising lead in the 33rd minute when Crowe scored. Maritimo, a side that competed against European giants like Benfica, Porto and Sporting Lisbon in their domestic league, struggled to break down the Irish side and it looked as though Sporting Fingal would pull off one of the greatest European results a League of Ireland club had ever produced. That was until the 78th minute when Maritimo finally found the net through former Portugal under-21 international, Esteves.

The home side seemed to find another gear after that and took the lead in the 85th minute through Algerian international, Abdelmalek Cherrad. A 2-1 defeat away from home would still be a fantastic result, but Sporting Fingal were not content with that and in the 87th minute they equalised through Lorcan Fitzgerald. It looked like Fingal were going to come away with a historic European draw until heartbreak in the 95th minute when Maritimo's Brazilian forward Tcho scored the winner to give the Portuguese side the advantage in the tie. The second leg was played at Dalymount Park, the home of Bohemians FC, due to Morton Stadium not being up to UEFA standards. The tie took place on 22 July 2010 in front of 2,150 fans. But whatever hope Sporting Fingal thought they had of overturning the first leg defeat was quickly extinguished when Maritimo took the lead in the 20th minute when Alonso put away a penalty to make it 4-2 on aggregate to the Portuguese side. It remained 1-0 going into the break and Fingal had chances to reduce the deficit but failed to hit the net.

It was the Primeira Liga side who scored again in the 67th minute to all but end Sporting Fingal's European campaign when another Brazilian, Marquinho, made it 2-0 on the night and 5-2 on aggregate. It would have been a harsh scoreline on Fingal, but they didn't give up and a late surge saw Eamon Zayed score two quickfire goals, the first coming in the 81st minute and the second in the 89th to make it 5-4 on aggregate and leave Fingal needing only one goal to force extra time. The League of Ireland outfit pushed but with their desperation to get an equaliser, they left themselves open and Maritimo took advantage and caught them on the break. Kanu (no not the former Arsenal man, but another Brazilian), scored in the 95th minute to end the tie at 6-4 to the Portuguese side. Sporting Fingal went out but could take confidence going into their debut season in the League of Ireland

Premier Division and expectations were at an all-time high for the club.

Back to domestic action and Fingal were more than holding their own in the Premier Division. They finished a respectable fourth out of the ten clubs competing. They also gained qualification for the 2011 Europa League. They even managed to remain unbeaten against the eventual champions, Shamrock Rovers, in the four games they played against them, drawing three and winning one.

But by November 2010, worrying signs started to show that Sporting Fingal were in trouble. In fact, it was worrying times for everyone in the Republic of Ireland. There was an economic crash and many had been hit heavily financially, with property developers going bust. One of those people was the joint owner, Gerry Gannon, who could not fund the Sporting Fingal project anymore and had to pull out altogether. It left Fingal with no real financial stability, with their attendances still too low to keep them financially independent. The Fingal County Council were not prepared to invest any more money into the club, concluding that their cash would be better spent elsewhere due to the financial crisis that was going on at the time. Attempts were made to try to keep the club going, but in the end, they were in vain and in February 2011 the club announced they could no longer pay their players' wages.

The final straw seemed to be the club's withdrawal from the Setanta Cup, a tournament that was played between the League of Ireland sides and the Northern Ireland Premier Division sides. The club were due to play Lisburn Distillery but failed to compete in the tie. Their withdrawal saw them replaced by UCD. A few days later it was announced that Sporting would not be applying for a League of Ireland licence and therefore pulled out of the league altogether.

There were suggestions that they would compete in the A Championship but those plans never materialised and Sporting Fingal FC were gone from the footballing world in a professional capacity.

2.

FC Amsterdam (The Netherlands)

FC AMSTERDAM were founded on 23 June 1972, after two clubs, Blauw-Wit and DWS, merged. Blauw-Wit Amsterdam, which translates into English as Blue White, got their name because of their club colours. They had been founded in 1902 and had originally had a big rivalry with Ajax, with both clubs sharing the Olympic Stadium between 1928 and 1972, while before that the Blauw-Wit played at the Old Stadion from 1914–28. They played a total of 52 competitive derbies against Ajax, known as the Stadsderby, winning 16, drawing 13 and losing 23 against their old foe. The club then merged with DWS but still remain as an amateur club until this day.

DWS had a more colourful history, having been renamed a couple of times. AFC DWS were founded on 11 October 1907, by three men named Robert Beijerbacht, Theo Beijerbacht and Jan van Galen. The club were originally named Fortuna but soon changed their name to Hercules. It wasn't until 22 March 1909 that the name was changed to Amsterdam DWS, with the DWS standing for Door Wilskracht Sterk, which translated means 'Strong Through Willpower'. DWS went on to enter professional football in 1954, playing their home games at the Olympic Stadium in Amsterdam. In 1958 they merged with BVC/Amsterdam into a club named DWS/A, but in 1962 the name of the club changed again and reverted back to DWS.

It was 1964 when DWS did something no other Dutch club has managed to do, in gaining promotion and then winning the Eredivisie in back-to-back seasons. The 1964/65 season saw the club reach the quarter-finals of the European Cup, losing 2-1 on aggregate to Hungarian side Vasas ETO Gyor, drawing 1-1 in the first leg in front of 46,915 at the Olympic Stadium and losing 1-0 in the second leg at the Martirok utja Stadium with Povazsai scoring an 87th-minute winner for the Hungarian side, breaking DWS fans' hearts.

A fun fact about DWS is they are the last club to win the Dutch Eredivisie title to not wear a predominantly red and white coloured home jersey, with PSV, Ajax, Feyenoord, AZ and FC Twente all doing so in their own league triumphs.

In 1972 the club merged with Blauw-Wit Amsterdam and then later, Volewijckers joined up in 1973/74, to form FC Amsterdam. DWS continued as an amateur football club and celebrated their 100-year anniversary in 2007.

In the 1973/74 season the club finished a respectable fifth out of 18 clubs in the Dutch top division, which qualified them for the 1974/75 UEFA Cup. The first round saw them ease past Maltese club, Hibernians, 12-0 on aggregate (5-0 at home and 7-0 in the away leg). The attendance for the home leg was a mere 3,007, compared to their city rivals, Ajax, who were playing in the same competition and in that same round had an attendance of 29,000 for their 0-0 draw against English side Stoke City.

The second round saw FC Amsterdam take on the mighty Inter Milan, with few people giving the Dutch team a chance. However, they proved everyone wrong, beating Inter 2-1 at the San Siro thanks to a brace scored by Nico Jansen. The home leg ended in a 0-0 draw, but again the attendance was quite low, with only 8,667 people watching one of the club's greatest achievements. The third round was a much easier affair with the club defeating German side Fortuna Dusseldorf 5-1 on aggregate, winning 3-0 in the home leg (Husers with a brace, and an own goal), while beating Fortuna 2-1 at the Rheinstadion, with goals coming from Husers and Jansen. This set up a quarter-final tie with another German side, Koln, but it wasn't going to be as easy. This German side proved to be too strong for FC Amsterdam and thrashed them 5-1 in the first leg at the Mungersdorfer Stadion in front of 25,000 spectators. The home leg at the Olympic Stadium ended in a 3-2 loss, with Koln going 3-0 up. Jansen scored two in the second half to make the score look respectable on the day but Amsterdam's European adventure was over, losing 8-3 on aggregate.

That season was to be the peak of FC Amsterdam's achievements and they were relegated in the 1977/78 season from the Eredivisie to the Eerste Divisie. The club finished ninth in their first season back in the second tier. They were only four points off a play-off spot and were hopeful that the next season they would be challenging for promotion. But that wasn't to be the case as the club finished 16th, only three points above the relegation places, having won just nine of their 36 games that term.

The next campaign would be the last for FC Amsterdam. Although finishing in a higher position than the previous season, 13th, the club saw their attendances dwindle due to lack of success and they withdrew from the league and disbanded. In their short history as FC Amsterdam, the club had players such as Jan Jongbloed, the Dutch goalkeeper in the 1974 World Cup, Geert Meijer, who went on to play for city rivals Ajax for three seasons and Nico Jansen who was regarded as their best ever player, scoring 41 times in 78 appearances for the club. He went on to play for Feyenoord, scoring 43 times in 68 appearances for them.

In my search for a former fan or an expert on Dutch football I was directed towards plenty of names that could help me. But one name kept being mentioned and that was Martijn Schwillens, author of many football books. One that really stood out to me was *Verdwenen Maar Niet Vergeten* which roughly translates as *Forgotten Clubs of the Netherlands*. I got in touch with Martijn and his knowledge and insight into FC Amsterdam was just as I expected – brilliant.

What was your inspiration for writing your books about football clubs?

Martijn Schwillens: Ever since I was a kid I was fascinated by the rankings of the Dutch Eredivisie and Eerste Divisie, the only two professional levels in the Netherlands. When I first got interested in going to football myself (late 1980s), I quickly noticed a few teams were missing in the rankings including FC Amsterdam and a couple of new teams had replaced them, such as FC Emmen and RKC Waalwijk. Furthermore, I grew up with the stories of my father going to Fortuna '54, the first ever professional football club in the Netherlands (mind you, not the oldest, but we didn't start a professional football league until 1954). This club later merged with Sittardia into Fortuna Sittard, the team I still support.

FC Amsterdam are one of the clubs you write about. What was your view on that club? Can you tell me anything about their fans that you may have learned in your research?

Martijn: FC Amsterdam played their last ever match in front of a mere 500 spectators on pitch two of the Olympic Stadium in Amsterdam. However, the club were formed after a merger of DWS Amsterdam and Blauw-Wit and DWS were well supported, with more than 10,000 fans going there every fortnight. Therefore, most FC Amsterdam fans were fans of the former. However, after getting relegated after a couple of years (the merger did not bring in bigger numbers at home matches and the club were funded by one man: De Stoop) the demise of FC Amsterdam happened quickly. Most fans turned to Ajax, or distanced themselves from football in Amsterdam altogether. Mind you, in the early 80s Ajax only drew 14,000 people.

Like my native Ireland, the Netherlands have had a few 'Forgotten Clubs' as well. Who were your favourite club that you wrote about or found the most interesting?
Martijn: I have visited every 'forgotten professional club' that went bust after 1992. The club I liked best was SC Veendam. Their stadium, De Langeleegte, was well known by football supporters all over the country. Veendam is a very distant town in the north-east of the province of Groningen. Even from the middle of the Netherlands it will take you 2.5 hours to get there. I also liked RBC Roosendaal and Haarlem though.

Can you tell me any interesting or original fact you came across when researching/writing about FC Amsterdam?
Martijn: What springs to mind is that a lot of FC Amsterdam (DWS) supporters, all being older than 50, have hardly ever been to Ajax. The club is still being missed by a small number of football-minded people in the capital. Ajax is also a nationally supported team. Most season-ticket holders do not come from Amsterdam but from all over the Netherlands.

Amsterdam is such a big city, and its people love football so much. Can I ask, why is there only one professional

club in the city? Or at least one major one. For example London has loads, even Dublin has six professional football clubs.

Martijn: Unlike Ireland, Britain or Germany, the Netherlands has a closed pyramid, so there are hardly ever amateur teams getting into the professional ranks (Achilles '29 gave it a run for five years and then went bust). The Second Division is a semi-professional league, but the champions opt to stay there. Therefore, teams are not getting relegated from the First Division. AFC Amsterdam became the champions a couple of years ago but they wanted to stay semi-professional too, so Amsterdam will not have a second professional team, as AFC Amsterdam are by far the best amateur side in the city. Eindhoven (two) and Rotterdam (three) have more clubs in one city though.

Can you ever see another Amsterdam club rivalry again? A major derby in the city in the future?

Martijn: In fairness, I cannot see it happening. As long as the Dutch FA does not allow teams going up from the Second Division to remain semi-professional, teams will opt to stay in the amateur ranks. Unfortunately! And if it would happen, a big city rivalry will never be the case. AFC Amsterdam are even popular among Ajax fans, whilst FC Amsterdam (or DWS) were seen as a big rival and were even hated, seen from an FC Amsterdam fan's perspective. The real rivalry will always be Feyenoord–Ajax.

3.

KSK Beveren (Belgium)

THE ORIGINAL Beveren club, Standaard Beveren, was founded in 1922 by a local businessman named Paul Verhaert. They became a member of the Belgian Football Association and were given a federation registration number of 'Matricule 737'. The original club stayed as part of the association until May 1931, when they fell into financial trouble and dissolved. This would be the first time the club had parted ways with its original form. But three years later, on 23 July 1934, a pub landlord in Beveren was asked to get a team together to play against another football team from the nearby municipality of Temse. The team from Beveren, who were called Standaard Beveren on the day of the match, won 2-1, and so it was decided they would form a football club but call it KSK Beveren. They applied to be part of the Belgian Association of Football on 5 September 1935 and received their official registration number, 'Matricule 2300'.

Straight away, the newly formed side picked up two titles back-to-back in their local league, and moved to a new stadium called the Velodrome in 1938. It was owned by a local brewer and businessman, Frederik Thielemans, and the stadium's name was eventually changed to the Freethiel Stadium in his honour. But during the world wars, football in Belgium was badly hampered, like in the rest of Europe, and football leagues were created on an emergency basis. SK Beveren started competing again in their top provincial league in 1945, when the Second World War had ended. It took three years before they would be promoted to the national divisions, under the guidance of new chairman, Louis Verhaert. In 1949 the club went up after defeating Herzele.

With the club now in new, unprecedented territory, they had to wait three years before being promoted from the Belgian Fourth Division. It was a feat that saw the club use mainly local talent, instead of importing footballers from different municipalities. They gained promotion through the play-offs with a 2-1 win over Willebroek. But their progress stalled for the next eight years, with the club playing in the Belgian Third Division from 1952 until 1960, regularly fighting for survival and struggling to come to terms with the level of quality they were now facing.

In the 1959/60 season their luck finally ran out and the club finished 15th, meaning they were relegated back to the Fourth Division. Instead of feeling sorry for themselves, the club regrouped and planned, and in doing so decided that giving local youth a chance was their best way of gaining promotion again. Indeed, it proved to be the right choice because after three years the club gained promotion to the Third Division again. Amongst the players that got them back up were prolific striker Robert Rogiers, winger Jaen Janssens and centre-midfielder Wilfried van Moer. Janssens would go on to earn seven caps for the Belgian national team and score one goal for them, while Van Moer would make 57 appearances for the Belgium and also manage them in 1996.

The 1963/64 season proved to be one of the most successful in the club's history, as Beveren romped to the Fourth Division title, winning it by 16 points, ahead of second placed Brasschaat. They went the whole season unbeaten and scored an incredible 111 goals in the process.

The next season saw them finish third but they went on a cup run that year, reaching the last 16 stage, only to be knocked out by First Division club, Cercle Brugge. The following season, 1965/66, saw them once again finish third. It was just a taste of what was to come as they finally gained promotion to the Second Division when they became Third Division champions in 1966/67, after clinching a point away to Zwevegem, with a late goal Rogiers securing a 2-2 draw and promotion. Beveren didn't stop there, however, and in their first season in the Second Division, they won it, under the guidance of their new coach Guy Thys, a man who would eventually lead the Belgian national team to their only major tournament final to date, when he guided them to the 1980 European Championship Final, only to be defeated 2-1 by West Germany in Italy. Beveren clinched the title with a 3-2 win over UR Namur.

The 1968 season, and their first in the top division in Belgium, started off with a 1-1 draw against Sint-Truidense VV. Jean Janssens wrote his name in the Beveren history books, scoring the club's first goal in the First Division. It didn't take long for the team to get their first win in the top flight, when in just their second game, and their first at home, they beat Daring Molenbeek 2-0. It caught the imagination of the Beveren public, who turned out in their thousands to watch the team play at the Freethiel Stadium. A record attendance of 18,000 watched Beveren lose out to Belgian football giants Anderlecht, 2-1. The club finished a respectable 13th that campaign. The next season would prove to be even better, with the club finishing sixth, with the help of prolific goalscorer Robert Rogiers. His 16 goals in total saw him become joint top goalscorer in the league that season.

That summer saw the club participate in the Intertoto Cup, although that year there were no knockout phases and therefore no winner was declared. Beveren competed in Group 9, with three other teams. They were Polish club Odra Opole, Swiss club La Chaux-de-Fonds and Denmark's Boldklubben 1913. The Belgians finished second in the group, behind Odra Opole, winning two, drawing two and losing two.

The 1969/70 season once again saw progression on the field, with a fourth-place finish under the management of Ward Volkaert meaning they qualified for the Inter-Cities Fairs Cup, the equivalent of what today we call the Europa League. The club once again competed in the Intertoto Cup or what was also known as the Rappan Cup, and were placed in Group B4, alongside German side Werder Bremen, Sweden's club Oster, and LASK from Austria. Beveren finished third in the group, managing to only win one game. But it was their European exploits in another tournament that caught everyone's attention that year.

The club met Austrian side Wiener Sport Club in the first round of the Inter-Cities Fairs Cup and beat them at the Sportclub-Platz in Vienna, 2-0 on 16 September 1970. The goals were scored by Rogiers and Janssens. The return leg saw the Belgians run out easy winners on the night as they put three past the Austrians without reply, leaving the tie 5-0 on aggregate in Beveren's favour. It set up a second-round tie against Spanish giants Valencia. Not many gave Beveren a chance to get any type of result, but the Belgians were to surprise everyone and on 22 October 1970, they pulled off one of the greatest victories in the club's history when they beat Valencia at the Mestalla Stadium in front of 45,000 people. The goal was scored by De Raeymaeker in the 77th minute and it gave the Belgian club the advantage going into the second leg. Even though Beveren were 1-0 up in the tie, most people fully expected Valencia to sweep them aside in the second leg. That wasn't the case and the game, played in front of 20,000 spectators at the Olympic Stadion in Antwerp, saw the Belgian side progress after drawing 1-1 on the night and winning 2-1 on aggregate. Once again, De Raeymaeker scored the goal against Valencia in the 60th minute to put Beveren 2-0 up on aggregate. A late goal by Forment for the Spanish side in the 84th minute proved to be a mere consolation as Beveren progressed to the next round, where they would meet English side Arsenal. This time, the quality of the opposition was too much for Beveren, and they lost the first leg at Highbury, 4-0. They fared much better in the second leg, drawing 0-0, but the damage had been done in London and they were eliminated from the competition.

The club stayed in the First Division for years, having success in the Belgian Cup in the 1977/78 season. It meant they qualified for the 1978/79 European Cup Winners' Cup, and they went on another European adventure. First, they faced Northern Irish side Ballymena United, who they beat 3-0 in both the home and away legs. The second round saw KSK Beveren face Croatian side NK Rijeka. After drawing 0-0 in the home leg, Beveren won the second leg 2-0 to progress to the quarter-finals. It was there they met Italian giants Inter Milan. The first leg was played in the San Siro, in Milan, and the two sides played out a 0-0 draw. The advantage was with KSK Beveren going into the second leg; with their fans behind them, they felt confident they could pull off a result. And that is what they did. On 21 March 1979, Robert Stevens scored the only goal of the night in the 85th minute to ensure SK Beveren would be going through to the semi-finals to face Barcelona.

On 11 April 1979, KSK Beveren travelled to the Camp Nou, full of confidence that they could once again pull off a shock result. However, they suffered a setback in front of a crowd of 70,000 when they conceded a penalty in the 65th minute. Rexach stepped up and slotted the kick away to give the Catalan club the advantage going into the second leg. That was played two weeks later, on 25 April, in front of a crowd of 20,000 fans. It was a tight affair and KSK Beveren had their chances to equalise but failed to do so and in the 85th minute they conceded their second penalty in the tie. This time Krankl stepped up to take it and he made no mistake, putting Barcelona 2-0 up on aggregate and sending them through to the final, one they would eventually win against German club Fortuna Dusseldorf.

The club underwent a name change again in 1978, this time to SK Beveren. It proved to be a lucky omen, because in 1979 they won their first ever First Division title, beating Anderlecht by four points, winning 19 games, drawing 11 and losing just four all season. It also meant that they qualified for the 1979/80 European Cup. They met Swiss club Servette in the first round on 19 September 1979, losing in the first leg in Switzerland, 3-1. The second leg was played on 3 October at the Freethiel Stadion. Beveren took an early lead when Albert tucked away a penalty in the 18th minute, but Servette equalised when Italian, Berto, scored in the 37th minute, leaving the tie 4-2 in the Swiss club's favour. That is how it ended, and SK Beveren were eliminated.

The club went on to win their second First Division title in the 1983/84 season, again pipping Anderlecht to the title. They finished the campaign having won 22 games, drawn seven and lost just five and once again they qualified for the European Cup. This time they managed to get past the first round, beating Icelandic side IA, 7-2 on aggregate, drawing the first leg away from home 2-2 and winning the second leg in Beveren, 5-0. It set up a second-round tie with Swedish club IFK Gothenburg. The first leg in Sweden ended 1-0 to the home side, meaning Beveren would have to win the second leg, which they did, 1-0 in normal time, thanks to a goal in the 76th minute from Creve. It sent the game into extra time. With the away goals rule still in play, if IFK Gothenburg were to score then SK Beveren would need two more. Unfortunately for the Belgians, that is what happened and in the 99th minute, Pettersson put the Swedish side 2-1 up. Beveren came back and scored again, making it 2-1 on the night and 2-2 on aggregate through a Gorez penalty in the 100th minute, but it wasn't enough and IFK Gothenburg progressed on away goals.

The next season, the club undertook another name change, this time referring to themselves as KSK Beveren. They continued to compete under this name and had relative success, especially in the Belgian Cup, coming runners-up in 1984/85 and again in 2003/04 when they were defeated by Club Brugge, 4-2 at the King Baudouin Stadium in Brussels. But only three years later the club found themselves in financial difficulties and nearly lost their professional licence, which would have seen them relegated back down to the Third Division. They successfully appealed the decision and continued playing in the Jupiler League until the 2007 season when they finished bottom, having only won five games all season, drawing ten and losing 19. It was the start of a dramatic fall for the club who found themselves in the Third Division for the 2010/11 season as they did not apply for a professional licence due to financial difficulties.

This is where the story of KSK Beveren gets controversial, as from 2010 the club decided it was best to merge with another football club, KV Red Star Waasland, becoming KV Red Star Waasland-Beveren, and moving to the stadium of defunct club Sint-Niklass. But the matricula number that the newly merged club used was that of KV Red Star Waasland. A group of fans from KSK Beveren decided to start a new club under the name KSK Beveren and began life in the lower divisions of Belgian football. They are called YBSK Beveren and are currently the only Belgian football club that are 100 per cent fan-owned. Both clubs claim to be the rightful heir of KSK Beveren.

I got in touch with the Belgian Football Podcast to find out more about KSK Beveren, while also speaking to a fan of YBSK Beveren, to find out what it is like to be the only 100 per cent fan-owned club in the country. Both their insights into the history of the club and players were excellent. First up is Scott Coyne, one of the members of the Belgian Football Podcast.

Thank you for taking the time out to answer these questions on KSK Beveren and Belgian football. The first thing I must ask is why Belgian football? How did you get into it?

Belgian Football Podcast: The Belgian Football Podcast is the No.1 English language podcast covering Belgian football. It was founded three years ago by Ben Jackson (@benjack94). Ben was quickly joined on the team by me, Scott Coyne (@scott_coyne @coyneconsultant) and Joris Becq (@Joris_Becq) who is actually Belgian and a Genk fan! It has grown significantly in its three years and we have plans to expand further.

KSK Beveren is a complicated club for a number of reasons with a complicated history. What can you tell the readers about KSK Beveren that they may not know?

Belgian Football Podcast: KSK are a significant club, with two championship wins and two Belgian Cups to their name. The club's heyday was in the late 1970s/early 1980s. In 2010 the club effectively folded and the club in existence today is 100 per cent fan-owned.

So many great players have come from Belgium throughout the years, with this latest crop being dubbed the 'Golden Generation'. In your opinion, is that set to continue?

Belgian Football Podcast: The current Red Devils side is overburdened by the 'golden generation' tag. The generation coming behind this one is equally impressive if not more so, so who is to say whether it might be the next generation that go that step further. The future of Belgian football at a national level is bright.

KSK Beveren are a club that went up and down the leagues in their history. It seems they had their best success when giving local youth a chance. Is this a common thing Belgian clubs do or do they turn to foreign imports like in other leagues?

Belgian Football Podcast: Most Belgian clubs have a strong youth system and policy. The academies are generally strong. Belgium really values youth development in its football culture – it is important and can be across clubs and leagues, it is not exclusive to Beveren.

The club had a few former players that would be considered decent, Yaya Toure being the standout name. In my research a player named Robert Rogiers seemed to pop up a lot. He seemed to be a prolific goalscorer yet there is very little written about him. Can you enlighten the readers about him?

Belgian Football Podcast: He is probably well known because he played in Europe for KSK during their Fairs Cup run in the late 1970s. He made his debut aged 16 and scored 48 goals in 174 appearances for KSK. He was capped twice by the Red Devils [Belgium] as well.

Another star player that caught my attention who played for Beveren was Wilfried van Moer, a former Belgian international player and manager, who sadly passed away in 2021. Winning the Belgian Golden Shoe three times is no mean feat. What can you say about him?

Belgian Football Podcast: Van Moer is arguably Beveren's most famous player. He was outstanding for the national team and played during the final of Euro 1980 in which Belgium narrowly lost 2-1 to West Germany. He also won the Golden Shoe on three occasions as well – this is the yearly award for Belgium's best player – and made 169 appearances for KSK and also managed the national team very briefly.

Finally, I know it is a complicated situation with there being two clubs claiming to be the original KSK Beveren, with Waasland-Beveren being the merger and KSK Beveren being fan-owned now. I won't ask you who is the rightful heir as it's an unanswerable question, but where do you think the future of football in Beveren is heading? Will there be another merger or is this how it will stay? Two separate clubs who may one day meet in the same league?

Belgian Football Podcast: There are plans for a merger, but we think they will not be successful; there is too much animosity and a split in the Beveren community. There are also other teams in the same geographical area [Antwerp province]: Lokeren, Lierse, Waasland-Beveren, Antwerp, KV Mechelen and even Racing Mechelen.

Stijn Kluskens, a man who runs the KSK Beveren Twitter account, gave me an in-depth insight into KSK Beveren, past and present.

Thank you for taking time out to answer my questions on KSK Beveren, one of the more complex stories I have had the pleasure to write about. First of all, you are 100 per cent fan-owned and, to my knowledge, you are the only Belgian club to have that status. What are the pros and cons of being fan-owned?

Stijn Kluskens: Personally, I think the biggest advantage is that you have the certainty that the individuality/soul of your club is preserved. No sudden rich guy that pops up who can change the logo, the colours. No crazy merger situations, no fear that your club has to move 100km further, and above all the club can really mean something to the community. You give football back to what it was made for: the supporter!

And, you know everything about the club and there are no more secrets. You know that the club will not do crazy things and you can help decide how and where you want to grow as a club. I feel even more connected to the club than I used to be. And nobody can be angry about the small things like ticket and drink prices because you can decide/vote. If something bothers you, just send an email and it can be discussed at the next meeting, it's that simple!

But, it comes with a price: no rich owner means no big budget. So, you have to be more patient for success on the field and work really hard for it. It also becomes a lot harder to do that as a professional team, but not impossible at all. Then you will have to work differently, but the essence of the story must remain the same.

KSK Beveren have had some really good players over the years, most notably Wilfried van Moer, who went on to manage the Belgian national side. What can you tell me about him and how he is regarded by the KSK Beveren fans?

Stijn: I did my research [source book *KSK Beveren part 1*] for the details because I am too young to have watched him play. But the name, the reputation of Van Moer is legendary in the town! If you are a Beveren supporter, you know Van Moer! You know our little general! Van Moer is without a doubt the most successful player ever produced by the famous youth academy of SK Beveren. He won everything there is to win in this football country: golden boots, league titles, cups, and the respect of football critics on both sides of the language border.

Who, in your opinion, is the best player to have played for KSK Beveren and who is your favourite player to have pulled on the Beveren shirt? It can be the same player if you like.

Stijn: Favourite player: without a doubt Heinz Schönberger. One of the best football players to have played on the Belgian football fields. A true ball virtuoso who you couldn't get off the ball without making a foul, and also a wonderful person who still lives in Beveren.

Best player: Lambert Smid. A technically very gifted footballer with great pace and stamina. He also had an excellent right foot and was the playmaker in the midfield for six years but was also not afraid to do the dirty work. He always played with a big heart and gave 200 per cent of himself every game! A man that everybody loved.

What is the vision for KSK Beveren? Where do you see the club in five years' time?

Stijn: A stable, healthy, fan-owned club that plays just below professional football, that contributes to the local community, that offers affordable and good youth football at all levels. And to secure and continue the history and future of KSK Beveren.

What is your favourite moment in the history of KSK Beveren? Whether you were actually there or not.

Stijn: Inter Milan, 21 March 1979, the quarter-final of the European Cup Winners' Cup. The very small amateur team from Beveren had drawn 0-0 in Milan and could dream of a football fairy tale. And so it happened in minute 85 of the return game! Hofkens with the legendary move and Stevens blasts us to the biggest party ever in Beveren! Those songs are sung to this day! Those stories come up every summer on a nice evening with a bottle of wine.

Finally, KSK Beveren are a Belgian club that clearly have a passionate fan base (I've watched the fan videos). Is there anything you would like to add or tell the readers about KSK Beveren?

Stijn: The past of KSK Beveren deserves to have a bright future. KSK Beveren stand for tradition, pride and future and we want to ensure the future of the club by giving football back to the supporter with fan participation as a fan-owned club.

4

Wacker 04 Berlin (Germany)

WACKER 04 Berlin originally started out as Reinickendorfer FC West when they were founded on 25 July 1904. The club then merged with Tegeler FC in 1908 and renamed themselves SC Wacker 04 Tegal. The club's colours were purple and white, and they played at the Wackerplatz. The club competed in the Oberliga Berlin-Brandenburg, the top-flight division of the Prussian Province of Brandenburg, which included Berlin. They remained competitive throughout the 1920s, never really challenging for the title, but never getting relegated either.

In 1933 they moved to the Gauliga Berlin-Brandenburg league, the highest division in the provinces of Brandenburg and Berlin, both in the German state of Prussia. The first season saw Wacker relegated, but they bounced back in 1934, gaining promotion at the first time of asking. They didn't last long in the top flight and were relegated during the 1939/40 season. It seemed that Wacker were a bit of a yo-yo club as they once again gained immediate promotion and remained in the First Division until World War Two ended and so did the Gauliga Berlin-Brandenburg division, as it was disbanded in 1945.

Wacker competed in the newly formed league, the Oberliga Berlin, but not as SC Wacker 04 Tegal. Instead, the club took the name SG Reickendorf-West. They stayed in the division until 1956 when they were eventually relegated. But just as before, the club gained immediate promotion, and played in the Oberliga until 1964, when the league formats were changed again, and the Bundesliga was formed. Wacker (as I will continue to refer to them) went on to play in the Regionalliga Berlin, one of five regional leagues set up: Berlin, North, South, South-West, and West. The five league champions of each region and the runners-up from the North, West, South and South-West groups went on to play in a promotion play-off to decide who would gain promotion to the Bundesliga. The Berlin group was only given one place because it had significantly fewer teams competing in it.

The first season of the Regionalliga Berlin saw Wacker 04 finish third, winning 15, drawing four and losing eight. The 1964/65 season saw Wacker finish fourth in the ten-team group, and way behind the three above them, winning nine games, drawing four and losing 13. They finished a total of 17 points behind third-placed SC Tasmania 1900 Berlin, a club who gained promotion to the Bundesliga that year. Hertha BSC had their licence revoked and therefore were expelled from the Bundesliga, leaving a space open. With Tennis Borussia Berlin losing in the promotion play-offs and the second-placed Spandauer SV declining the chance to be promoted, it went to the third-placed team.

The 1965/66 season saw an extension of the Regionalliga Berlin to 16 clubs, making the prospect of winning it even harder than before for Wacker. Add in Hertha Berlin's inclusion, a club that were far superior to all others in the Berlin region at the time, and Wacker had to be content with yet another fourth-placed finish. Hertha Berlin were, of course, the champions of the division, only losing once all season. However, they failed to gain promotion back to the Bundesliga via the play-offs and would yet again be competing in the Regionalliga Berlin the following year.

The 1966/67 season provided the same outcome, with Hertha Berlin finishing top. Wacker 04 Berlin had to settle for sixth spot. The 1967/68 season saw Hertha Berlin, who had failed once again to gain promotion to the Bundesliga via the play-offs, finish top of the division again. This time, however, they would be successful in the play-offs and gain promotion back to the Bundesliga, leaving the Berlin division wide open for the next season. Wacker 04, who had finished fourth that season, had high hopes for the following campaign, and were looking to push for promotion to the Bundesliga themselves.

But it wasn't to be in the 1968/69 season, as they finished fourth once again. The signs were still encouraging as they finished as the second-highest scorers (93). The following season saw the division reduced to 14 clubs from 16. This didn't help Wacker's cause and they finished in fifth place. However, in the 1970/71 season, they finally qualified for the play-offs, finishing second in the Berlin division, behind Tasmania 1900 Berlin by ten points and just one point above third-placed Blau-Weiss 90 Berlin. They were placed in Group 2 of the play-offs, but it proved to be too much of a step up as they finished bottom of the pile, winning only one game.

This only made the club even more determined to reach the promised land of the Bundesliga and in the 1971/72 season they topped the Regionalliga Berlin by just one point. In fact, the top four clubs that year were only separated by three points. After their previous experience of the play-offs the year before, they were better prepared; however, they were not good enough once again, finishing fourth out of the five clubs in their group.

The 1972/73 season saw the club gain qualification for the play-offs for the third year in a row, coming second in the Berlin Division, but once again they found themselves out of their depth, finishing bottom of Group 2 and only winning one game. The 1973/74 season was like a game of Russian roulette, with the teams who came first and second being the only ones who would not be relegated to the Oberliga Berlin, as German football was looking to re-organise its football pyramid, with the introduction of the 2 Bundesliga. Of course, finishing second as Wacker 04 Berlin did that season, also meant they would qualify for the play-offs and have a chance of gaining entry to the top division, the 1 Bundesliga. But once again they failed in their attempt, finishing fourth out of the five clubs in Group 5 and they had to settle for a place in the newly formed 2 Bundesliga.

The 2 Bundesliga was split into two different divisions, the North and the South, with the winners of both divisions gaining promotion to the Bundesliga while both second-placed clubs played each other in a play-off. Wacker Berlin didn't have to concern themselves with any of this, finishing in 13th out of the 20 clubs in the North division. The 1975/6 season saw the club flirt with relegation, finishing only a point above the drop zone. But it was just a reprieve as the next season, 1976/77, saw them relegated to the Amateurliga Berlin when they finished 18th out of 20.

They didn't stay in the Amateurliga Berlin for very long, becoming champions in the 1977/78 season and gaining promotion back to the 2 Bundesliga North division. However, in true Wacker 04 Berlin style, they were relegated again, coming dead last in the 20-club division.

It would be the last time Wacker 04 Berlin would compete at such a high level, with the club falling down the divisions for the next decade, playing their football in the Third and Fourth Divisions of German football. In the end, in 1994, while playing in the Verbandsliga Berlin, the Fourth Division, the club was declared bankrupt and therefore dissolved, meaning that there was no more Wacker 04 Berlin. The fans, however, continued their support elsewhere and joined up with BFC Alemannia, who then briefly unofficially renamed the club BFC Alemannia 90 Wacker, but reverted back to their original name in 2013.

5.

Jutrzenka Kraków (Poland)

JUTRZENKA KRAKÓW was founded in the year 1909 and was a Jewish minority Polish football team based in Kraków. At the time, it was seen as one of the most important Jewish sporting teams in Europe, alongside Hasmonea Lwow, Hakoah Czernowitz and their big city rivals, Makkabi Kraków. The fans and players of the club were connected to the Bund political party, a secular Jewish socialist party formed back in 1897, while their rivals Makkabi Kraków were aligned to the Zionist movement and political parties. This caused tension between the two football clubs and the matches between them became known as the 'Holy War', a term that has since been adopted by the two biggest clubs in Kraków today, Cracovia and Wisła.

Jutrzenka wore black and white stripes as their colours and played their home games in the place Wisła call their home today. Ironically it was Makkabi who had a strong alliance with Wisła back in the day, with Wisła seen as having a somewhat anti Semitic view as a football club, with their policy to not sign any non-Catholic players to their side. Naturally, Jutrzenka aligned with the more democratic Cracovia. The rivalry between the four clubs was more than just football, with political, religious and social aspects all being involved in their disdain for one another.

Back to the football: Jutrzenka had little to no success on the field. Their best season came when they finished second to Wisła Kraków in the 1920s in the A-Class League, the highest level of football in Kraków at the time. It was considered a success as they finished ahead of the much bigger and better-supported Cracovia, who finished third. However, Jutrzenka do have a place in Polish footballing history for being one of the founding clubs of the first Polish soccer league. The league was founded on 1 March 1927, and was independent from the Polish Football Federation until it finally recognised the league on 18 December 1927.

The first league title went to Wisła Kraków, while Jutrzenka finished 14th and last in the table. It meant they dropped out of the league and therefore had the 'honour' of being the first Polish team to be relegated from the Polish football league. It would be their only appearance at such a level, with the club playing their football in the lower and local divisions for the rest of their existence. And that existence lasted until 1939, when the club was dissolved after the German armed forces invaded Poland.

The club didn't re-emerge after World War Two and that was the end of Jutrzenka Kraków, a club that many may have forgotten, but one that still holds a place in the history of Polish football, not least for being the pioneers of the 'Holy War', but also having the unwanted accolade of being the first Polish club to get relegated from the Polish football league.

One of the most notable players to have pulled on the Jutrzenka jersey was Polish-born Jozef Klotz. Born in 1900, in Kraków, Klotz had a Jewish background. He came up through the ranks of the Jutrzenka youth team and played for the club for 15 years before moving to another Jewish minority team, Maccabi Warszawa. He was a centre-back but holds the record of scoring Poland's first international goal, which came in their third game, against Sweden in Stockholm on 28 May 1922, which Poland won 2-1. It was one of only two appearances he made for the Polish national team, the other coming in a 3-0 defeat to Hungary on 14 May 1922, in his home city of Kraków. Klotz retired at the age of 30, although it's not known if he remained playing with other clubs in lower divisions. He died in the Warsaw Ghetto, in 1941, when he was murdered by the German Army, having been imprisoned there since 1940. In 2019, Josef Klotz was honoured by the Polish Football Association.

When I went looking for someone to speak to about Polish football and its history, one name kept being mentioned. It was Ryan Hubbard, author of *Partition to Solidarity: The First 100 Years of Polish Football*, a brilliant read for anybody interested in Polish football, or football in general. It was a coin flip as to whether to put this interview in this chapter or the second Polish club I write about further on in the book. Ryan didn't disappoint with his input. Here is what he had to say.

Thank you for taking time out to answer my questions on Polish football and Jutrzenka Kraków. It was one of the shortest chapters I have written in the book, but still one of the most fascinating ones. The club has been gone since 1939, but were one of the founders of the Polish football league. What can you tell me about how the Polish football league was formed and the history of it?
Ryan Hubbard: The Polish football league was established on the back of a very tumultuous time in the country's history. Not even ten years earlier, Poland was merely a distant memory on the map of Europe – its historical lands swallowed up by the empires of Russia, Prussia and Austria-Hungary.

Prior to the re-establishment of the Polish state in 1918, the few 'Polish' clubs which had been created – most under a push for Polish autonomy – actually fell under the umbrellas of their respective empires. But after 1918, efforts were doubled to bring them all together for a national competition.

At first, the competition was very fragmented. Links between the different regions – which had been in separate countries for more than a century – were simply not established, while the end of the First World War did not bring an end to all hostilities in central and eastern Europe. It was decided that, for the first five seasons, regional qualifying tournaments would be played to establish a regional champion. Those champions would then take part in a national tournament, to ultimately decide the Polish champions.

In Kraków, Cracovia and Wisła were the dominant teams, with the former even winning the first national championship in 1921. Jutrzenka yo-yoed up and down the table over the early years, but remained the only other constant presence in the regional competition.

By 1927, the majority of Polish clubs – pushed by the likes of Wisła and Czarni Lwów, who felt that the current structure didn't satisfy those cities which had more than one strong team – began to favour a national league system. In April, this new system began outside of the auspices of the PZPN [Polish Football Federation], and without the participation of Cracovia, whose president at the time was also a high-ranking PZPN official. With their absence, a position in the league was instead offered to Kraków's third club, Jutrzenka.

In my research, the 'Holy War' came up, with Jutrzenka and Makkabi Kraków being the original derby which this name came from. What can you tell me about this game, back then and in modern days between Cracovia and Wisła?

Ryan: The rivalry between Jutrzenka and Makkabi was, indeed, the original '*Święta Wojna*', or 'Holy War' in Kraków. Despite the two being the city's Jewish clubs, the rivals' hatred of each other was unquestionable.

Jutrzenka were considered to be the left-wing, anti-Zionist Jewish club, whilst the views of the Jewish Zionists Makkabi were diametrically opposed. While tensions did exist between Jewish and non-Jewish clubs, sometimes they actually co-existed very well.

Jutrzenka soon realised they had much more in common with Cracovia – described as a 'club for all' – than their Jewish rivals. Makkabi, meanwhile, saw themselves as much closer to Wisła. Perhaps these alliances were even some of the first instances of club friendships within Polish football.

The term 'Holy War' in regard to the rivalry between Cracovia and Wisła is thought to have been first coined in the mid-1920s. Cracovia's Jewish player, Ludwik Gintel, is said to have encouraged his team-mates by shouting: 'This is our Holy War!' With the increasing dominance of the two clubs, the term stuck.

There were quite a few Jewish clubs in Poland back then. I think I named four of them in the chapter and they were known as Jewish minority clubs. Are there still Jewish minority football clubs in Poland?

Ryan: There are now very few, if any Jewish-minority clubs remaining in Poland. World War Two absolutely decimated the country's Jewish population, with those who weren't killed emigrating at the earliest opportunity.

The likes of Jutrzenka and Makkabi, as well as clubs of other minorities (such as Ukraina Lwów and 1.FC Kattowitz) were disbanded as the borders of central Europe shifted. In their place, new Polish clubs sprang up and under the Soviet structure, clubs aligned themselves more to industry than religion.

Politics also played a huge part in how these football clubs were run and who were their fan bases. Is this still the case nowadays?

Ryan: Politics does still play a minor part in Polish football fandom, although perhaps to an ever-decreasing degree.

During communist rule, clubs found themselves attached to different industries: Legia Warsaw were the army club, Wisła Kraków belonged to the militia, Górnik Zabrze were the mining club, and Lech Poznań were the main club of the railways. The army and mining clubs had the most financial and political clout, and therefore found themselves able to attract the best players. This often caused resentment among fans of other clubs. Teams such as Polonia Warsaw – perhaps one of the most liberal, anti-communist, Polish nationalist clubs in the country – found themselves attached to the destitute railway industry, and began plummeting down the leagues.

Nowadays, some of these attitudes and views still remain amongst older generations; but amongst those younger, who knew nothing of the communist system, they have begun to fade. Certain fan groups are known for their political views (Ruch Chorzów's Silesian nationalism, Legia's right-leaning tendencies), but nowadays the club and their supporters as a whole are no longer defined by their views.

Polish football has always been seen as being followed by fanatical supporters, so it is quite surprising to see that there have been so many clubs that have dissolved throughout the years in Polish football. What are the main reasons for this in your opinion?

Ryan: Political and cultural changes in Poland were usually the reason for many clubs disappearing from the map, but nowadays it is often cashflow problems which cause clubs' dissolution. In recent years we've seen a number of former Polish champions drop into the financial quagmire, and either plummet down the division, or be forced to start again at the very bottom.

Many clubs fell into chaos after the fall of communism, as their government subsidies dried up. Górnik Zabrze and Ruch Chorzów, both 14-time Polish champions by the late 80s, suddenly couldn't cope without their backing, and haven't won a title since.

Poor ownership has also led to the downfall of clubs such as Widzew Łódź and Polonia Warsaw, while several others struggled after demotion due to their part in a match-fixing scandal which engulfed Polish football.

Fortunately, there have been a number of improvements in the Polish football system in recent years, and such incidents seem to be happening much less often.

Some great players have played in Poland or have come from Poland. I mentioned Jozef Klotz, a player who played for Jutrzenka for 15 years and became Poland's first ever goalscorer in an international match. What can you tell me about him?

Ryan: Klotz was born on the second day of the new century, in Austro-Hungarian-occupied Kraków. The son of a shoemaker, Klotz began studying medicine, although he soon quit his studies to volunteer in the early days of the new Polish Army, and fought in the Polish–Bolshevik war between 1918 and 1920.

Jozef was a part of Jutrzenka Kraków from the club's establishment in 1910, while his younger brothers all joined the club in various different disciplines. It was while playing for Jutrzenka that he received a call-up to the Polish national team for its second match (a 3-0 defeat to Hungary), and then again for a trip to Sweden a few months later.

In Sweden, he wrote his name into Polish football history, with a well-taken penalty to give the White Eagles a 1-0 lead. Poland eventually won for the first time, 2-1. It was the last time that Klotz played for the national team.

In 1925, Klotz married a Catholic woman and then transferred to Warsaw, where he turned out for the capital's Jewish club, Makkabi. Unfortunately, little more is known about his career.

Klotz lived in Warsaw until his death, in 1941, in the city's Jewish ghetto. Although the exact details of his murder aren't known, it's likely he was killed in a mass execution by Nazi soldiers.

My last question is a multiple question really. With the introduction of the Europa Conference League, there will be more clubs playing European football, and I envisage Polish clubs will look at this as a way of picking up a European trophy. Maybe even looking a little bit higher and being competitive in the Europa League. But do you think they can reach a higher level? Maybe compete in the Champions League in the future? What do you see as success for Polish clubs in the future and what do you think they can achieve?

Ryan: Unfortunately, Polish success in European competition still seems to be some way off. The addition of the Europa Conference League may give more opportunity for Polish teams to play in Europe, but the strength of the teams in the latter stages of the competition is still likely to be too strong for Polish clubs at the moment.

For Polish football, European success at the moment would be to see more than one club participate in the group stages. It's been more than a decade since Legia and Wisła both reached the Europa League, and since then, even one team progressing through the qualifying rounds has been difficult.

If Poland can get back to seeing more than one team qualify on a regular basis, it will do wonders for the strength of both the clubs and the league as a whole. The coefficient will improve, and the country may even get to a point where one of its clubs is guaranteed a spot in the group stages without having to go through the qualifying rounds. Unfortunately, that still seems a way off.

6.

FC Partizan Minsk (Belarus)

FOUNDED IN 2002 as MTZ-RIPO Minsk, the club was formed after two clubs in the city of Minsk merged. They were the well-established Traktor Minsk, a club who were originally founded in 1947 and have since been re-founded in 2015, and academy side Trudovye Rezervy-RIPO Minsk. The idea behind the project was that it would be a professional club with the financial resources Traktor Minsk brought to the table and the potential of creating their own talent in the school of football brought to the table by Trudovye Rezervy. It was an immediate success, with the club winning the Second League in 2002, gaining promotion to the First League for the 2003 season. They continued their progress, finishing second that season, only losing out to Lokomotiv Vitebsk in a play-off for the title, after the two sides finished on the exact same points tally, 70. MTZ won 22 of their matches, drawing four and losing just four all season. In fact, Minsk had a better goal difference than their rivals but the league felt a play-off at a neutral venue would be the fairest way to decide who would be crowned champions. Vitebsk won the game 2-1, played at Baranovichi.

MTZ still gained promotion to the Belarusian Premier League and many saw them as dark horses going into the 2004 season. However, they were brought back down to earth that year, finishing 14th, and having to play in a promotion/relegation play-off against the 15th-placed team, who had been their title rivals the year before, Lokomotiv Vitebsk. The two clubs had finished level on points once more, and again Minsk had the better goal difference, but the Belarusian FA still felt that the fairest way to decide who got relegated was to play a one-off game at a neutral venue. Just like the season before, Baranovichi was the venue picked for the match, but unlike the season before, MTZ came out on top, winning the game 4-1, with goals from Zelmikas (15th minute), Mkhitaryan (34th), Fedorchenko (55th) and Parfenov (61st). Yeremeyev replied in the 66th minute for Vitebsk but the game had long been over.

Too add to the joy of avoiding relegation, MTZ also won the Belarus Cup, causing a huge upset, beating BATE Borisov 2-1 in the final at the Dinamo Stadium in Minsk. After going a goal down in the 28th minute from a Lebedzew strike, few would have given MTZ a chance of a comeback. But that's exactly what they produced, hitting back just before half-time, when the Ukrainian, Fedoro, found the back of the net in the 42nd minute. The sides went in level at half-time, and it left the 15,500 fans anticipating an exciting second half. Many expected BATE to come out blazing, but MTZ were not to be broken and it was the newly promoted side who took the lead in the 73rd minute thanks to forward Artem Kontsevoy. Borisov had no reply and MTZ won their first major trophy in the club's short history. With the cup win they also gained qualification to the 2005/06 UEFA Cup first round. With their success and their place in the Belarusian Premier League secured for the next season came attention from investors. This, to some, could be seen as the beginning of the end for the club.

They made their European debut against Hungarian side Ferencvaros in the Central-East Region qualifiers. The Belarusian side won the first leg away from home, 2-0, but lost the second leg at home, 2-1. It was enough to see them through, 3-2, on aggregate and in the next round they faced Czech side, FK Teplice. After drawing the first leg at home, 1-1, they lost away 2-1, ending their European journey that season.

But it was the off-field situation that most MTZ fans were concerned about as news emerged that Russian-Lithuanian businessman Vladimir Romanov had bought the club, adding to his portfolio that included Scottish club Hearts and Lithuanian side FC Kaunas. It saw many players being loaned between the three clubs. At first, it seemed as though the project was working and the 2005 season saw the club finish third, only one point behind their city rivals, Dinamo Minsk, a club they had shared a fierce rivalry with since their entry to the Belarusian Premier League. The rivalry ran deeper than football, with political agendas and alliances being a part of the animosity between the two clubs' fans. The third-place finish saw MTZ once again qualify for European competition, this time the Intertoto Cup.

Their European adventure started against Kazakhstani side Shakhter Karagandy, with a 5-1 win in the first game, away from home. The tie had already been all-but won, but MTZ were made to sweat when they were pushed all the way by Karagandy in the second leg, losing 3-1 in Minsk. It set up a tie with the newly formed FC Moscow, who had only been founded in 2004. (They have since been dissolved, in 2010.) The Russians won 3-0 on aggregate and once again MTZ were knocked out in the second round of a European competition.

The 2006 season saw the club just miss out on playing in Europe for the third time, as they finished fourth, one point behind third-placed Shakhtyor Soligorsk. That season three MTZ players finished among the top seven goalscorers.

They were Vyacheslav Hleb, brother of former Arsenal and Barcelona winger Alexander Hleb, Artem Kontsevoy and Oleg Strakhanovich.

The 2007 season saw the club finish fifth but they still qualified for the 2008 UEFA Cup due to their triumph in the Belarus Cup. It was their second major trophy and they won it by beating Shakhtyor Soligorsk in the final. The Minsk club ran out 2-1 winners in a game that was decided by a Strakhanovich goal in the 83rd minute. MTZ had taken an early lead in the fifth minute thanks to Hleb, and it looked like that would be enough to secure their second Belarus Cup until Strypeykis equalised in the 82nd minute. Almost instantly MTZ hit back and held out to lift the trophy at the Dinamo Stadium.

For the third time in their history, the club would be competing in European competition, but this time they would knocked out in the first round. It was Slovakian side Zilina who dumped them out at that early stage, winning 3-2 on aggregate. It didn't affect their confidence when playing domestically however, and they finished the 2008 season in third place, gaining qualification for the now renamed Europa League. That season saw the club win 17, draw six and lose seven. Their success was once again thanks to the goalscoring exploits of Artem Kontsevoy, who finished third top-goalscorer with 15 that season, only one behind the joint top scorers, Gennadi Bliznyuk and Vitali Rodionov, both of BATE Borisov, who had won their third title in a row.

With the newly formed Europa League format in place, MTZ played their first-round match against Montenegrin side Sutjeska Niksic. They drew the first leg away from home, 1-1, and the second leg in Minsk ended in the same score after 90 minutes, meaning the tie went to extra time. It was Mikalay Ryndzyuk who struck the winner and his second of the game in the 111th minute to set up a second-round match against Ukrainian side Metalurh Donetsk.

MTZ were outplayed and outclassed by their opponents, losing 3-0 at the Metalurh Stadium in Donetsk. The second leg seemed to be an uphill task but MTZ gave it a go and made Metalurh worry when they took the lead in the 16th minute thanks to Brazilian Nicolas Ceolin. But the hope of a comeback was to be short-lived as Metalurh scored in the 36th minute to all but end the tie as a contest. The Ukrainians went on to win the match on the night thanks to a goal from Henrikh Mkhitaryan, who has played for Manchester United and Roma. It would be the last time MTZ would play in European competition, but they and their fans weren't to know that at the time.

The 2009 season saw a dramatic fall on the field with the club narrowly avoiding relegation by just a point. They only won eight games all season, drawing six and losing 12. It was only a stay of execution though, as the 2010 season saw the club, under their new name Partizan Minsk, finish 12th and bottom of the league. They did, however, bounce back straight away and the 2011 season in the Belarusian First League saw the club finish in second place, behind Slavia Mozyr. It meant Partizan Minsk would have to play in a promotion/relegation play-off match against the team who finished 11th in the Premier Division. That team would be FC Vitebsk, who had also undergone a name change (they have had a few throughout the years). The two clubs had played each other in play-offs before, but they were one-off matches at a neutral venue. This time, it was to be a two-legged affair with the winner gaining their place in the 2012 Belarusian Premier League. Partizan won the first leg at their home ground, Traktor Stadium, 2-0 with goals from Shappyatowski and Makas. The second leg at the CSK Vitebsky was a much tighter affair. Vitebsk took the lead in the 27th minute through Sjesarcuks and narrowed the aggregate margin but Partizan restored their two-goal advantage three minutes later when they were awarded a penalty. Maskas stepped up and slotted it away to put Partizan Minsk on their way back to the top flight. But Vitebsk were determined to go down fighting and Artsyom Skitaw's goal in the 55th minute made for a nervous ending for the Minsk club. However, they managed to hold out and when the whistle blew, they were confirmed as the club who would be competing in the Premier Division in 2012. Well, that was the plan.

The 2012 season was just about to start, when it emerged that Partizan Minsk's owner, Vladimir Romanov was to abandon the club, having run into personal legal problems. (Hearts fans will know all about these problems as well.) As a result, Partizan no longer had the financial backing they once enjoyed and were unable to acquire the licence needed to compete in the Premier Division and so they had to withdraw their application, leaving only 11 clubs to compete in Belarus's top division that season. The club fell down the leagues and found themselves playing in the Minsk Championship, an amateur league, finishing only fifth that season. In 2013 they renamed themselves again as Partizan-MTZ Minsk and re-joined the second league in a bid to revive themselves and climb back up the ladder; however, it was a short-lived dream. After finishing 11th in the third tier in 2013, the club withdrew from the league midway through 2014. They folded and were never to play again in the Belarusian football pyramid.

7.

FC Lantana Tallinn (Estonia)

FOUNDED IN 1994 after the Belov family bought the now defunct club, Nikol Tallinn, FC Lantana Tallinn entered the Estonian football league. For the first few seasons the club wore black and white stripes but changed their colours in 1998 to sky blue and royal blue stripes.

In their first season, they came second in the preliminary round of the league, under the name Lantana-Marlekor, winning 14, drawing three and only losing one game all season. Coming second gained them qualification for the Championship Tournament, where the top six would compete for the title. In the Championship they also finished second, one point behind Flora, winning seven, drawing two and losing one game. They were helped by their prolific striker Maksim Gruznov, who scored 11 goals that season, becoming joint-third-highest goalscorer overall. Their impressive second-place finish in their first season prepared them for an eventful 1995/96 campaign.

Their form also produced a run all the way to the final of the Estonian Cup. They started their journey in the second round, winning that tie with ease, beating Kopli Tallinn 10-0 away from home. The third qualifying round consisted of a two-legged affair with JK/Kalev. Once again FC Lantana proved to be too strong for their opponents, breezing past them 14-2 on aggregate, winning the first leg away from home 6-0, and the home leg 8-2. It set up a semi-final match against JK Trans Narva, with the scores being a lot closer than the previous rounds. Lantana came out of the two-legged affair victorious, winning 2-1 at home and 1-0 away. So, for the first time in their history, they would be playing in the Estonian Cup Final, and it would be against Estonian giants FC Flora Tallinn. Attendance for the game was only 600 and Flora won the match 2-0 with goals from Marko Kristal and Ricardas Zdancius to see the favourites lift the trophy.

As Flora had already qualified for European competition as league winners, Lantana took their place in the Cup Winners' Cup. However, their European adventure in 1995/96 didn't last long, and they were knocked out by Latvian club DAG-Liepaja, in controversial circumstances. Drawing the home leg 0-0, they won the second leg 2-1, only for it to be overturned to a 3-0 loss as the Estonian club were deemed to have fielded an ineligible player.

Lantana (they dropped the Marlekor part of their name) topped the league in the preliminary round. Once again, they qualified for the Championship Tournament. Just like the preliminary round, Lantana topped the league by quite a few points, seven in total, ahead of Flora, which meant they lifted their first league title and their first major trophy. Once again, Maksim Gruznov finished as the club's top scorer, but this time he was joint-highest with his team-mate Andrei Borissov, as both scored 12. In the league, they only finished behind Flora striker Lembit Rajala, who scored 16 goals.

The club once again qualified for European competition, but this time it was at a higher level, in the UEFA Cup and their European exploits lasted a little bit longer, with the club reaching the second qualifying round. In the first qualifying round they beat Icelandic side Iprottabandalag Vestmannaeyja, winning the home leg 2-1 and drawing the away leg 0-0. This set up a second-round qualifier against Swiss side FC Aarau. This proved a step too far for the Estonians and they fell to defeat; despite winning the home leg 2-0, they lost 4-0 away, losing on aggregate, 4-2.

The 1996/97 season proved to be just as successful as the last one, with the club adding to their silverware won from the previous season. Once again, they topped the preliminary round, finishing ahead of Flora. They went on to win the Championship Tournament and this qualified them for the Champions League first qualifying round for the next season. Once again, they ended up being Estonian Cup finalists, but once again they lost, 3-2 to Tallinna Sadam at the Kadriorg Stadium in Tallinn.

In the Champions League, they met Finnish side Jazz and lost 3-0 on aggregate: 1-0 in the first leg and 2-0 in the second leg. The 1997/98 season saw the club finish third in the league, winning four, drawing three and losing three. This would be the last time the league would have a preliminary round with a new format coming in for the next season. Finishing third, FC Lantana qualified for the Cup Winners' Cup for the following season. They faced Scottish side Heart of Midlothian in the first round of qualifying and they were thrashed 6-0 on aggregate, losing the home leg 1-0 and the return 5-0. They also got to the Estonian Cup Final for the third time and for the third time they lost, once again to Flora Tallinn, who ran out 3-2 winners on the day.

The 1998 Meistriliiga proved to be the same as the previous one, without the preliminary round. FC Lantana finished third for a second season in a row, winning seven, drawing four and losing three. Finishing third qualified the club for the UEFA Cup this time and they faced Georgian outfit FC Torpedo Kutaisi in the first round. Once again, FC Lantana were beaten heavily, 9-2 on aggregate, losing

5-0 at home and 4-2 away. Their domestic form also took a dip, finishing sixth out of eight clubs in the Estonian Premier Division. They only finished three points above Lelle, who were forced to play in a relegation play-off match. It was to be the last season for FC Lantana, as the club was wound up and dissolved for good. (Through my research it seems it was done for financial reasons, but this is not 100 per cent confirmed.)

Answering my questions on FC Lantana and Estonian football are the lads from the Estonian Football Podcast, two Englishmen who have a passion for Estonian football. Their knowledge of the game in Estonia is second to none and that is proven from listening to their podcasts and reading their previews and opinions on the Estonian league. Here is what they had to say:

Cheers lads for giving the readers an insight to Estonian football. My first question is one I'd say you get asked a lot, but why Estonian football? Is there a link to it or was it just a random interest you picked up?
Estonian Football Podcast: We decided to head out to Estonia just for a city break in 2018 and stumbled across an abandoned stadium with the Levadia badge on it, so decided to check out the other stadiums nearby. We looked at the league every now and then, and eventually just started to follow it with more interest, and in lockdown we were bored so decided to talk about it.

FC Lantana Tallinn weren't around for a long time but were around for some good times. What can you tell us about the short-lived, yet successful club that was FC Lantana Tallinn?
Estonian Football Podcast: From following Estonian football, we've learnt it's very weird and especially back in the 90s

probably fairly corrupt (if anyone can correct us on that then great). Lantana existed from a prototype club called Nikol Tallinn (who were TVMK). TVMK were bought out by the Nikol company in 1992 and from this point TVMK's history technically ended and Nikol Tallinn were born. Nikol only existed for two years before they themselves became bought out by the Belov family and a new club, Lantana Tallinn, was born. In the six years that Lantana competed in the top flight they finished in the top three for five of those seasons and won the league back-to-back in 1995/96 and 1996/97. Mixed form after this led to Lantana being wound up for financial problems in 1999.

FC Flora Tallinn are probably the best-known football club from Estonia. (I know of them as they have played against a few Irish clubs in recent years.) What is the height of expectations for an Estonian club like them in Europe? I'd assume with the introduction of the Europa Conference League they will want to do well in that competition?

Estonian Football Podcast: We love the Conference League: what a competition for these 'smaller' clubs to get a taste for European action. We think after what Flora did in 2021 [winning one group-stage match in the Conference League] that is the common goal now for Estonian teams, when it comes to Europe. But for improvements in the future, the league needs more funding from the EJL [the Estonia, FA] to make it more competitive to attract better players. Right now you have Flora, Levadia and maybe Paide and Kalju who have the chances for Europe. The rest are not so good, many still have part-time contracts, despite the league going 'fully pro' in 2020. The Premium Liiga lost two teams due to financial problems in 2022, so there's still so much work to do for the league to improve, for teams to be more competitive in Europe.

Who are the stars to watch out for in the Estonian league at the moment? Are there any players that will catch our eye in the future? Maybe even make a big-money move to one of the so-called bigger leagues in Europe?

Estonian Football Podcast: Many players are heading to Italy for youth football. Oliver Jurgens currently plays for Inter Milan and looks to be a real talent, as well as Martin Vetkal who's at Roma. You have Karl Hein who's just had a loan spell at Reading from Arsenal and Maksim Paskotsi who's at Tottenham. Those that are currently playing in Estonia, I'm just going to mention young players here: Danil Kuraksin for Flora, Robi Saarma for Paide. We could name so many more, but we'll just stick with two. It's difficult to say just how far these players will go, but it's fun to watch them play in Estonia.

Who is your favourite Estonian player and who is the best Estonian player to ever play the game? It can be the same answer of course.

Estonian Football Podcast: We have a different favourite player; one is Marten Kuusk who is playing for Ujpest in Hungary and the other is Vladislav Kreida who is currently at Flora, after his loan in Ukraine was paused due to Russia's war. The greatest Estonian football player is either Joel Lindpere or Ragnar Klavan – probably Klavan as he's won Estonian footballer of the year seven times, which is a record.

Estonian football at an international level, how are they looking in regard to challenging for qualification for a major international tournament in the next few years? I know a few years ago they played in a play-off match against the Republic of Ireland and lost, so that was close, but they haven't been close since. Is there any hope

for Estonia to be playing in a European Championships or even a World Cup anytime soon?

Estonian Football Podcast: Probably not. They have a long way to go; they have improved over the last 12 months but more improvement is needed. With the World Cup increasing to 48 teams for the next tournament, then of course it's possible. And with the Nations League a new route to qualification, it's possible. As we said before, the EJL need to fund more for Estonian football, and until that happens, it will be difficult.

Finally, do you think we will ever see FC Lantana again, and can you tell our readers one or maybe more than one interesting fact about Estonian football?

Estonian Football Podcast: FC Lantana are done, they are bankrupt. Interesting fact: pretty much anyone can compete in the Estonian Cup, even under-19 teams. An example in this year's competition, Flora's under-19s lost 14-0 to Flora's first team and Tulevik beat their under-21s 10-0. It's a crazy league, there is usually some kind of nonsense going on in the background and sometimes it's just laughable. It's a predictable league, but at the same time it's not.

8.

FC Amkar Perm (Russia)

FOUNDED IN 1993, FC Amkar Perm were based in the Russian city of Perm. They took their place in the Russian professional league in 1995, finally making it to the Russian Premier League in 2004. The club was originally formed to represent the Perm Inorganic Fertiliser Company. This is where the name of the football club came from, as the word 'Amkar' is a translation of two Russian words, *amiak*, meaning ammonia and *karbamid*, meaning carbamide. These are the two substances that were used in the fertiliser plant.

The club's first team mainly consisted of employees when they first started off in 1994, but they soon started adding quality to their team from other surrounding cities, with former professionals joining the club. In their first season they swept up every trophy they could win in the region of Perm, including the league and cup double. The next year they applied to join the Russian leagues and got accepted. They were included in the Russian third tier in 1995.

Joining the professional leagues didn't seem to halt FC Amkar Perm's success and with the help of some former Zveda Perm players, the club qualified for the second tier by coming second in the sixth group of the third tier (Russian football has a very complicated tier to tier promotion and relegation system). In 1998 they played the biggest game in their history to date when they hosted Spartak Moscow at their Zvezda Stadium, in the Russian Cup. The sold-out stadium saw 25,000 witness Amkar beating Spartak 1-0. That year the club finished top, scoring 100 goals in the process and reaching the Russian First Division.

Amkar finished respectably in the top six in their first four seasons in the division. They even managed a cup run in 2001/02, but lost 1-0 to CSKA Moscow in the semi-final. It was only a matter of time before the club realised their ambition to get to the Russian Premier Division and their time finally came when they had to beat Fakel Voronezth on the final day of the 2003 season. Amkar took their chance, which saw them promoted to Russia's top tier for the first time in their history.

Adjusting to the dizzy heights of the Russian Premier Division, Amkar finished a respectable 11th (2004), 12th (2005) and 13th (2006). In the off-season, before their debut in the Russian Premier League Amkar had recruited players of high quality, including the likes of Vladimir Leonchenko and Andrei Lavrik. They even went on another cup run, but once again were beaten in the semi-final by Khimki, losing 2-0 on aggregate.

In 2005 they had an entertaining season, with plenty of goals and memories made for the Amkar fans, including wins against Russian giants Zenit St Petersburg and Dynamo Moscow. They may also remember a loss to Lokomotiv Moscow when they were 3-0 up at half-time only to throw it away in the second half and lose 4-3. But Amkar were not really known for their goalscoring, rather their defending. In 2006 the club went 15 matches without conceding a goal. This record was then beaten by them in 2007 when they went 17 games without conceding a goal. This helped the club qualify for the Europa League and would ultimately go down as the most successful season in the club's 26-year history.

In the second round of the Europa League, they met English club Fulham. They lost the first leg 3-1 at Craven Cottage and won the home leg 1-0 but unfortunately this meant they went crashing out early on and so their European adventure ended. The club also struggled domestically and were in danger of being relegated from the Premier Division. Survival was achieved, thanks to the return of head coach, Rashid Rakhimov.

Once again, in 2010, the club reached the semi-final of the Russian Cup, under unusual circumstances. They had received a bye in the quarter-finals after FC Moscow were dissolved. Amkar lost in a penalty shoot-out to Zenit St Petersburg after a 0-0 draw in normal time. The club struggled again in the league but managed a 14th-place finish to secure their spot in the Russian Premier Division yet again, but it came at a price. Martin Kushev, an Amkar cult hero and the club's top goalscorer in the Premier Division, announced his retirement from the game.

The next season saw Amkar volunteer themselves to join the Russian First Division, stating that due to financial circumstances they could not compete in the Premier Division. The club's supporters rallied and tried to get support and funds together. They didn't succeed but the introduction of a new chairman, Gennady Shilov, replacing outgoing chairman, Valery Chuprakov, saw the club retract their request to join the First Division and continue to play in the Premier Division.

They gave younger players a chance and were competitive without ever really challenging for the title. The club stabilised over the next few years until 2018, when the Russian Football Union revoked FC Amkar Perm's licence to compete in the Premier Division for the 2018/19 season. This meant they could not compete in the Russian National League either and on 18 June 2018 club president Gennadi Shilov announced the club was dissolving.

However, the club and their fans have now created a phoenix club, one that plays in the lower leagues of Russian football.

I spoke to Alex McGuinness, an Irishman who was born in Perm so naturally has grown attached to the club that represents his town of birth. He even runs a Twitter account to promote the club and all their matches and club news, such is his dedication and support for the newly founded Russian club.

How did you start following Amkar Perm?

Alex McGuinness: My local team is Dundalk and when Dundalk played Zenit in the UEL in 2016 I grew an interest in Russian football after I came back from Russia. [Alex went to the away game v Zenit]. I knew I was born in Perm so I started supporting Amkar Perm. They were in the Premier League at the time and were a good mid-table side with a strong defence.

Who is your favourite player to have played in the red and black of Amkar Perm FC?

Alex: My favourite player is probably Belorukov, who was a strong defender and a great servant for the club for so many years and probably Amkar's most famous ever player.

What has been the best thing about following Amkar Perm FC?

Alex: The fan base: the fans are truly so passionate about the club and they are the reason why Amkar is back from the dead.

Where do you see the club in five or ten years?

Alex: With the way things are looking at the moment, with Amkar being state-owned, I hope they can return to the

Premier League in a few years, and if not, hopefully the second tier of Russian football. It's exciting.

Do you think the club will ever get back to the level they were at before they dissolved?
Alex: Yes, Amkar can get back to the top, [they are] not the first club to go through this. Arsenal Tula for example have fallen this badly and still got back to the Premier League.

If there was one thing you could add to the club right now, what would it be and why?
Alex: I dream of a new stadium as the current stadium only holds 17,000 but if they would renovate the stadium that would be great; but if I was realistic, it would be a healthy, good future for Amkar.

Finally, can you tell me an interesting fact about the history of the club?
Alex: When Amkar Perm formed, Perm was known to have a good trade partnership with the city of Milan in Italy and this gave Amkar its famous red and black stripes. Amkar became Perm champions, which led them to climb the Russian leagues to the Premier League, where they stayed for 18 years.

9.

Kayseri Erciyesspor (Turkey)

KAYSERISPOR – the club which later became Kayseri Erciyesspor – had a strange start to life. The club was formed in a merger between three clubs in the city of Kayseri, in 1965. Those three clubs were Erciyesspor, Sanayispor and Ortaanadoiuspor. The reason for this merger was the request of the then Turkish Football Federation president, Orhan Sefik Apak, to all amateur clubs to merge in their respective cities to form one big club to represent their city in the 2. Lig (Second Division of Turkish football). The new club, Kayserispor, submitted the relevant paperwork, officially being founded on 1 July 1966.

They competed in the 2. Lig in 1966/67. Their first manager was Erdogan Gurhan and the club competed in the Beyaz Grup (White Group). The other group was known as the Red Group. The club's first official goal was scored by Yener, against Ankara Toprakspor. Their first season saw the club finish in ninth place, with nine wins, nine draws and 12 losses, scoring 21 goals and conceding 33. That season, the White Group was won by Bursaspor, while the Red Group was won by Mersin Idman Yurdu, who were champions of the league that season and gained promotion.

After a few seasons competing in 2. Lig, in the 1972/73 season they finally gained promotion to the Turkish First Football League, winning the White Group and beating the Red Group champions Adana Demirspor to become the champions. The club's first season in the top division saw them finish 11th out of 16 clubs.

The following season was not as successful, in fact it was as bad as it could get, with the club finishing rock bottom of the league. It meant they were relegated back to 2. Lig once again. The following season saw them reach the semi-finals of the Turkish Cup (Turkiye Kupasi), beating giants Galatasaray in the quarter-finals, but losing in the semi-finals to Adana Demirspor. The 1978/79 season was also an entertaining one for the Kayserispor fans as they saw their club score 66 goals, playing a brand of football under their manager Tamer Kaptan that was pleasing on the eye.

The club wouldn't stay long in the Turkish Second Division and gained promotion in the 1978/79 season via the play-off system. They had come runners-up in White Group and faced Ankaragucu, who they beat 3-0 to gain promotion once again to the Turkish First Football League. But, again, their time in the top division was short-lived, and they were relegated straight back down the following season, finishing 15th. Amazingly that season the club had only lost one game at home, and that was to eventual league champions Trabzonspor, 1-0. But it was the seven 0-0 draws that were to be their downfall in the end, and their lack of goals, 15 in total that season, that would resign them to playing their football in 2. Lig once again.

It wouldn't be until the 1984/85 season that they would gain promotion for the third time in their history, winning Group B (the 2. Lig had now been split into three groups, having been split into four for a few seasons) and becoming overall league champions. But again, they were relegated the following season, coming rock bottom.

They competed in the Second Division up until the 1988/89 season, when they were relegated to the Turkish

Third Football League. This was no surprise as the club had been a complete circus act, setting a record for most managers in a single season, hiring and firing no less than eight of them. It took two seasons before they were promoted back to the Turkish Second Division (1990/91) and they gained back-to-back promotions, winning Group C in 1991/92 and moving up to the Turkish First Football League once again. Their first season back proved to be a successful one, when compared to their last stay in the Turkish top flight, as they finished 12th out of 16, beating the drop by three points. The 1993/94 season was much the same, with the club finishing 12th out of 16 again and narrowly staying out of the relegation places by three points.

The 1994/95 season saw the expansion of the league to 18 clubs and Kayserispor finished in a respectable 11th position. The 1995/96 campaign proved to be too much for them and they finished inside the relegation places, 16th, just two points away from safety and saw their stay in the Turkish First Division come to an end. But in true Kayserispor style, the club managed to get promoted back straight away the following season, and were then relegated in the 1997/98 season, this time on goal difference – Genclerbirligi and Gaziantepspor both had minus-five goal differences, a much better figure than Kayserispor's minus-18. It was their defence that let them down that season, as they conceded 60 goals in that campaign.

They would remain in the Second Division for the rest of the decade and wouldn't be promoted to the Turkish Super Lig until the 2003/04 season. The following season, 2004/05, they finished 14th out of 18, avoiding the relegation places by two points. But that wasn't the most bizarre or most shocking thing to happen that campaign.

Before the start of the 2004/05 season, in a bizarre turn of events, the two teams in Kayseri decided to switch their names, their managers and even their chairmen. The club now became known as Kayseri Erciyesspor. They even changed their kit colour to blue and black. This is where it gets a bit confusing in the history of this club. While Kayserispor continued to play in the Turkish Premier Division, Kayseri Erciyesspor were in the 2. Lig, trying to reach the heights of their city rivals and in the 2005/06 season both were competing in the Turkish Premier Division, with Kayserispor finishing fifth, gaining entry into the Intertoto Cup second round, while Kayseri Erciyesspor (the club we have been looking at) finished a respectable tenth. Both clubs possessed prolific goalscorers with Kayserispor's Gokhan Unal finishing the season as the league's top scorer with 25, and Kayseri Erciyesspor's Cenk Isler finishing third with 20 goals. The games between the two were tight affairs with Kayseri Erciyesspor coming out on top, drawing 0-0 with their city rivals at home and beating them 2-1 away.

The following season saw Kayseri Erciyesspor relegated from the Turkish top division, finishing 17th out of the 18 clubs. Their city rivals finished in a comfortable fifth place and also took the bragging rights on each of the matches they played against each other that season, winning 1-0 at home and 4-0 away. It wasn't all bad for Kayseri Erciyesspor that season as the club managed to go on a cup run, all the way to the final, where they lost to Besiktas, 1-0, when Brazilian striker Bobo scored in extra time.

It wasn't until the 2012/13 season that the club would gain promotion back to the Turkish Premier Division and despite some heavy defeats, including a 5-0 thrashing at the hands of Trabzonspor at home, they managed to avoid relegation, finishing 14th. On top of the success of staying up, their city rivals, Kayserispor, were relegated that season, finishing rock bottom in 18th. Kayseri Erciyesspor also held bragging rights, defeating Kayserispor 4-0 and drawing 1-1 in the matches played against them. But once again, Kayseri Erciyesspor failed to build on their success and were relegated in the 2014/15 season.

This was the beginning of the end of the club. They finished 17th that season and their collapse after that was dramatic and resulted in four consecutive relegations, leaving the club in the Turkish Regional Amateur League for the start of the 2018/19 season. However, the club withdrew from the league that season and therefore became no more.

Turkish football fan, Emin Urcan was the man who informed me about Kayseri and assured me it was the most interesting story that I would read about in Turkish football history. He wasn't wrong. I asked him a few questions about them and Turkish football.

Firstly, thank you for directing me to the story of Kayseri Erciyesspor. Such an interesting story. What is your opinion on the club?

Emin Urcan: In my humble opinion, they were the second team of Kayseri, especially if we were to talk about the last 14 years. Except for the 2013/14 and 2014/15 seasons, when Kayseri Erciyesspor were the better side. Kayserispor were relegated in the former season, and jumped back as 1. Lig champions the following season. Coincidentally, the former (2013/14) was Erciyesspor's first season back in the top flight after seven years of absence, and in the latter (2014/15), they were relegated to 1. Lig.

How do Turkish football fans see that club? Are they missed or were they hated?

Emin: I'm not exactly sure about the answer, but the only place they're mentioned nowadays is the history books, occasionally as a sidenote. As for the rivalries, other than the Kayseri derby with Kayserispor (which was not that prominent compared to that of the local derbies in, say, Adana or İzmir), the other rivalry was with Sivasspor. It was mainly due to the 1967 Kayseri Atatürk Stadium disaster, which claimed 43 lives. The animosity, apparently, had died off by the 1990s. Last but not least, though it is a personal theory at best, I think they had an antipathy towards Beşiktaş because of the outcome in the 2006/07 Turkish Cup Final, in which the Kayseri side lost – they nevertheless made it to the UEFA Cup (despite having been relegated!) owing to the Black Eagles already qualifying for the Champions League as runners-up of the league behind Fenerbahçe, who won the league in what was their 100th anniversary.

There have been quite a few Turkish clubs that have dissolved over the years and a number recently. In your opinion, what is the reason for this?

Emin: In most cases, it is down to financial instability, even more so in recent years as a consequence of the hyperinflation of Turkish lira. Sometimes it occurs thanks to a dodgy person/people. Other times, it is due to broken promises and failed projects. It does not help that the results on the pitch are atrocious, either. I'd also wager that all this happens partly because of the incompetent people in charge of Turkish football. I firmly believe we need a major overhaul in our football, starting with a brand new football league pyramid and reducing the number of professional clubs and introducing semi-professionalism to Turkish football. I could go on and on.

Turkish football is always seen as a bit crazy from outside of Turkey. Are the games that intense with the fans or is it all built up for show? There seem to be more fierce rivalries in Turkey due to the closeness of major cities.

Emin: It is definitely not for the spectacle. The people here are, I cannot stress this enough, utterly passionate – regardless of sport. The intensity you'd see or witness as an outsider happens for two reasons. The first is that the match in question could be a derby (or a big match) of sorts. You would know about the intercontinental derby between Galatasaray and Fenerbahçe. You should definitely watch an İzmir derby. Although the main culprits, Göztepe and Karşıyaka, haven't faced each other since 2016 because of differing fortunes, a match in 1981 saw 80,000 fans turn up at İzmir Atatürk Stadium. This is a Guinness World Record for a non-top-flight game in terms of attendance. I should also point out that [at the time of replying] Altay and Göztepe played each other just last Friday, with Altay winning the match via a last-gasp winner from the 37-year-old Portuguese stalwart Marco Paixão. The second reason behind this passion on the pitch, as well as the terraces, is that the match in question might be crucial for a league title, European places, promotion/relegation. Occasionally, controversial moments before, during or after a match could well lead to that.

I have searched far and wide to try and find out why the two clubs swapped names, managers and chairmen and still don't know why they did it. Is this a mystery of Turkish football or can you explain why it happened?
Emin: I can't really answer that. Maybe it is a mystery. Still not sure at all.

Finally, in your opinion, is there a problem in Turkish football in regards the bigger clubs getting bigger and richer and leaving the smaller clubs behind? Turkish football has always been dominated by a select few clubs. What do you believe can be done to make sure that there

are no more 'Forgotten Clubs' in the future of Turkish football?

Emin: There definitely is a problem in that regard, and it is just the tip of the iceberg if you look at it from a wider angle. I believe wholeheartedly that the TFF, our football federation, applies double standards, especially for those in the top two tiers (and more specifically, the Big 4 [Besiktas, Galatasaray, Fenerbahçe and Trabzonspor]). The fact that we have only had six different top-flight winners since 1959, when the Süper Lig was established, speaks volumes about the misfortune of others. Gaziantepspor, for example, were so close to winning the whole bloody thing in the 2000/01 season – they finished third that year. Look where they are now. Gone!

Anyway, with the current board (and the government!) in charge, I can't see a change happening anytime soon. Unless lower league and amateur clubs are funded by the TFF, not many of them will see the light at the end of the tunnel. As I had noted before, we need a major overhaul in our football pyramid. Do you know how many clubs play in our top four flights (which also happen to be professional)? There are 133! (Including Kastamonuspor, who had to withdraw from 2. Lig due to floods that took place there and were subsequently reprieved from relegation.) The next highest number I know is the one in Russia, with 112 clubs in its top three professional divisions. Even England has only 92!

10.

Dangerous Darkies/Mpumalanga Black Aces FC (South Africa)

THE DANGEROUS Darkies were founded in 1991 and were based in Nelspruit, a city in north-eastern South Africa. The city of Nelspruit is now known as Mbombela and was one of the host cities of the 2010 FIFA World Cup. The club competed in the National Soccer League (NSL) which at the time was South Africa's top football league, until it merged with the National Professional Soccer League (NPSL). That organisation had been a league for black players from 1973–77, then it merged with the National Football League (NFL) which had previously only had white players compete in it. In the NPSL, clubs were known as 'white' or 'black' teams. The 'white' teams were allowed have only three black players play for them at the time. There was then another split as clubs formed their own league, known as the National Soccer League.

The Dangerous Darkies only played in the league for two years and weren't that successful. In their first year, 1991, they came 19th out of 24. But they did avoid relegation to the second tier and that was their main objective in their debut season.

The next season saw the Dangerous Darkies finish bottom, 22nd out of the 22 teams that competed. That was it with regards to top-flight football for the Dangerous Darkies and they merged with another club in Mpumalanga,

Witbank Aces. The merger saw the renaming of the club to Mpumalanga Black Aces FC. This is their complicated story.

They were originally formed back in 1937, by dairy workers. They were a relatively unsuccessful club with very few honours to showcase. They had won minor trophies, such as the BP Top Eight Cup in 1980, the Bob Save Super Bowl in 1993, and the Premier Soccer League (PSL) promotion/relegation play-offs in both 2008/09 and the 2012/13 seasons. They only competed in the PSL for four seasons and in the 1996/97 season, when they were known as the Witbank Aces, they came 18th out 18. This saw them relegated to the National First Division.

It wasn't until the 2009/10 season that the club, now known as the Mpumalanga Black Aces, played in the PSL again. They barely stayed up, finishing 15th out of 16 clubs. This meant they had to play in a promotion/relegation play-off, which they won and staved off another relegation.

The following season was full of drama for the wrong reasons for the Black Aces. On 20 September the club sacked their manager, Aiki Ayoimamtis, after a poor run of results. Neil Tovey was brought in to try to help the club avoid relegation. He didn't do any better and he was sacked on 24 December, Christmas Eve. Paul Dolezar was brought in as the third manager that season for the Black Aces. The Serbian failed to turn it around and he was also sacked, on 22 February. The club never recovered and finished bottom of the pile in 16th place. This saw them relegated to the National First Division once again.

The Black Aces didn't exactly set the National First Division alight, finishing 13th out of 16 clubs. They would have finished even lower had Carara Kicks had an 18-point deduction that season for fielding an ineligible player, getting relegated in the process. But 2012/13 saw a huge improvement from the Black Aces and they finished in third place, earning them a shot at promotion via the play-off tournament. The Black Aces won it and returned to the South African Premier League once again.

The 2013/14 season was marred by yet more controversy as several games were boycotted by various clubs at the start of the season, leaving some clubs playing more than others. The Black Aces didn't care in the end though as they had achieved what they set out to do, and that was return to the top tier of South African football.

The club didn't disappoint in the 2013/14 season on their return to the South African Premier League, finishing a respectable seventh out of 16. They just missed out on a CAF Confederation Cup qualification spot by three points. The next season saw another decent finish, with the club coming tenth out of 16. However, the 2015/16 season proved to be one of their best, finishing fourth and equal on points with Platinum Stars who finished third and in the CAF Confederation Cup qualification spot. Both teams were level on goal difference as well as points and so it went down to goals scored and unfortunately for the Black Aces, they had scored four fewer than their rivals. (Black Aces scored 37, while Platinum Stars scored 43.) Interestingly, Platinum Stars had one point deducted that season for playing an ineligible player, Siyabonga Zulu. Had it been a harsher penalty, things would have panned out differently. The other highlight of that season for the Black Aces was Collins Mbesuma becoming their top goalscorer for the season, with 14.

That was to be the end of the Black Aces, or at least that name as the club were bought by Cape Town City, who were owned by John Comitis, and relocated from Mbombela Stadium to Cape Town Stadium. Cape Town City had been founded back in 1962 but went bust a few years back and this was Comitis's attempt to resurrect them. His plan worked as Cape Town City are still an established South African Premier Division side or a DSTV Premiership side if you want to be entirely correct.

I spoke to Hugo who runs the African Insider Twitter account, and he was able to tell me a little bit about the Black Aces, more about their story and gave me an insight into how South African football is run.

First, thank you for taking the time out to answer my questions. Tell me, what is it about African football that you love so much?

Hugo: African football is an expression of pure passion, channelled into one medium. Unlike Europe, Asia or the Americas, there isn't much money in it. The support is genuine, and the players and staff are approachable.

The Dangerous Darkies, or the Black Aces were a strange club to cover in that they never really won anything other than a few promotions. I tried researching it but couldn't find any fan base or even a blog about them. Did they have a fan base at all?

Hugo: The Black Aces had a dedicated fan base, being one of the oldest teams in the country. The team folded many times, most notably in 2002, contemporarily during the advent and propagation of the internet in South African circles. You won't find many blogs for a dead club.

In my research, point deductions, player ineligibility and clubs boycotting games seemed to happen a lot. Is this just a feature in South Africa or is it widespread in all of the African league?

Hugo: It's common everywhere, even in Europe. It's inversely proportional to teams' funds. When money is on the line for players who need it, clubs will take whatever measures necessary, professional or not. Among the rich, fully professional clubs, the mindset exists but it is seldom seen in the top African leagues, minus Linafoot (which itself has a disparity issue).

The Black Aces are now known as Cape Town City and still play in the South African League. Have they improved on what they once were?

Hugo: As a brand, 100 per cent. They're also producing a lot of youth thanks to collaborations with Manchester City, who have been touted to add them to their CFG [City Football Group] soon. However, they face staunch competition with Stellenbosch, local rivals owned by one of the world's richest men.

Can you give the readers any interesting facts on South African football that they may never have heard before?

Hugo: Honestly, I wouldn't know what's considered interesting or not! How about this: Vincent Julius was the first black player to play in the South African NFL. Other teams protested, but it was eventually permitted to avoid further economic and sporting sanctions on the country.

Africa is such a big continent, with so many nations and so many national leagues. In your opinion which leagues are the best for quality, entertainment, and just outright madness?

Hugo: For median quality, the Botola Pro 1 [Moroccan league] is there. Top-class coaches, stadia and players. Egypt comes a close second but too many fan-less company teams spoil the broth. One for disport would be Ghana's PL. The Premier Soccer League is also of high standard.

Finally, there are so many clubs I could have picked from the continent of Africa to cover regarding them being

a 'Forgotten Club', and I do cover one more club from Africa in the book. But in your opinion, why are there so many 'Forgotten Clubs' in Africa? Is it purely a financial thing or are there other reasons?

Hugo: Finances and colonialism form the antecedent for 'Forgotten Clubs'. If a club doesn't have enough money, they fold. If a Second Division club has money but has an impatient owner, they buy another club's league place. If a benefactor is bored, he will stop funding a club and it dies. Same with colonialism. Once a specialised population goes (such as the King's Army Rifles in East Africa, Rhodesians, Pied-Noires, Lusophone settlers), the clubs created that serve their disparate communities just cease to function.

11.

La Paz FC (Bolivia)

LA PAZ Football Club was founded on 30 May 1989, under the name Atletico Gonzalez. Founder, owner and president of the club was Mauricio Gonzalez, who named the club after his father, Walter Gonzalez. More about Mauricio Gonzalez will be revealed later, but he was keen to have a successful and competitive football club in La Paz. The club wore the colours red and blue, which emulated that of Spanish club, Barcelona. Their colours had a more in-depth meaning to them, with each colour representing something. Red symbolised the club's passion and love for sport, while blue represented the perennial blue skies over the city of La Paz as well as showing the loyalty of their fans. The white the club wore in their shorts and socks as well as in their away kits, symbolised the snowy mountaintops of Mount Illimani.

They would play their home matches at the Hermando Siles Stadium in La Paz, a location that has been the centre of dispute due to its high altitude, with other club sides and international sides claiming it gives Bolivia, and it gave La Paz, an unfair advantage. In fact, it is recorded as the highest point at which football is played in a stadium. Because of this and the ambitions the club had, their motto was '*Plus Alus*', which translates as 'Higher'.

It wasn't until 2003 that the club finally gained promotion to the Liga del Futbol Profesional Boliviano,

the top division in the Bolivian football pyramid. They did
so by winning the Simon Bolivar Cup, a competition for
clubs from around the country aiming to gain entry to the
top flight. La Paz defeated Real Santa Cruz in the final.
The first leg of the tie ended in a 2-2 draw: La Paz took
the lead with a goal from Rodney Porcel in the 19th minute
only for Santa Cruz to equalise in the 32nd minute thanks
to a goal from Justiniano. It didn't take long for La Paz to
retake the lead, as they did so in the 36th minute with a goal
from Alex Vallejos. They took their advantage into the half-
time break, but Santa Cruz equalised early in the second
half when Cespedes struck in the 47th minute. It remained
2-2 and it would go down to the second leg to decide who
would win the cup and gain promotion. The second game
wasn't as exciting as the first and after 90 minutes it ended
0-0. And so it went to a penalty shoot-out in which La Paz
came out 5-4 winners. It was La Paz's goalkeeper, Gustavo
Gois de Lira, who scored the winning spot kick and so in
2004 they were to compete in the Bolivian Premier League
for the first time in their history.

The club's first season in the Bolivian Premier Division
was one that surprised a lot of people as they finished seventh
in the first half of the competition, known as the Opening
Tournament. This was won by Bolivar, who topped the
12-club league. La Paz had opened the campaign with a
2-0 win away to Central Union at the IV Centenary on 15
February. Their second game, another away game on 22
February against Wilsterman at the Felix Capriles, ended
with a 5-1 defeat and brought the '*Azulgranas*' back down
to earth. This, along with 'the Engineers', was one of La
Paz FC's nicknames.

Their first official home game in the top flight ended in
defeat to Bolivar, 2-0. It was technically a home match for
both sides as they shared the huge 42,000-seater stadium,

the Hernando Siles. Because of La Paz's seventh-place finish, they entered Group A in the second half of the season, but they struggled to find form and finished bottom of the group.

The 2005/06 season saw the league format change, with three tournaments to be competed in that year. They were the Adaptation Tournament, the Opening Tournament and the Closing Tournament. The Adaptation Tournament was a simple league format, where each team played each other home and away. Twelve teams competed and the winner would qualify for the 2006 Copa Libertadores as the number one ranked Bolivian club. La Paz were seventh in the final placings.

The Opening Tournament was in a two-group format, Group A and Group B. Both groups consisted of six teams, with the top three in each group qualifying for an extra mini-tournament, the Hexagonal Final. There, each team would play each other home and away with the team who came out top winning the title and qualification for the 2007 Copa Libertadores. La Paz competed in Group B and finished second with 19 points. They only finished behind Bolivar, who didn't lose a game. It meant La Paz would compete in the Hexagonal Final, where they finished fourth in the group.

With one more tournament to go, La Paz were feeling confident they could do well in the Closing Tournament. It had the same format as the Opening Tournament, with all 12 clubs competing against each other twice, home and away, with the top team after 22 games declared the champions. However, it was a disappointing end to the season for La Paz, who finished 12th out of the 12 clubs. They finished eighth in the overall standings, which were calculated from all three tournaments, meaning they would compete in the top flight the following season. It was clear that La Paz wanted to progress and start to challenge at the top of the table, or at least try to win one of the tournaments that were on offer.

The Opening Tournament in 2007 saw them finish third in their group, behind Real Potosi and Bolivar. This gave them confidence going into the Closing Tournament and it showed in the group stages when they finished top of Group B and qualified for the final stage. They finished second, just behind San Jose, setting up a two-legged final to decide who would be crowned champions. The first leg was played in La Paz and the two sides could not be separated, drawing 2-2. The second leg, played on 12 December 2007 at the Jesus Bermudez Stadium, was a tight affair, with both teams going for victory. In the end San Jose triumphed, winning the game 1-0 and 3-2 on aggregate. It meant that to qualify for the 2008 Copa Libertadores, La Paz had to beat Bolivar in a two-legged affair. The first leg was played at the Felix Capriles stadium and La Paz, the away team, won 2-1. A draw in the second leg would be enough to qualify them for their first South American Cup, but they did even better, winning the second leg by the same scoreline as the first, 2-1.

Their run in the 2008 Copa Libertadores ended in the first round when they were beaten by Mexican club Atlas, 2-1 on aggregate. It was their first taste of continental football, and they were determined to have another opportunity to play at that level. And they reached their goal after finishing runners-up in the Opening Tournament 2008, only behind University. They continued their good form that season, finishing second in Group B in the Closing Tournament, behind Real Potosi. But in the next phase they were comprehensively beaten by Blooming, 6-2 on aggregate: La Paz had beaten Blooming 2-1 at home, but then lost the away leg 5-0. It didn't stop La Paz finishing off the season strongly and when they competed in the play-offs, they went into them full of confidence. After beating San Jose in the first phase, they went into the quarter-finals and faced Blooming. This time the result went in La Paz's favour, and they beat Blooming in a penalty shootout after they drew the tie 3-3 on aggregate.

The semi-finals saw them once again face San Jose, who had gotten through thanks to what we would call 'the back-door' system. Once again, La Paz beat San Jose, but this time it was decided on the away goals rule. In the first leg, La Paz played at home and drew 1-1. The second leg was also drawn, but this time it was 3-3, meaning La Paz went through. It set up a final meeting with Real Potosi. It was played over two legs and Potosi won both games, 1-0, winning the overall tie, 2-0 on aggregate. It meant La Paz had missed out on their first major title in Bolivia. However, they did end up top of the overall table through results from all the tournaments they played in during that season. Unfortunately, no title is given for such an accomplishment.

La Paz would compete in the 2009 edition of the Liberators Cup. They were drawn against Paraguayan club, Cerro Porteno, and it proved to be a mismatch as the Paraguayans beat their Bolivian opponents twice, 2-1 and 2-0 to progress to the next round. The 2009 domestic season saw La Paz finish sixth in the Opening Tournament. The Closing Tournament that year didn't see La Paz do anything of note, finishing bottom of Group B. It was a disappointing season for the club, and they failed to qualify for any continental tournaments for the following year.

The 2010 season saw a restructuring of the Bolivian football league system. The Opening Tournament was now played with two groups of six clubs, known as 'the Hex Groups', Hex A and Hex B. The top three of each group would then qualify for the Hex Winners' Group while the remaining six clubs, the bottom three of each group, would enter the Hex Losers' Group. La Paz competed in the Hex B and finished in fifth place.

This meant they would be competing in the Hex Losers' Group, where they finished fourth. It was another disappointing Opening Tournament and they were hoping to have a better Winter Tournament. This was a simple knockout, with each club drawn against another and then playing a two-legged match to decide who progressed. There was still a chance if you were defeated, as the two best losers would also go through as eight teams were needed to make up the quarter-finals. La Paz were drawn against San Jose, but unfortunately that is as far as they would get in the Winter Tournament. They drew the first leg 3-3 away from home on 16 June 2010. It set them up nicely for the second leg, that would be played on 19 June, but they were easily dispatched by San Jose who beat them 4-1 at the Hermando Siles Stadium, meaning La Paz were knocked out. Not only that, the heavy second-leg defeat meant they didn't qualify as one of the two best losers and so their Winter Tournament participation ended early. Their Closing Tournament performance didn't set the world alight either, as they finished tenth, winning just seven games, drawing five and losing ten. Another disappointing season for the *Azulgranas*, something that they would try to change in the following campaigns.

The 2011/12 season saw the league format change once again, with the season split into three tournaments, the Adaptation Tournament, the Opening Tournament and the Closing Tournament. La Paz were simply in decline at this point, both on and off the field and it showed with the last-place finish in the Adaptation Tournament. They fared a little better in the Opening Tournament, competing in Group B with five other clubs, but finished fifth and failed to qualify for the quarter-finals, missing out by one point, behind The Strongest. The Closing Tournament was now the only thing they could try and be successful in that season; however, that wasn't to be the case as they finished tenth in the table and so suffered the disappointment of another season that saw no qualification for a continental tournament.

Their poor performances throughout the season saw them finish 11th in the overall table, which meant they had to lay a promotion/relegation play-off against Destroyers. The tie would be played in a best out of three format. La Paz won the first game 6-1 at home, and many thought they would easily win the second game to secure their place in the Bolivian First Division for the next season. However, Destroyers came back fighting and won the second game at their home ground, the Ramon 'Tahuichi' Aquilera, 3-1. It came down to a tie-breaker leg, which was won by La Paz, 1-0, in the neutral venue, Felix Capriles. Argentinian Alejandro Molina scored the deciding goal in the 41st minute to secure La Paz FC's place in the Bolivian First Division for the following season.

But it was only a matter of time before La Paz would struggle to hold on to their top-flight status, and it didn't take long for them to be relegated. The season after their promotion/relegation play-off, 2012/13, the club found themselves finishing bottom of the table in both the Opening and Closing Tournaments. They were automatically relegated. It was the beginning of the end for La Paz, and financial difficulties finally caught up with them. With their relegation, their support dwindled, and their debts began to rise. It was all too much for the club and on 21 September 2013, the club dissolved and disappeared from Bolivian football, unable to compete even at the lower levels of the pyramid.

12.

Barra Futebol Clube (Brazil)

BARRA FUTEBOL Clube, also known as Barra de Teresopolis, or Barra for short, was a football club that competed in the Brazilian football league and was based in Rio de Janeiro state. The club was founded on 8 June 1939 and wore the colours red, black and white. They played their home games at the Pitucao in Teresopolis which had a capacity of 4,000.

The club played at amateur level until 1993 when they professionalised the football department, competing in the Campeonato Carioca Third Level, the third tier of the annual First Division competition for clubs in the state of Rio de Janeiro. The highest level the club ever reached was Serie C in the 1995 season – Serie C was the third level of the Brazilian football pyramid and 108 clubs competed in it, hoping to gain promotion to Serie B. However, only two clubs could go up out of the 108 and Barra began their long journey towards that desired destination on 27 August 1995.

The 108 clubs were split into 32 groups, some of which had four clubs competing while some only had three. Most groups were drawn to suit the geographical challenges that faced the clubs competing, as Brazil is one of the largest countries in land mass. Barra competed in Group 6, alongside three other clubs, Rio Branco-ES, Estrela de

Norte and Campo Grande. Both Rio Branco-ES and Estrela de Norte were from the Espirito Santo state, while Campo Grande were from the Rio de Janeiro state like Barra.

The first matches in the group saw Barra travel to Campo Grande, at the Estadio Italo del Cima on 27 August. Campo ran out 1-0 winners, while Estrela beat Rio Branco 3-1 in the other fixture on the same date. Barra's second game was another away match, this time to Rio Branco at the Estadio Kleber Andrade on 31 August. Barra picked up their first win of the group, triumphing 2-0, while Estrela and Campo Grande drew 1-1 at the Estadio Sumarie. Playing their first three games all from home, Barra travelled to the Estadio Sumarie to play Estrela on 3 September 1995. The game ended 1-1, leaving Barra on four points halfway through the group. Rio Branco picked up their first points by beating Campo Grande 3-1 at home. With their next three games all at home, Barra were in pole position to qualify from the group.

The fourth set of group games took place on 10 September, with Barra playing their first home game at the Pitucao. Their opponents were Campo Grande. They won the game 2-0, putting them top of the group. Estrela beat Rio Branco in the other game. The next fixture versus Rio Branco took place on 14 September. Many expected the home team to run out easy winners, but that wasn't the case as Rio Branco pulled off a surprise 1-0 win. It meant it went down to the last games of the group, and Barra would have to get at least a draw against Estrela. But they went one better and on 17 September they beat Estrela 1-0 to not only qualify for the next stage, but to top the group as well. Rio Branco also qualified for the next round, finishing second after beating Campo Grande 1-0 in their final group game. Barra had finished the group with a record of three wins, one draw and two losses.

It set up a second-phase match with Vitoria Futebol Clube. The first leg was played at the Pitucao and was an uneventful 0-0 draw. The second leg, played away at the Estadio Salvador Venancio da Costa, also ended in a draw, however it was 2-2, meaning Barra progressed to the third round courtesy of the away goals rule. There they would face Esporte Clube XV de Novembro, a club from the Sao Paulo region. However, they proved to be too strong for Barra. Despite a close first leg played at the Pitucao, ending 1-0 to Esporte, the second leg proved to be somewhat of a mismatch. At the Estadio Barao de Serra Negra, Barra were well beaten, 4-0 on the night and 5-0 on aggregate, to end their quest for promotion to Serie B. The club from Rio de Janeiro had done their state proud that year, being the number one ranked team from there, ahead of other clubs like America Football Club, Bayer Esporte Clube and of course Campo Grande.

It would be the only time Barra Futebol Clube would attempt to climb the Brazilian football pyramid and they ended back playing in their regional league of Rio de Janeiro, up until 1996, when the club closed their professional football department after a dispute over why they were not promoted to Serie C. They announced they had been dissolved and that was the end of Barra Futebol Clube.

13.

Sportivo Palermo (Argentina)

FOUNDED ON 18 May 1908, Sportivo Palermo took their name from the neighbourhood they were created in, Palermo. Their shirt colours derived from their crest, blue and white. They played amateur level football and in 1915 when they merged with Atlas Club, they joined the Argentine Football Federation. They began to compete in the Fourth Division of the Argentinian football pyramid and kept the name Sportivo Palermo, despite the fact Club Atlas were a successful amateur club. It was thought that the younger players of Sportivo Palermo were better in quality and so the name Club Atlas disappeared.

The club remained at amateur level after the merger and played their matches at Caseros in Buenos Aires. They competed in the Fourth Division (1915), Third Division (1916) and then the Segunda (1917–19). They won the 1917 Segunda Division championship, topping their group, Section A, North, with a record of 25 points and qualifying for the final tournament, which they won, gaining promotion to the Intermediate Division.

In 1920 they made the step up to the top flight and it was around this time the club decided to merge with another club. In fact, it was more of a takeover, as they absorbed Asociacion Atletico Eureka or Eureka Club as they were sometimes known. Eureka Club had played for three seasons, reaching the top flight of Argentinian football, only to be unable to complete the 1919 season. This resulted in them merging with Sportivo Palermo, a club who were right beside them in regards location and had, themselves, just been promoted.

Their first season in the top flight, in 1920, saw the club finish tenth. That season also saw them gain the unwanted record of having the biggest away defeat, losing 6-0 to Sportivo Almagro. It was also a season of controversy, with their league losing two clubs mid-season. Sportivo Palermo played in the Asociacion Argentina de Football (AFA), but there was another league in Argentina at the time known as the Asociacion Amateurs de Football (AAmF). Both Lanus and Sportivo Almagro left the AFA season to join the AamF League. Boca Juniors won the AFA that year whilst their fierce rivals, River Plate, won the AAmF.

The 1921 season saw Sportivo Palermo finishing ninth out of 11, although Platense did not finish the season. In 1922 Sportivo Palermo moved back to Palermo and that season saw a big improvement, to the extent that they nearly won their first title, only missing out by three points to Huracan. Sportivo Palermo finished second, above Boca Juniors, who were third. The 1923 season saw the club drop to 16th in what was now a 23-club league, expanded from the previous season, when there had only been 17 clubs competing. The new clubs to join the AFA included Palermo, who had been relegated from the AAmF league the season before. The other clubs to make their AFA debuts that season were All Boys, Argentina de Banfield and Sportivo Villa Urquiza. Argentino de Quilmes also returned to the top flight having been relegated in 1918.

For the 1924 season, Sportivo Palermo made the switch to the AAmF and finished 14th out of 24. The 1925 season saw them improve their position to seventh and then in 1926 they finished eighth. It would be the final season before the two associations merged and it saw several clubs being relegated, all from the AFA. In 1927 the Argentine Primera Division emerged, with 34 clubs competing in the league that year. There was also no relegation, so the bottom four teams, Tigre (31st), San Isidro (32nd), Estudiantes (33rd), and Porteno (34th) were given a reprieve. Sportivo Palermo finished a respectable eighth and San Lorenzo won the first Primera title.

The 1928 season saw the league expand to 36 clubs, with teams only playing each other once, as had been the case the previous season. Unlike the 1927 campaign, there was the possibility of relegation, and this happened to Liberal Argentino and Porteno. Sportivo Palermo finished 19th, winning 11, drawing 11 and losing 13. There was the weird scenario that any of the founders of Asociacion Amateur could not be relegated unless they finished in the bottom four twice – basically, they were given a lifeline, but it did not apply to the clubs that had competed in the AFA.

The 1929 season saw another restructure of the league format as many thought the 36-club league was too much and wasn't fair, as each team only played each other once in the season. Instead, the league would be split into two groups, from the now 35 clubs that competed. The top two of each group would then play each other in a final stage tournament to declare who was the overall Argentine Primera Division champion. However, the season was full of controversy, with numerous games being abandoned. Huracan, the defending champions, withdrew from eight games in total that season and finished 14th in their group. Sportivo Palermo competed in Group B, which was won by Boca Juniors, albeit they had to play a play-off match with San Lorenzo to decide who was the eventual winner of the group. After losing to Boca, San Lorenzo were to play a third-place play-off with River Plate but they failed to turn up to the match, so the game was awarded to River Plate. Sportivo Palermo finished ninth out of 17 in the group. The overall championship was won by Gimnasia y Esgrima, the first title in their history, although many will point to the fact that a lot of games were not played that season. Once again, there were no relegations, with Colegiales gaining promotion to the Primera.

Once again, a restructure of the format of the league took place and the Argentine Primera Division reverted to a 36-team league, with each club playing each other once. But like the previous year, match abandonments and clubs just not turning up to matches marred the season that saw Boca Juniors crowned champions. Sporting Palermo finished a miserable 31st. Relegation was brought back in, and Honor y Patria and Argentino del Sud were the unlucky clubs who finished 35th and 36th, with the latter setting one of the worst points tallies for a season ever seen in South American football, finishing with just four points.

It would seem there was a theme in Argentinian football that every season had to have some sort of controversy connected to it and 1931 was no different. Originally, 34 clubs were to compete in one league, like the previous season, but after 19 games had been played, a group of clubs decided to break away and form a new, professional league known as Liga Argentina de Football. It included 18 clubs in total, with Boca Juniors, River Plate, San Lorenzo, and Racing being among those to make the switch. However, Sportivo Palermo stayed with the AFA, which remained an amateur league. They finished eighth that season out of the 16 clubs that remained, winning six, drawing three and losing six. It was the 1932 season which turned out to be one of the worst in Sportivo Palermo's history as the club finished bottom of the AFA league, winning ten, drawing four and losing 18. They were relegated to the Segunda by just one point.

But without fail, there was a twist in the tail for Sportivo Palermo and once again they looked to merge with another club: this time it was Club Atletico Palermo. The merger lasted two seasons, with the club, under the name Atletico y Sportivo Palermo, finishing the 1933 season in 16th, winning just six games, drawing two and losing 11. The 1934 season was a huge disappointment, with the club finishing bottom in 23rd place. It was the final season in which the clubs played as a merged club and both went their separate ways, to the Third Division of the Argentinian pyramid.

But Sportivo didn't play in any more official tournaments until 1956, when they re-emerged to take part in the Primera D championship, also known as Tercera de Ascenso. The club didn't last long in the Primera D and were promoted instantly after finishing second to the champions, Almirante Brown.

Sportivo jumped up and down between the Third and Fourth Divisions, playing in the Third Division until 1960 when they were relegated, gaining promotion back to the Third Division in 1963 and remaining there until 1970, when they were relegated again. From the 1971 season up until 1983 they remained in the Fourth Division, before they left the Argentine Association and soon after dissolved as a football club.

14.

Atlanta Chiefs (USA)

ATLANTA CHIEFS were founded in 1967 and were one of the members of the National Professional Soccer League (NPSL) in which they competed for one season, before joining up with the United Soccer Association to form the North American Soccer League (NASL). They were backed and created by Dick Cecil, who was the vice president of the baseball side the Atlanta Braves, and was inspired by the excitement and interest the 1966 World Cup had created over in England. Of course, this was helped by the fact the host nation won the World Cup that year. Nevertheless, Cecil saw it as an opportunity to expand his sporting knowledge and help utilise the assets at his disposal, mainly the Atlanta Stadium, which he would use to host the Atlanta Chiefs' home games and create extra revenue. The Chiefs played there from 1967 to 1972, except for the 1970 season when they played at Tara Stadium. The club colours were red (home) and white (away).

In their first season, in the NPSL, the club finished fourth in the Eastern Division, meaning they failed to qualify for the play-offs. They averaged an attendance of 6,961. The following season proved to be a huge success and in the first season of the newly formed NASL, they were crowned champions, after coming first in the Atlantic Division and winning the play-offs against the San Diego Toros in front of a bumper crowd of 15,000 at

Atlanta Stadium. It was the first time a sports team had won a championship in the city of Atlanta and no other team would match that until 1995 when the baseball team Atlanta Braves won the World Series.

The 1969 season saw no play-off game being played due to the lack of clubs involved. Atlanta finished second overall in the regular season, but attendances had dropped by almost 50 per cent from the first season. In 1970 the club finished second in the Southern Division but failed to qualify for the play-offs. Attendances didn't improve either despite another solid season. However, they had a successful season in 1971, in which the club won the Southern Division and came runners-up in the play-offs. 1972 saw an increase in attendances because of the success in the previous season, but the club failed to emulate that success in what was a short season playing-wise. Only 14 games were played, with the Chiefs winning just five of them, drawing three and losing six, finishing third in the Southern Division.

The 1973 season saw the Atlanta Chiefs change names to the Atlanta Apollos after they were sold to the owners of the Atlanta Hawks and they played their home games at Grant Field. But this did not help the club succeed on the pitch and they experienced their worst ever season. The club were removed from the championship and the franchise folded.

That was it for the city of Atlanta as regards soccer until the football club was revived in 1979. The Colorado Caribous, a soccer team from Denver, were relocated to Atlanta, after being purchased by Ted Turner for around $1.5 million. Dick Cecil, the original owner of the Atlanta Chiefs, was also involved. Their first season back saw the club record 12 wins and 18 losses, finishing fourth in the Central Division, National Conference and failing to qualify for the play-offs. It did, however, see a big increase in average attendances from previous years, which was cause for optimism that this time the club would be successful. However, the 1980 season turned out to be terrible. While they finished fourth, the crowds dwindled as the public grew disinterested in a side that failed to produce on the pitch.

The following season saw the club improve dramatically and they secured the Southern Division title and qualified for the play-offs but only got to the first round. Despite the improvement and the slight increase in attendances, Turner saw a decrease in profits and decided to pull the plug on the franchise, seeing the club go out of existence for the second time in their history, and this time for good.

Although the Atlanta Chiefs were gone from the footballing world, the name 'Chiefs' would live on. Former Atlanta Chiefs player, Kaiser Montang, went home to South Africa and founded the football club, Kaiser Chiefs, taking his name and the club he played for in the USA and merging them. They, of course, are one of the more successful clubs in South Africa and are well known across the world. As such, indirectly, the Atlanta Chiefs are also responsible for the naming of the music band, the Kaiser Chiefs.

I spoke with Stephen Brandt, a soccer fanatic, who pointed me in the direction of the Atlanta Chiefs and assured me that I would find their story interesting. He was not wrong.

First of all, thank you for alerting me to the story of the Atlanta Chiefs. Can I ask, what do you find so interesting about that particular football club?
Stephen Brandt: Well, I wrote a long piece on them in *The Football Pink* many moons ago. The number of cultural references that come from this club is amazing. South

Africa's Kaiser Chiefs was named after them, when Kaiser Montang went back home. Plus that band was named from there. Jomo Sono also played with the Chiefs after the Colorado Caribous came to Atlanta. He went back home and renamed the Highlands Park club the Jomo Cosmos.

American soccer has such a stop-start history, with the NASL and so many soccer clubs coming and going. Can you tell me why that is, in your opinion?

Stephen: While the sport had been around since the 1800s, American businessmen didn't like anything that was foreign to them. Baseball was segregated until the 40s, the NFL was the same, and basketball was worse. So, no one really knew the sport. It was seen as a quick buck and that's it. Problem is, the league never followed up after Best, Marsh, Pele and Cruyff all came in. Apparently, the Philadelphia franchise had looked into bring in Maradona before he went to Barcelona. They also tried to get Kevin Keegan to come over. Once the money started running out, the clubs went poof.

So many world-class players have played in America: Pele, George Best, Johan Cryuff, Eusebio and more recently David Beckham, Kaka, Robbie Keane, Zlatan Ibrahimovic. Do you think this has been a good thing for American soccer or do you see it as those players just looking for a final payday?

Stephen: Great players go where the money is. How many great players came to England in the 90s? Many. It's just what the game is. Some have stayed. Beckham never left, Pele spent a lot of time here. Cruyff loved it. It's a good place for stars to go and not be hounded. Here a good-looking Brit is normal.

Atlanta itself has had a few teams over the years. Would that area be soccer mad or is it just a case of 'Let's see if we can get the public interested?'

Stephen: It's very soccer mad. It's basically had the sport at some level above university since the 1970s. Look what Atlanta United has done. It's in the south, and players from South America will love it there. It's why Toronto never does well, it's freaking cold in Canada.

In your opinion, is the MLS now11 better equipped to stop football clubs from dissolving or will this still be an issue for some MLS clubs?

Stephen: Well, we did see Chivas USA go under in the last ten years so it can happen. With the pandemic, I expect at least one more down the road to have to go bust.

So many stories to be told and the Atlanta Chiefs proved to be an interesting one, but can you tell me anything that you, yourself found out about them? Any interesting fact that you may have come across?

Stephen: There are a couple. Phil Woosman, who set the club up in its first time is one of many, many former Aston Villa players to come over to the NASL. Heck, the Portland Timbers team was basically the B squad of Villa. Also, the Chiefs beat Manchester City a couple of times, annoying future Crystal Palace manager Malcolm Allison.

The MLS now seems to be thriving, more and more people are taking an interest in it and there seem to be more clubs joining. Inter Miami and Austin FC are examples of newly joined clubs. How big do you think MLS can get?

Stephen: St Louis and Charlotte are the next two in line. I think it's fine right there. I'm sure MLS will look at Las Vegas and Phoenix later too.

This may sound like a negative question, but in the context of the book it must be asked. What football club do you think will be the next to dissolve in the United States, if any should, and why?

Stephen: Well, the Cosmos come and go so often I expect another era of them. With the pandemic, it'll be some small team in a lower league going poof.

15.

Galt FC (Canada)

FOUNDED IN 1881 (although it has been cited in some places that they were founded in 1882), the football club Galt FC was based in Ontario, Canada. Back in the early 1900s there was no national league that Galt FC competed in so they would go on tours to play their football matches. There was, however, the Ontario Cup, which they won on three occasions in their short history. The first success came in 1901 and was quickly followed up with a second success in the competition the next year. In fact, the club won the trophy on three occasions, all in a row as they picked up their third Ontario Cup in 1903. As a result of their success the club decided to go on a tour of Manitoba. In 25 days, they managed to win 16 of the 17 games they played, drawing the other one. Remarkably on that tour they only conceded two goals, scoring 46 in reply.

Again, this success didn't go unnoticed, and the club were chosen to represent Canada at the 1904 Olympic Games that were being held in St Louis, USA. Only having to play two games, both against American sides, they won them both comfortably, winning 7-0 against the Christiaan Brothers College and beating St Rose 4-0. John Gourlay captained the side that took home the gold medal for Canada. This success drew even more attention to soccer in Canada and a match against an English side touring Canada at the time, named the Pilgrims, was set up. The

Pilgrims were an amateur touring football side who would regularly visit Canada and the US to play. They were led by a man named Fred Milnes, who came from a wealthy family. This enabled him to sign only amateur forms when joining a football club, which enabled him to play for whoever he liked. He set up the Pilgrims FC and they spent most of their time playing in the US. This game, against Galt FC, had caught the imagination of the public and was dubbed 'the Championship of the World' by the media, after Galt's success in the Olympic Games. The game itself was played at Dickson Park in front of an estimated crowd of 3,500 and it ended in an exciting 3-3 draw.

As said before, there was no official championship in Canada at the time but that didn't stop the side from declaring themselves champions when they defeated Montreal Westmount in two games in 1905. The first game was held in Montreal on 13 June when Galt ran out 2-1 winners. The second fixture, which took place in Galt on 3 July, saw Galt win 2-1 again. In both games, the same names appeared on the scoresheet for the Ontario side. Fred Steep and Alexander Hall both scored one goal each in both games.

Unfortunately, that's where the story ends with Galt FC, and the club disappeared after 1910. During my research I found an excellent article written by Canadian soccer history blogger, Andy Wilson, with details of all the players that played for Galt FC and even the years they played, with details on some of the players.

I interviewed Andy, who is the creator and editor of the Canadian Soccer History Archives and online magazine *Canadian Soccer Sentinel*; he gave me an insight to this old club and Canadian soccer in general. He is constantly promoting the game over in Canada and his online magazine is a great read, if you have an interest in football in different leagues and countries around the world. Andy knows his stuff. Here is what he had to say.

Thank you for directing me in the way of Galt FC and their history. Can I ask, how or when did you find out about them?

Andy Wilson: When I moved over to Canada from England in 2009 I was trying to find out more about Canadian soccer and was astounded to find that the history was huge and yet it was virtually impossible to find anything. I started to research it myself and came across them purely by chance during one of my scattergun searches.

You clearly have a passion for soccer, but is it hard to maintain that passion in a country where it is not the dominant sport?

Andy: My passion for football will always be there. Being born and raised on Merseyside it is ingrained in you. My first ever match was standing on the Kop at Anfield and my first wage packet bought my first season ticket to our local club, Tranmere Rovers, so it will always be my passion. The passion for soccer in Canada is there and is only growing. The emergence of the Canadian men's team and the gold medal for the women have helped immeasurably to grow the fan base. Put that with the formation of the Canadian Premier League and the fan base is growing. Hockey will always be the number one sport but football is huge.

Canadian football is on the up, with the foundation of the Canadian Premier League in 2019 proving that. Where do you see the sport going in the next few years and what do you think can be done to get more people involved in it?

Andy: One big hope is that the women's game gets a professional league. It's such a shame that we only get to see our top women's players on TV for the most part. Personally, my hope is for solid growth of a pyramid. We have step one with the CPL and MLS but no step two and only step three leagues in Ontario and Quebec. British Columbia launched a step three league last summer and step four and below is massive on a local level.

Canada are co-hosting the 2026 World Cup, so I can only imagine the excitement that is building up over there. What can we expect from Canada as a host country and do you have hopes that the national team can compete at the tournament?

Andy: We are proving that we are more than capable at CONCACAF level and it would be amazing to see us compete against others. I firmly believe we could hold our own against a good number of countries. Canada were the most improved country in the world in 2021 and rose to 40th in the FIFA rankings.

Galt FC are one of the oldest clubs to feature in this book, being founded in the late 1800s and dissolving in 1910. Do you know why they dissolved and disappeared?

Andy: Unfortunately, after such a short and storied existence the disappearance of Galt is still quite the mystery. All that I really know is that they were dissolved in 1910. There is no mention of how and why that I have found (yet).

Can you ever see Galt FC appearing again in some shape or form in Canadian soccer? There are only eight teams now in the Premier League – surely there is going to be expansion?

Andy: Galt is now known as Cambridge. If the CPL expands there maybe they will use the name? I don't know. There is a youth team known as Galt but I'm unsure if they are even still around to be honest. For me, the name should be left alone as one of those glorious teams in history.

Do you have any interesting fact about Galt FC that you discovered in your research of them?

Andy: One fascinating thing about them was that they won the 1904 Olympic gold medal, although there were no medals presented. Just as fascinating is that there were a few other Canadian teams due to take part and one of the reasons for teams withdrawing other than money was that they were always getting beaten by Galt so didn't see it worth their while to travel to St Louis. They were pretty much the Invincibles of their time. They even did a tour of the neighbouring province of Manitoba in 1903 and only conceded two goals in 17 matches, winning 16 and drawing one 0-0.

16.

Canberra Cosmos FC (Australia)

CANBERRA COSMOS were founded in 1995, a franchise created in the community, backed by the ACT Soccer Federation, which runs football in the Australian Capital Territory, and was also helped by other local clubs in the area. The idea was to build a professional side in the area to compete in the National Soccer League. The club's colours were originally dark blue tops and shorts with the away kit being all white. This changed when their kit brand changed, and they turned to all red kits for their home attire while wearing all yellow for away matches. They played their home games at the Canberra stadium.

The project seemed to be a no-brainer, with Canberra being the capital of Australia and there being an appetite for a football club like the Cosmos to be created in the area, this coming from the local football clubs and the local government as well. And so, they were admitted into the NSL for the 1995/96 season with high expectations. Their first season ended in a respectable ninth position, out of 12 clubs, finishing ahead of the likes of Wollongong, Newcastle Breakers and the Gippsland Falcons.

One of the most notable players to play for the Cosmos in their first few seasons was former Australian international and captain, Paul Wade, who had played for the Socceroos 84 times, scoring ten goals. Wade himself was born in Cheshire in England but had moved to Australia at the age of 11 and gained Australian citizenship. He played for a few Australian clubs but will be most remembered for playing with South Melbourne, who he made a total of 212 appearances for, scoring 12 goals between 1987 and 1995. He is currently Australia's second-most-capped player, behind Alex Tobin who has 87 caps. He never played in a World Cup tournament but did play in two Olympic Games, in 1988 and 1992. He won silverware with the Socceroos in 1996 in a tournament known as the OFC Cup, involving nations from the region. Australia and New Zealand were given byes into the semi-final while the smaller nations like the Solomon Islands, Fiji, Papua New Guinea, New Caledonia and Vanuatu had to qualify by competing in the Melanesia Cup. The winners of that tournament would play the winners of the Polynesia Cup – contested by nations such as Tahiti, Tonga, Western Samoa and American Samoa – in the OFC semi-final. The Solomon Islands and Tahiti won their respective tournaments and met in the semi-final, while Australia played their two-legged semi-final against New Zealand. After a 0-0 draw in the first leg in New Zealand, Australia ran out 3-0 winners in the second leg, with Wade scoring the second goal. Australia went on to win the OFC Cup by beating Tahiti 6-0 in the first leg in Tahiti and 5-0 in the second leg in Australia.

In their debut season, the Cosmos were also thankful to have had local talent in their squad, helping them win eight, draw 11 and lose 14, with a goal difference of minus 13, after scoring 48 and conceding 61 goals. They had managed to attract an average attendance of 2,934 to the games and had been on a cup run, getting to the semi-finals before being knocked out. Things seemed to look positive for the Cosmos going into the 1996/97 season, despite their local talent being snapped up by other NSL clubs. The likes of Michael Musitano and Alex Castro were gone by the time the season started. It was to prove to be a terrible one on the field for the Canberra Cosmos, who finished bottom of the league, winning only two games, drawing five and losing 19. They were also on the end of some heavy defeats, and a first-round knockout in the cup. Despite their poor form on the field, their average attendance rose, albeit not by much, to 3,176 a game.

With the 1996/97 season behind them, the club tried to look forward with new players, and a new manager was appointed. Former Everton player, Mick Lyons, who had managed the club from the very start, stepped down in May 1997 and the club appointed Branko Culina as manager. He added players like former Hibs man Gordon Hunter to his side, among others. They also had a huge boost financially off the field, announcing a new sponsorship deal with computing company Novell ahead of the new season. Things were looking good for the Cosmos; however, the positive vibes did not translate on to the football pitch, with the club finishing bottom again, 14th out of 14 clubs. Once more, they were on the end of some heavy defeats, most notably an 8-0 thrashing by Wollongong. The club were in turmoil and attendances started to drop off with the public becoming disillusioned by the whole project.

Not surprisingly the poor season on the field led to the departure of Culina and saw the appointment of former Australian international coach, Rale Rasi, for the 1998/99 season. It was an eye-catching appointment as Rasic had been appointed coach of the Australian national team in 1970 at the age of 34 and had led them to the World Cup finals tournament in 1974. Rasic was not one to hold back his words either, and after he was sacked by the Australian Soccer Federation, he claimed it was because he was not seen as a real 'Aussie' as he was born in Yugoslavia (Bosnia and Herzegovina as it's known today). He also claimed that he taught the Australian players how to sing the Australian national anthem.

His fiery character combined with the team's poor form at the start of the season, saw Rasic having disagreements with the Cosmos board and with only seven weeks gone into the season he left the club, in November 1998. Australian coach Tony Brennan took charge until January 1999 as caretaker manager and in the same month the club hired Scottish football coach and former Canberra City and Canberra Croatia player Tom Sermanni. Familiar with Australian football, having coached clubs like Sydney Olympic FC and the Australian women's national team, Sermanni seemed like a decent appointment at the time, but he couldn't prevent the club from finishing bottom of the league that season, 15th out 15. Off the field, the attendances dwindled again, to an average of 2,337.

The new season saw the club feeling optimistic that they could improve on the pitch, and they did, finishing 14th out of 16 clubs. However, it was off the field that problems started to arise. The Cosmos were still not attracting the support they thought they would get and even though their average attendances had risen that season to 2,428, they became financially unstable and on 30 June 2000 administrators were appointed to oversee the club's financial affairs. But the off-field problems didn't seem to affect the players as they finished a respectable 11th out of 16 clubs in the 2000/01 campaign. Nevertheless, their manager Sermanni departed in March 2001. The writing was on the wall for the club at this stage as they still didn't have enough support to keep going. The appointment of Milan Milovanovic to replace Sermanni was just until the end of the season, and he was in turn replaced by former Uruguayan striker Antonio Alzamendi in July 2001, but it became apparent that there were serious problems within the club when his contract was quickly terminated in the following weeks, before the season started.

While financial pressure grew from within the club, Soccer Australia were also putting on pressure from the outside. They proposed big changes to the NSL, wanting to reduce the league's numbers from 16 clubs to 12 for the 2001/02 season. Clubs like Carlton and Eastern Pride folded, which meant that two others had to be dismissed as well. With their financial state, Soccer Australia saw Canberra Cosmos as an easy pick and alongside Brisbane Strikers, they were excluded from the 2001/02 season before it started. Appeals from both clubs took place as they felt the decision was unfair and the process was unjust. The Australian soccer board gave in and reinstated both of them. The Cosmos had been given a lifeline and they quickly appointed new coaching staff and a new manager, former Tahiti national team manager, Leon Gardikious. The club even connected with English club Swindon Town, in a plan that would see both clubs exchange players on loan and do business in regards to off-field sponsorships. But their financial problems persisted and the Cosmos were unable to recover from their first exclusion. They could not afford to pay the fee to participate in the NSL and so Soccer Australia excluded them once again from the league. The Cosmos gave up and the club dissolved in September 2001, never to play another game again.

17.

Okinawa Kariyushi FC (Japan)

FOUNDED IN 1999 by the Kariyushi Hotel Group, located in Okinawa, the aim of Okinawa Kariyushi FC was simple. To become a J-League football club within the next few years and establish themselves among the elite in the Japanese game. The club wore orange and marine blue as their home colours, which were deemed the colours of Okinawa. White was worn as their away colour and occasionally they wore green for their third kit. They played their home games at Naha City in Okinawa.

Originally put in the Okinawa Prefecture Division 3, they won the league and the Okinawa Prefecture Social League Games TV Cup. The challenge to get to the J-League (JFL) wasn't going to be an easy one, but in 2002 they won the Kyushu Football League, winning all 18 of their games, although one game was won by a penalty shoot-out. There are no draws in the Kyushu League and if the scores are level at the end of the 90 minutes, a game goes to penalties. This title win enabled Okinawa to move to the Regional League Final Tournament, which gave them a chance to get promoted to the JFL. It was all looking promising, with the services of Ruy Ramos as a player and technical director secured just a few seasons before. The club were building up something positive, or so it seemed.

The first setback came when they were knocked out in the preliminary round of the Regional League Final

Tournament, stopping their progress towards the JFL for another year. The tournament, which is now known as the Japanese Regional Champions League tournament, was set up as a pathway for football clubs from nine different regions in Japan to try and enter the JFL and subsequently the J-League. Nine different leagues take part. They are the Hokkaido Soccer League, the Tohoku Member-of-Society Soccer League, the Kanto Soccer League, the Hokushinetsu League, the Tokai Adult League, the Kansai Soccer League, the Chugoku Soccer League, the Shikoku Soccer League and the Kyushu Football League.

That was just the beginning of the bad news, as Ramos left the club at the end of that season after having a disagreement with board members over the direction in which the club were heading. Not only did Ramos leave but he took most of the playing squad with him, and created a whole new club, FC Ryukyu, who still play their football in Japan's J-League. Okinawa Kairyushi looked to be on the brink of folding. This all happened, despite the club winning the Kyushu championship.

In 2003 the club recruited and rebuilt, on and off the field. They hired director Hisaku Kato and a whole new playing squad. Their aim was still to join the JFL and get to the dizzy heights of the J-League. It was a successful year once again in the Kyushu League, with the club taking the title, winning 16 games, two by penalty kicks, while the two games that they did lose were both in penalty shoot-outs.

They failed to win the Kyushu League for a third time in a row in 2004, finishing runners-up that season, winning 14 (one courtesy of a penalty shoot-out) and losing three. It was a remarkable feat considering what was happening to the club. In 2004, the club started to show off-field cracks again and the club's director, Kato, announced that the sponsorship deal Kariyushi had was discontinued. It meant the club were unable to pay their players anymore and they put all 27 on the transfer market, effectively for free for other clubs to pick up. They dropped into the National Football Championship, finishing off the season, which to the club was seen as a victory. The dream of playing in the J-League was further away than it had ever been. But the club decided not to give up, and once again, they dusted themselves down and made another attempt to make it to the big time.

In 2005 the club competed in the Kyushu League once again, but this campaign was far from a decent one, as they finished eighth out of the ten clubs, winning just three games (one by penalties) and losing 12 (two by penalties). They were nowhere near the club they had been only a few seasons earlier, and it was clear that the policy of using players from their youth academy was going to require patience if it was going to pay off. The next two seasons saw a slight improvement, with the club finishing fifth in 2006, winning nine and losing seven, and sixth in 2007 (winning nine, losing eight, one by penalties). The 2007 season saw a change in management and in came Nakamoto Hiroshi. While dropping one place in the table in the 2007 campaign, the club seemed to stabilise and signs of improvement were evident.

It was in 2008 when things seemed to get back on track for the club that had won the Kyushu League twice already. They won their third title that year, winning 15 games (one penalty shoot-out) and losing only two. This meant the club qualified for the Regional League Final Tournament, but once again they failed to progress past the preliminary round. The good times seemed to be back and to prove it wasn't just a flash in the pan, the club replicated their title success in the 2009 campaign, winning 12, courtesy of three penalty shoot-out wins, and only losing once all season. Again, they qualified for the Japanese Regional League Final Tournament and again they failed to get past the preliminary round.

That was to be the end of Okinawa Kariyushi's attempt to break into the JFL. In fact, it was the end of the club, as on 10 December 2009, they announced they would be dissolving by the end of January 2010. The project that they started back in 1999 only lasted 11 years, but it became clear that it was no longer financially sustainable. Quotes from the president, Shigeru Yuanaga, stated the club were paying around 60 million yen a year on expenses that included players' wages and the operating of the club in general. (423,240 Euro or 444,480 US dollars.) He also made comments that he felt some of the players they had signed were just using the club as a holiday home, while not being good enough to gain promotion to the JFL, the main aim of the club when it was founded.

18.

Jiangsu Suning FC (China)

THE ORIGINAL Jiangsu Football Club was founded in April 1958 as just an amateur, provincial team, by the local government at the time. The first competition they took part in was the 1959 Chinese National Games, the first time the event took place under the People's Republic of China. The club finished 12th. In 1960, they joined the top tier of Chinese football and finished 19th out of 25 clubs. The next season saw the club finish tenth, but this was not an improvement from the previous season as they only played seven games, winning none, drawing three and losing four. The 1962 season saw the club finish 19th.

By the 1963 campaign, the league had expanded to 39 clubs and the Chinese Football Association decided to trim it down to just 20 for the following year. Jiangsu came seventh in their group, which relegated them from the league. They did not participate in the 1964 season at all. They did remerge in 1965 to play in the second tier, where they once again finished seventh in their group, but Chinese football then stopped for several years due to the Chinese Cultural Revolution.

It wasn't until 1973 that football resumed, and Jiangsu took their place in the top tier once again, finishing 11th. Playing more games in the 1974 season (22) the club finished 21st. In 1976 they finished a respectable ninth and in 1977 15th. But 1978 was to be a disastrous season, when they finished 14th and found themselves relegated to the second tier, where they remained for quite some time. It would be a full decade before Jiangsu were back in the top tier. The 1987 season in the second division ended with them finishing fifth and securing promotion, only to be relegated the following year in, back down to the second tier after finishing 14th.

In 1994 the club were involved in the top tier of Chinese football again. This time it was a different league. After winning the 1992 Second Division title, the club were guaranteed a place in the newly formed Chinese Jia-A League. Joining the league saw the club undergo a name change, and they were now known as Jiangsu Maint. But that season saw them struggle on the field, finishing bottom of the league in 12th. It resulted in the club being relegated to the Chinese First Division, and they also had troubles off the field as they struggled financially. They were helped by different companies in the local area and managed to stay afloat but did not manage to avoid relegation to the third tier of Chinese football when they finished bottom of the Chinese First Division in the 1996 season.

However, their stay in the third tier didn't last long and they won promotion straight away, winning the title. They remained in the Chinese First Division for some time, even undergoing another name change. On 7 January 2000, the club changed their name to Jiangsu Sainty after being taken over by the Jiangsu Sainty Group. This proved to be a bad move as the club were embroiled in a bribery scandal. Numerous players and officials at the club were said to have been bribed to lose a match against Chengdu Wuniu on 6 October 2001. The match finished 4-2 to Chengdu but foul play was uncovered and sanctions were brought in against those involved. The Chinese FA also stepped in and made Jiangsu re-apply for a league licence the following year. The club got their licence on the condition that they would rid themselves of any corruption.

On the field the club would remain in the Chinese First Division for years to come until the appointment of Pei Encai. The Chinese manager guided them to the Chinese League One title in 2008, topping the league by 16 points, winning 24, drawing two and losing three games that season. They were also helped by the goals from the Brazilian strike partnership of Magno Ferreira (15) and Marcio Barros (13). Tan Si, the Chinese striker, also chipped in with ten goals.

Their first season back in the Chinese Super League saw the club finish a respectable tenth out of 16 clubs. However, that season was marred by match fixing which saw the clubs who finished seventh, Chengdu Blades, and ninth, Guangzhou GPC, relegated. The 2010 season was much the same for Jiangsu Sainty, finishing one place lower than the previous season in 11th out of 16.

The next season saw the club managed by Serbian-born Dragan Okuka. There was an immediate improvement and they finished fourth in the table that season, missing out on qualifying for the Asian Champions League by just three points. Their success was mainly down to their strikers, Romanian Cristian Danalache, who scored 13 that season and Serbian striker Aleksandar Jevtic, who scored 11. The 2012 campaign proved to be even better, with the club finishing second, just four points behind title-winners Guangzhou Evergrande. The two clubs recorded the highest attendance of the season, with 65,769 people watching a 1-1 draw at the Nanjing Olympic Sports Centre, the home of Jiangsu Sainty. The club had finally qualified for the Asian Champions League and striker Cristian Danalache topped the goalscoring charts with 23 goals that season.

In the 2013 season the club competed in their first Asian Champions League (ACL). They were drawn in Group E with South Korean side, FC Seoul, Thai outfit, Buriram United FC and Japan's Vegalta Sendai. They played their first match on 26 February 2013, against FC Seoul, losing heavily 5-1 at the Seoul World Cup Stadium in front of 6,231 people. Their first home match of the competition saw them play out a 0-0 draw against Vegalta Sendai in front of 35,756 on 12 March 2013. They finally got their first win in the competition, beating Buriram United 2-0 in front of their own fans on 2 April. Goals from Lu Bofel and Sun Ke in the first half were enough to put the Chinese side in pole position to qualify out of the group. But on 10 April in the return leg, Buriram got their revenge. This time it was the Thai side who won 2-0, with goals coming from Suchao and Charyl at the New T-Mobile Stadium. Jiangsu lost their next game to FC Seoul at home, 2-0, and despite beating Vegalta Sendai in their final game, 2-1, they were knocked out of the competition by goals scored. Buriram United had scored more and went through with table-topping FC Seoul.

Their domestic form took a hit, with the Asian Champions League journey taking its toll, and the club finished 13th, only one point out of the relegation places. The 2014 season saw a slight improvement with the club finishing eighth. They also reached the Chinese FA Cup Final for the first time, where they lost out to Shandong Luneng Taishan over two legs. They lost the first leg 4-2 at the Jinan Olympic Sports Centre Stadium. Despite winning the second leg at home 2-1, thanks to goals from Antar and Eleilson, they went down 5-4 on aggregate.

In 2015 the club once again saw a name change, this time to Jiangsu Guoxin-Sainty, due to the merger that had happened back in 2011 when Jiangsu Sainty International

Group merged into the Guoxin Group, forming the Jiangsu Guoxin Group. The Guoxin Group effectively became the owners of the club. Back on the field, they finished in ninth place but qualified for the Asian Champions League once again due to their success in the Chinese FA Cup. They had won their first major trophy, beating Shanghai Greenland Shenhua 1-0 over two legs. The first leg, which was played at the Nanjing Olympic Sports Centre was drawn 0-0 as was the second leg, played at the Hongkou Football Stadium in Shanghai. The final was decided in extra time when Brazilian-born Croatian international Sammir scored in the 110th minute to give Jiangsu and their Romanian manager Dan Petrescu the trophy. The club would play in the final of the Chinese FA Cup the following season, but wouldn't be as successful, losing to Guangzhou Evergrande Taobao over two legs in the final. The first leg ended 1-1 while the second, played at the home of Jiangsu, ended 2-2 meaning that Guangzhou won the cup on away goals.

The club were on the rise, and new owners and investment from the Suning Group saw them change their name again to Jiangsu Suning. It was a huge move that saw the club become one of the wealthiest in Chinese football. It enabled them to attract players like Brazilian and Chelsea midfielder, Ramires. They competed in the 2016 Asian Champions League, drawing South Korean side, Jeonbuk Hyundai Motors, Japanese side FC Tokyo and Vietnam's Becamex Binh Duong FC in Group E. Once again, the Chinese club failed to get out of the group, finishing third, below Jeonbuk Hyundai Motors and FC Tokyo. However, their domestic form didn't suffer this time around as they finished second in the 2016 Chinese Super League season and qualified once again for the ACL. Brazilian Alex Teixeira finished as the club's top goalscorer that season with 11. It proved to be third time lucky for Jiangsu Suning as they finally qualified for the knockout stages of the Champions League, topping their group that consisted of South Korean side Jeju United, who came second, Australians Adelaide United and Japanese side Gamba Osaka. But the last 16 was the furthest they would go and it was another Chinese club, Shanghai SIPG that would knock them out, winning 5-3 on aggregate (2-1 in the home leg and 3-2 away). Jiangsu Suning failed to impress in the Chinese Super League in the 2017 season and finished 12th, winning seven games, drawing 11 and losing 12.

Without Champions League football distracting them in the 2018 season, the club improved their domestic form, finishing fifth, but missing out on qualification for the 2019 Asian Champions League by five points. The 2019 season saw them go one better and finish in fourth place, but unfortunately for the club only the top three were awarded qualification to the Asian Champions League that season due to Tianjin Tianhai leaving the league.

But the best was yet to come from Jiangsu Suning and in 2020 the club finally won their first Chinese Super League title. In a changed format, where the season was split to create a championship play-off round with the top four clubs from the regular season competing for the title in the end, Jiangsu Suning beat rivals Guangzhou Evergrande 2-1 in the final, with goals from Eder and Alex Teixeira securing their first title.

It seemed that the club, who have had so many name changes, and so many ups and downs over the years, were finally going to become a dominant force in Chinese football. However, that was not the case, and the writing was on the wall when they had to make another name change on 1 February 2021, becoming Jiangsu FC, leaving out 'Suning'. It was said that this was done because of new regulations set by the Chinese FA that each club should have a neutral name and not the name of a sponsor. But by the end of the month the club had been dissolved, including their youth and women's teams. The parent company, Suning Holding Group, announced the decision with immediate effect, stating financial difficulties as the reason.

I spoke to Xiaoou, a Chinese football fanatic, about Jiangsu and Chinese football. He was the man who told me to look at the story of Jiangsu, stating it was one of Chinese football's most interesting stories and he wasn't wrong.

The sudden dissolving of the club, just after winning the Chinese Super League, is a strange one. They were owned by the Suning Holdings Group, who just ceased their footballing operations three months after winning the league. Was this a surprise to Chinese football fans?
Xiaoou: Fairly. First of all, nobody expected Suning, a very well-known electronics retailer, would suffer so much financial distress that it would wipe the football team out, especially as Inter Milan, also owned by Suning, is still coping fairly well. Then as you mentioned, the club just won the top flight. But Covid changed a lot of things and government policy diverged from history and became very tough on indebtedness, which was a big problem for Suning Group.

The club had the likes of Dan Petrescu and Fabio Capello manage them at one point, so they were able to attract big names. Why was that? Money? Reputation?
Xiaoou: The team was always fairly competitive in the league, having been top of the table 45 minutes before the end of the season in 2012. The scouting network was decent. The Inter connection certainly helped. Money was sufficient, but not always abundant, especially before

Suning came in. Nanjing is a city where foreigners can find a familiar life, unlike some other cities.

Doing my research on Jiangsu, I found that there were a few clubs in China that had dissolved over the years. Is this a problem in China? And if so, what do you think is the reason for it?

Xiaoou: Teams dissolve generally because the money runs out. Football is never a profitable business and outright dissolution generally happens in lower tiers of the league where the investors have a finite reservoir of patience. I don't think it is so much a problem as a symptom of a lack of real long-term plans. Most people get into football for a quick buck.

Chinese football hit the headlines over the past few years by attracting big-name players to the Chinese Super League, offering a lot of money in wages. People in Europe seemed to feel it was a cheap way to build a football league. How did Chinese fans see it? And how did you personally see it? Because Chinese football has been around for years, hasn't it?

Xiaoou: It all started with Evergrande, didn't it. They came at an opportune time when the reputation of football in China generally was at a low, in the late 2000s. They built their success with money and surprisingly good professionalism where the coaching staff are left to do their thing without much interference from the management (Lippi, and later Scolari). I think I speak for most fans when I say expensive foreign players, at Evergrande at least, were making local players better. The thing with most of the copycats is that they didn't build the coaching staff and other softer elements around their expensive players. Some of the teams were speculating they could curry political favours Most of them found it an easy way to skirt restrictions to do real estate deals where they have an excuse to grab land. A few businessmen were in it for personal egos.

The country of China is so big and has a massive population, but it hasn't done anything in regards the international stage of football. Can you see China making a big impact at a World Cup anytime soon? What are the reasons behind such a big country failing to qualify for the World Cup on so many occasions?

Xiaoou: The short answer is no. I'd be very, very, positively surprised if they can have a big impact on the international stage in the foreseeable future. And the reason is when we talk about population, we all talk about country population, but the Chinese football population is more like 10,000. If you compare it with Japan who have about a few million [people playing football] it is an extremely small talent pool. And the economist in me tells me that China is still a developing country relying on industrial investments to power the economy despite the overall size. The services and consumption economy are still very small so even in that regard there is just no good infrastructure to support the industry, so to speak, to develop (despite the fact that we are very good at hard infrastructure).

Can you tell me anything interesting about Jiangsu or Chinese football that the readers may not know?

Xiaoou: [Showing me an article of the 2006 World Cup qualifiers that China participated in.] China didn't advance because they messed up their own calculations regarding goal difference. In the last game they only realised they needed more goals in the 85th minute. It was really comitragic.

Finally, who is the best Chinese player to ever play the game of football in your opinion?

Xiaoou: If we exclude Lee Wai Tong, who was born in 1905 and whose legend spread mostly by hearsay, I daresay Zheng Zhi, who is coping with a barebone squad with Evergrande at the moment, is the benchmark to beat. Firstly, he played in Europe at a decent level for a few years, which beats most of his competitors. And compared with Sun Jihai or Hao Haidong, who I think would be other greats to consider, his good form lasted a good 15-plus years, which is more than they could manage. Even if you just think of the real medals he won – twice Asian Champions League as captain, an Asia Player of the Year (diluted as outland-playing players are no longer considered) and many league titles in the beginning and end of his career are beyond anyone else. In terms of personal ability I think Jia Xiuquan came close as a fairly prolific goalscoring defender, but he's not there in terms of actual achievements.

19

APOP Kinyras FC (Cyprus)

APOP KINYRAS FC were founded in 2003, when two clubs from the lower tiers of Cypriot football decided to merge. They were APOP Peyias FC and Kinyras Empas FC, thus the name APOP Kinyras FC. The APOP part of the club's name stands for Athlitikos Podosferikos Omilos Pegeias which translates to Athletic Football Club Peyia, while the Kinyras part of the name comes from the mythical king Kinyras who was founder of Paphos, the region APOP Kinyras FC come from. The club played in the colours of yellow and blue and played their home games at the Peyia Municipal Stadium.

They started their journey in the Third Division of Cypriot football in the 2003/04 season, when they immediately gained promotion. They won the title by beating their nearest rival, MEAP Nisou, by four points, winning 19, drawing three and losing just four games all season. Their promotion to the Second Division didn't stop their progression at all, with the club winning back-to-back promotions in only their second year of existence. The 2004/05 season saw the club finish top of the Cypriot Second Division, a league that had 14 clubs competing. APOP won easily, as they finished eight points clear of their nearest rivals, APEP. Their defensive record was impressive, only conceding 22 goals in total. They won two games 7-0, against Omonia and ASIL, both at home, and also had a

7-1 win away from home against Akritas Chlorakas, the side that finished bottom of the table.

The 2005/06 season saw the club reach the dizzy heights of the Cypriot First Division, in only their third season of playing; it was quite an achievement and didn't go unnoticed. However, it seemed that their rise up the Cypriot football pyramid had gone too fast, and their arrival in the big time had come too soon. The club struggled to adapt to the quality of the First Division and found themselves at the end of some heavy defeats, mainly away from home. They finished 12th out of the 14 clubs, meaning they ended up in one of the three relegation spots that season, finishing nine points from safety, with Olympiakos Nicosia not having to worry about being caught by APOP. The club went down, but it wasn't the worst thing that could have happened to them.

In the 2006/07 season they regrouped and came back stronger, winning the Cypriot Second Division, and gaining promotion at the first time of asking. They pipped Alki Larnaca by two points to clinch the title, and the second bit of silverware in the club's history. More importantly, they were back in the First Division, and this time they were aiming to stay a little bit longer. The 2006/07 season saw the return to form of their defence, only conceding 22 goals, while APOP also finished comfortably top of the scoring charts, with 65 goals.

The return to the First Division would be a bit different to their last visit to the top flight, for several reasons. First, the format had been changed. There would now be a first round, in which each team would play each other twice, home and away. The league was then split into three different groups: first to fourth would be placed into Group A, playing for the championship title. The next group consisted of the clubs that finished fifth to eighth, and they would play in Group B, with the winner of that group gaining qualification to the Intertoto Cup. The teams that finished ninth to 12th would play in Group C and battle it out to avoid the third and final relegation place, as the two bottom clubs, who had finished 13th and 14th in the first round, were automatically relegated.

APOP finished sixth, meaning they played in Group B, an improvement from their last stay in the First Division. This time they had won ten, drawn seven and lost nine games in the first round. It was decent form for a club that had just been promoted. However, their form dipped when playing in the group stages, and they finished bottom of Group B, and effectively came eighth that season. It was still a success as they had reached their goal of remaining in the top flight. But it would be the following season that would cement APOP Kinyras FC's place in Cypriot football history.

The 2008/09 season was much of the same, with the club finishing in sixth, placing them in Group B. They fared a little better this time around, finishing in seventh place, but it wasn't their league form that caught everyone's eye. APOP had gone on a cup run that would see the club create an underdog story that Cypriot football had never seen before. The first round of the cup was played against Omonia Aradippou, a club with a long history in Cypriot football, yo-yoing from the top tier to the Second Division. This two-legged tie was a close-run affair, with APOP taking the first leg 2-0 at the Municipal Aradippou Stadium. The tie seemed to be over, but the side from the outskirts of Larnaca came back into it and won the second leg in Peyia, 2-1. It meant that APOP won the tie 3-2 on aggregate. Few would have thought they would continue their cup run past the second round when they met AEK Larnaca, but once again they won the first leg away from home at the AEK Arena, 2-0. AEK Larnaca had won the

Cypriot Cup back in 2004, and were runners-up in 2006, so they had experience on their side. But APOP battled hard in the second leg and drew it at home, 1-1, meaning they went through, 3-1 on aggregate. The APOP fans were starting to dream that maybe they would see their club lift a major trophy.

Their next opponents would be one of the biggest and most successful clubs in Cyprus, Omonia Nicosia: a club that, before this tie, had won the Cypriot Cup 12 times. (They had won it a further three times, by the time this was written.) They had also won the Cypriot First Division 19 times (and twice more since 2008/09, at the time of writing). Many people didn't give APOP a chance, but they were not to be put down by others' expectations. In the end they beat Omonia 3-0 on aggregate; after drawing the first leg 0-0, they won the second leg with ease, 3-0, to progress to the semi-finals. There they would face the most successful club, APOEL, who had won 19 First Division titles up until that point (they have since won nine more, including the First Division title in 2008/09) and were the reigning cup holders having won it the previous year, for the 19th time (they have won it on two more occasions since, at the time this was written).

The first leg of the tie took place on 15 April 2009, at the Peyia Municipal Stadium, in front of over 3,000 fans. With home advantage, APOP didn't disappoint their fans and thanks to goals from Buyse (30th minute) and Vasconcelos (58th minute) they ran out 2-0 winners, with APOEL finishing the game with ten men after Pinto saw red in the 80th minute. But even with the two-goal advantage, APOEL were still favourites to progress, and APOP knew they would have to put in another big performance. The second leg took place on 6 May at the GSP Stadium, Nicosia. A crowd of just under 10,000 fans packed in to witness one of the great shocks of Cypriot

Cup history. But it wasn't the result that shocked people, as APOEL won the game 1-0 thanks to a penalty in the 16th minute, scored by Alexandrou. It was the fact APOP had managed to keep APOEL at bay for the rest of the game and secure their place in the Cypriot Cup Final for the first time in their history. Few could believe that they would be playing in the showpiece event on 16 May at the GSP Stadium, but that's what was going to happen, and their opponents that day would be AEL Limassol.

Not many people would have predicted what would happen in the final, which was played in front of a crowd of 15,000. Expectations that APOP could pull off a cup upset were probably limited to just their fans, as many saw AEL as overwhelming favourites. However, as the game wore on, it seemed as though APOP would hold their bigger and more successful counterparts to a draw and bring them to extra time. That was until the 84th minute when Angelos Efthymiou popped up to give APOP the lead. The unthinkable had happened and APOP were five minutes away from lifting their first major piece of silverware. You would have forgiven them for being a bit nervous for the remainder of the game, but those nerves were put to rest when Belgian Fangio Buyse scored a second in the 88th minute to all but secure the trophy for the underdogs.

The only sour note of the match was that Ivorian, Liri, was sent off in the 89th minute, but I am sure he got over that once he received his winners' medal. APOP had secured the first major trophy in their short existence and things were looking positive for the club. On a side note, Efthymiou, who scored the first goal in that game, went on to play for AEL Limassol the following season. The win also meant that APOP had qualified for the next season's Europa League, an added bonus to what was the best season in the club's short history.

Their first ever European game came against Austrian side, Rapid Wien, when they played them away on 30 July 2009. The match ended 2-1 to the Austrians, but APOP still felt they had a chance to progress, bringing them back to Peyia for the second leg. And they nearly did it, as they won the game in 90 minutes, 2-1, with goals from Edgar Marcelino and Sebastian Gonzalez. The tie, drawn 3-3 on aggregate, and with both sides having scored an away goal, went to extra time. Unfortunately, Wien managed to grab the winner, with Trimmel popping up to knock out the Cypriot side and end their European journey early.

It was back to domestic matters, and the 2009/10 season was one that the club entered with optimism. It turned out to be nothing spectacular, and the club finished in sixth place after the first round. Once again, they failed to impress in the group stage, finally finishing eighth.

But whatever positive vibes were around the club were soon gone in the next season, as they finished rock bottom in the first round, meaning automatic relegation. They only managed four wins all season, drawing seven and losing 15. If things were bad then, the following campaign was even worse. With rumblings and rumours that the club were in trouble off the field, and bankruptcy looming, on the field the club struggled again, and they were relegated in consecutive seasons, finishing 12th in the Cypriot Second Division in the 2011/12 season. They were relegated by just one point, but the was enough to see the club drop down to the Third Division. Their fans found it hard to believe that only a few seasons before they had been winning the Cypriot Cup and playing in the Europa League.

That wasn't to be the end of their downfall, as the club endured more humiliation, as scandals involving club officials and financial irregularities started to pop up, which concluded with the Cypriot FA relegating the club down to the fourth tier. But they would never play in that league, finally dissolving in 2012.

And so, the story of APOP Kinyras FC ends, but I spoke to a Cypriot football expert, who gave me more of an insight into the club, and the overall workings of Cypriot football. John Leonidou, Cyprus correspondent for UEFA. com, answered my questions:

Thank you for taking the time out to answer my questions about APOP and Cypriot football. The first thing I have to ask is what can you tell me about APOP Kinyras?

John Leonidou: APOP Kinyras Peyias, as they were officially known, were the merger of two teams from the district of Paphos – Evagoras and APOP. Throughout their history both those sides had been fairly small clubs languishing between the First and Second Division with little if any notable success in the top division. The merger – along with investment from local property business groups – aimed to put the district of Paphos on the Cypriot footballing map. Despite being a prominent city with a strong tourism stream, its own international airport and beautiful scenery, Paphos remained languishing behind the island's other big districts, namely Nicosia, Larnaca and Limassol, when it came to football.

They officially launched in 2003 and with some significant investment in foreign players and a new stadium, they moved up the divisions and were competing in the top division by 2007. In 2009, they became the first club from Paphos to win a major trophy, beating AEL 2-0 in the final. It remains one of the biggest upsets in Cypriot football history, especially after they had previously dispatched the other big favourites APOEL and Omonia. APOP also became the first team from Paphos to play in a UEFA tournament during a short-lived stint in the Europa

League qualifying round – losing 3-2 on aggregate to Rapid Wien. Following that defeat, the club's fortunes began to go downhill and by the time the banking crisis hit the island, APOP were already on their knees and relegated. The club was declared bankrupt and dissolved in 2012. Today, the sole representative of the Paphos district in Cyprus is Paphos FC.

In my research, I found that there have been 54 Cypriot clubs that have been dissolved. There could well be more. For such a small nation, what is the reason for this? Not enough fans? Bad financial management?

John: The main reason for this is really bad management and clubs exceeding their grasps when it comes to spending. Many Cypriot clubs – often under pressure from fans – don't plan for the long-term future and instead invest (sometimes over their budgets) in rafts of foreign players in what can only be described as a 'smash and grab' season for silverware. When boards come under pressure, they are usually quick to sack managers, fire players and replace them sometimes within four or five games. Bad management has very often landed clubs in huge financial difficulties that are many times too hefty to overcome.

I can remember watching the Republic of Ireland scoring a last-minute equaliser against Cyprus back in 2007. I think we only narrowly beat you at Croke Park in that World Cup qualifying group, 2-1. At the time, I remember thinking, 'Cyprus isn't a bad side.' Since then, I haven't really seen much progression. Can you tell us what you think on that subject?

John: If memory serves, it was 1-1 and Cyprus were very unlucky to concede a stoppage-time equaliser. I think it was also the same qualifying campaign that Cyprus beat Ireland

5-2 in Nicosia. Those were the good old days when Cyprus had it in them to spring some big wins and surprise results – including a 1-1 draw with Germany and further wins over Wales and Bulgaria. At the time, Cyprus had a generation of good attacking players – many of whom had played and prospered in Greece at the top sides. While they were strong going forward, they did have big flaws at the back and that was always their downfall. To put it plainly, there has been hardly any progress since then. Some have blamed the lack of chances Cypriot players are getting in their own leagues due to the high number of foreign players down the years. Others blame poor development standards for players that are 18 and over. Some also point the finger at the Cyprus FA, saying that they are unable to put a system in place (much like Belgium or Iceland) that would harmonise and enhance the national youth set-up on the island. The body of opinion is divided over who or what is to blame. I personally think it's a combination of things. What is apparent is that something has gone clearly wrong if the quality of the national team has taken big steps back instead of strides forward.

Sticking with the national side, with the introduction of the Nations League and more teams being entered in the World Cup for 2026, can you see Cyprus qualifying for their first ever international tournament soon?
John: With this current crop of players the answer has to be no. If the correct foundations are put in place and with a bit of luck, then I can see Cyprus perhaps challenging in maybe 10–15 years. There are talented young players on the island – gifted youngsters with raw talent. But then something goes wrong when they close in on adulthood.

Of course, at club level, Cypriot sides have played in the major European competitions already, with

APOEL Nicosia playing in the Champions League group stages and AEL Limassol playing in the Europa League group stages. With the introduction of the Europa Conference League, can you see Cypriot clubs being competitive and maybe even challenging for a European trophy?

John: Challenging would be a far fetch. APOEL went the furthest of any Cypriot side in 2012 when they reached the quarter-finals of the Champions League – a historic feat for such a small club. APOEL also reached the last 16 of the Europa League some years later. But Cypriot football simply doesn't have those kinds of funds anymore. Budgets have been significantly slimmed down, mainly due to FFP [Financial Fair Play] and their own budgetary constraints and so the quality of foreign players arriving on the island is nowhere near as good as it used to be. The onus on Cypriot sides is qualifying for the group stages with the grandest prize being the Champions League. Depending on the group, most Cypriot clubs will then focus on qualifying out of their groups.

Here in Ireland, Cypriot football has come under a little bit of a spotlight in recent years, with Jack Byrne, the League of Ireland's players' player of the year at the time, moving from Shamrock Rovers to APOEL, with Mick McCarthy also being manager at the time, after his second spell as Republic of Ireland manager. Of course, neither move was that successful, but how do you view the Cypriot football league's perception to the rest of the world?

John: In Cyprus, players and managers come and go all the time and despite heightened excitement when they first arrive, perceptions can quickly go south if things don't go according to plan from the off. There is little patience in

Cypriot football and a few bad results/performances could be curtains for players and/or managers. There was interest and excitement in Mick and Jack when they first arrived but the mood quickly dampened as results didn't go that well. In Cyprus, the fans like big names from other leagues – even if it is players way past their prime and in the twilight of their careers.

Finally, I always save this question for last. Who is your favourite player to have played in the Cypriot League? Who was the best player to ever play in the league, and who is the best Cypriot player of all time?

John: My favourite player to have played in the Cypriot League has to be Sinisa Gogic (the father of St Mirren midfielder Alex Gogic) who played mainly for APOEL and Anorthosis. From the former Yugoslavia and now a naturalised Cypriot, he arrived in the late 80s in Cyprus and was head and shoulders above anyone. He for me was the one player who could have gone on to have a successful career in any league – I believe he was that good. Strong, pacey, fantastic technique and a clinical finisher. He had all the attributes of a centre-forward. At 34, he signed for Olympiakos in Greece and was their top scorer in the Champions League.

The best player to ever play in the league is split between two players who dominated the local football scene in the 70s – forwards Sotiris Kaiafas of Omonia and Andreas Stylianou of APOEL. Both had big careers and are considered legends of Cypriot football.

If I had to pick my favourite Cypriot player of all time, then it would be Michalis Konstantinou: another forward who had a brilliant career in Greece with plenty of goals in the Champions League and has the most goals for Cyprus.

20.

KF Spartak Tirana (Albania)

FOUNDED IN 1950, as a team that represented the trade unions, KF Spartak adopted the colours blue and red while having the nickname '*Gladiatoret*'. In their first season in 1951, the club competed in the Karegoria e Dyte, the Second Division of Albanian football. The format had 48 clubs competing from the start, split into eight groups. The winners of each group went into the second phase, or the semi-finals, which consisted of two groups of four, with the top two of each group qualifying for the final group stage and competing to become champions. The four clubs that made it to the final group stage were automatically promoted. Spartak Tirana were placed in Group 4, winning the group that consisted of clubs like Dinamo Elbasan, Puna Librazhd, Puna Peqin, Spartak Elbasan, Spartak Kavaje and Spartak Peqin. As group winners they went to the semi-final stage, being placed into Group 1, alongside Puna Lezhe, Puna Shijak and Puna Rubik. They failed to progress, winning only one of their games, meaning they would be playing in the second tier the following season.

It wasn't until 1953 that the Second Division resumed, with the 1952 season not played, although the Albanian Cup and Albanian First Division went ahead. The new season saw a new format being brought in. Only 14 clubs competed in the competition, in two groups of seven. Spartak Tirana were placed in Group B, and won it comfortably, winning ten of their 12 games, drawing one and only losing once. This meant they progressed to the final, facing Group A winners, Puna Elbasan. There are varied reports from this game, some saying Spartak Tirana won 6-1, while others have said it was a much closer affair, with Spartak Tirana only winning 1-0. Whatever the score was, Tirana won the game and were crowned champions that year, the first piece of silverware in the club's history. It meant they would compete in the 1954 National Championship.

The Albanian National Championship was more straightforward, with a simple league format deciding who the champions of Albania would be. Spartak Tirana were nowhere near the title, finishing 11th out of 12 clubs, winning four, drawing five and losing 13. But as the league was looking to expand to 16 clubs in the 1955 season, they were spared immediate relegation. But it was only a stay of execution, as they finished 14th and in the final relegation place, only one point from safety. It was disappointing for the club to find themselves relegated back down to the Kategoria e Dyte so soon, but that's where they played for the 1956 season.

With the format changed to a league in the second tier, Spartak Tirana didn't spend much time wallowing in their disappointment after relegation the previous season. They won the league at a canter, finishing top by seven points from their nearest rival, Puna Fier. So, after one season, they were back in the National Championship, ready to compete with the big boys of Albanian football. It was a league that now only had eight clubs in it, half the number that competed the last time they were in the league. It didn't help their cause, and Spartak Tirana had one of the worst seasons in the club's history, going the whole season without winning a game, drawing just two matches and only scoring six goals. It meant they were once again relegated to the second tier.

But that isn't what happened. After the 1957 season, Spartak Tirana didn't play again and were dissolved, technically in the year 1959. It was widely recognised in Albanian football at the time that there were too many football clubs in the country and sports clubs reorganised themselves to get the most out of the facilities available to them. As a result, most of Spartak Tirana's players went to other clubs, but mainly to a club known as 17 Nentori, who are now called KF Tirana, and are the most successful club in Albania to date, with 53 domestic trophies to their name.

And so, Spartak Tirana remained defunct for decades, with no plans to resurrect the club until 2012, when a group of football fanatics felt it was time to bring the club back to life. The club entered the Kategoria e Trete (Third Division) Group A for the 2016/17 season. They immediately gained promotion, finishing top of the ten-team league. It saw the club promoted to the Kategoria e Dyte for 2017/18, and the quality of football didn't faze them as they finished a respectable fourth out of 14 clubs, although they were a massive 23 points behind the play-off positions and second-placed Veleciku. However, things were looking good for the club's second coming and another season in Albania's Second Division was something the club could look forward to, with a view to going one better and try and get into one of those play-off places.

That wasn't the case for the 2018/19 season. While the club finished closer in regards points to the play-off places, only ten points behind second-placed Luzi 2008, they were sixth out of the now 13-club group. Things seemed to be stable on the field, with the club not looking in any danger of relegation, but off the field, things weren't so great. The 2019/20 season saw the club drop even further down the table, into tenth place out of 13 clubs again, but things in Albanian football were not looking good, with three clubs dissolving after that season. Although two of them were the B teams of Tirana and Viliznia, another club, FC Kamza, withdrew and dissolved that year as well. Spartak Tirana were to follow almost immediately, with the club withdrawing from the league for the 2020/21 season.

Some would see this as the club folding once again, and technically, withdrawing from a league season is just that. However, the club continued to compete in the Albanian Fourth Division, finishing seventh out of eight clubs, winning just two games all season, both wins coming against the only club that finished below them, Osumi. They also faced a bit of controversy that season, being deducted three points for fielding an ineligible player against Eagle FA. At the time of writing, in the 2022/23 season, Spartak are still in the Fourth Division.

I got in touch with football fanatic, writer and co-editor of *KIT Magazine*, Phil Harrison, who is writing his own book on Albanian football and the country's communist past. He was able to give me an insight into Albanian football, how it is run, and why so many clubs, like Spartak Tirana, had or have dissolved.

Hi, Phil. Thank you for taking time out to answer my questions. It has been quite a challenge to find someone with knowledge about Albanian football, so I suppose my question is, why Albanian football?
Phil Harrison: It all dates to 1989 when England played Albania in Tirana. It was very much a Stalinised country. I remember the pictures on the BBC, with a woman on a wooden cart and a man walking out of a shop with a cabbage as if he had won the lotto. It looked very archaic, and it spiked my interest. So, I looked into Albanian

football and found there is very little written or reported about it, bar a few magazines, so I persisted with it [writing about it myself]. So, communism fell in 1991 in Albania and I've always been interested in communism, but it was always different in Albania, uglier than other countries. My principles are overall, if the country has a bit of football history that has been forgotten as such then I'm interested.

What can you tell me about Spartak Tirana? In my research, it just always felt there was no room for them in Albanian football, and that's why they have been dissolved at least once, and then withdrew and fell down the leagues, or is there something more to it than that?

Phil: They formed after the liberation of Albania. Quite adversely, they had two very famous managers, Adam Karapici and Loro Borici. For a club with a relatively small following, they had some big names involved. They were based right beside Blloku, which was an enclosed area where Albanians lived. They never had an official ground, like many Albanian clubs at the time.

The infrastructure in the SFH [Albanian Football League] in the early days wasn't great, it was a poor city to play football. There were no grounds to play football. Games were always played on a Sunday at 3pm with only one stadium in Tirana. (Spartak played in the inner regions of Tirana.)

In 1951 Albania became close allies with the Soviet Union and they sent in sporting experts to the country to improve Albanian football. But there was still not enough for all the clubs and Spartak were wound up as you could only have a certain number of clubs to play in the one stadium and they were left out.

In 1960, the Soviet Union and Albania split and any Soviet influence was frowned upon and ultimately was stamped out, so Spartak would have been targeted as they still had that Russian influence, the name Spartak being a stand-out reference.

Albanian football isn't the biggest or the most well-known around the world. Few would be able to name more than two or three clubs from there. Is there a reason for this? Are there other sports that come before football, a lack of investment in the sport or even a lack of interest from the Albanian people?

Phil: Basketball is a big sport in Albania with most clubs having basketball teams within them, but football is the biggest sport in Albania, so you can't really blame other sports for the lack of interest in Albanian football. There is probably still a lack of investment, as money still has to be invested into other areas in the country, while there isn't very much Western influence like businesses and stuff like that.

Obviously, the new national stadium being built has been fantastic. If you look at all of its best assets, the best Albanian players, they play in the better leagues around the world. Fans become kind of bored [when they can't watch the best players]. The standard back in the 1960s was great, but only one player in the national squad actually played in Albania, I think he was a goalkeeper.

Of course, with the introduction of the Europa Conference League, smaller nations and their clubs will have more of a chance to play in European competitions. Do you see this as an opportunity for Albanian football to put itself on the map, with clubs like KF Tirana now competing in those competitions?

Phil: It gives the club a platform, but from a wider perspective, does it improve the standard? Probably not, as all the really good players have migrated, and I don't think it will bring better footballers to the clubs or bring Albanian football up the ranks of European football, I don't think that will happen. It is very much an indigenous game in Albania.

In my research, a name that came up in regards to Spartak Tirana and Albanian football was a man named Loro Borici. What can you tell the readers about him?

Phil: Well, he was originally a footballer who played for Vllaznia Shkoder, which is in the northern area of the country. That area never really embraced communism and was always viewed with contempt by the Albanian government. Vllaznia were the oldest team in Albania, they were formed in 1919. They were the forefathers of Albania football. They didn't win the league for the first ten years, but when Borici played for them, they started winning. He then moved to Italy in 1940 and played for Lazio, until 1942, and was playing in the same attacking midfield area as Silvi Piola, Italian footballer of the year, so Borici couldn't break into that team, so he returned to Albania. At the end of the Second World War, in 1947 he played for Partizani. In between that time, he captained the Albanian side, who won one of two national titles, the Balkans Cup. They played three games, against Yugoslavia, Romania, and Bulgaria. They won two of those games and lost one. There was a real sense of excitement in that era. He then joined Spartak, under the management of Adam Karapici. He managed the Albanian national team; he had success with them in 1947. They had some minor success, drawing with Romania and Hungary. They also drew with Yugoslavia in 1948, the same season they won the Olympic gold medal.

Borici played for Partizani, one of the great teams of Albanian football. His goal ratio was 2.7 goals a game in 1951. However, Partizani didn't win the league or cup. Partizani scored 106 goals, and only conceded ten.

[Sidenote: Partizani are still the biggest club in Albania, while Dynamo's support has dwindled.]

He was a member of their golden team, then he left to join Spartak in 1957, when they had just been promoted to the top division. He stayed there until they were shut down in 1959/60. He was player coach at Spartak, and then he became player coach at Partizani, and had three spells as the national team coach.

He wasn't as successful a manager at Partizani as previous managers. Towards the end of his reign of being national team coach, he was known for having a very defensive style of football. It was known as 'Borici football' and wasn't great. One of his great achievements was that he led Albania to a 0-0 draw with West Germany in 1967, which stopped West Germany from qualifying for the 1968 European Championships, and enabled Yugoslavia to qualify. Albania should have won the game. The Albanian media still felt that if Borici was more adventurous they would have won, with a goal that wasn't given as it was declared not to have crossed the line by an Austrian ref.

Who is the best Albanian footballer to ever play the game?

Phil: Well, the player I would say is Panajot Pano. I have watched footage of this guy. He used to get on the ball, and he was progressive. He was known as '*Mbretit*' which means 'the King'. His parents moved to Tirana, and he became part of the youth academy at 17 Nentori (now known as KF Tirana), and he broke into the team, and he was part of the side that broke the dominance of Dynamo

Tirana. They beat Dynamo 4-0 in 1958, and a couple of weeks later they beat them in the cup. It was 0-0 but the referee added an extra 15 minutes to the game. When nobody scored the ref brought the game to a halt and declared Nentori the winners based on their corner-kick count, 8-4 on corners.

They beat Dynamo, the team of the police, and the Dynamo patrons didn't like this. Nentori were regarded as the 'hip' team of Albania, and they were one of the hated clubs in the country. However, the ministry of the interior wanted to break Nentori, who had a wealth of youngsters coming through. Players played for a club up to a certain age and then they were given national service. What this would do is wrestle the young players from their parent club to one of the bigger clubs when their national service ended, as they would be practically free agents by then. The bigger clubs would give benefits like nice houses and other things. Pano moved to Partizani where he became a legend and became known as *'Vogel e o Puskas'* which meant 'the little Puskas', not only because he was predominantly left-footed and he rarely did anything with his right foot. He was an aggressive and attacking player, rarely letting it go. He was an exciting player to watch. But the other thing is, he looked like Puskas.

He was hugely successful with Partizani as they went on to play in the Spartakiad, which was like a tournament between all the army clubs from the Eastern bloc, like Honved and CSKA Moscow. In 1967, in Vietnam, they reached and lost out to CSKA Moscow in the final but Pano was outstanding and was voted player of the tournament. It was a huge thing in Albania when they came back. His playing style, he was hungry for the ball and was hard to dispossess. He would be the player that Albanians regard as the best Albanian player to ever to play the game.

Albania's national team are usually seen as the whipping boys of their qualifying groups, whether it be a World Cup or European Championship campaign. Can you ever envisage a time when Albania may qualify for a major international tournament and what do they have to do to even get close to that goal?

Phil: They qualified before for the Euros, in 2016. They have won games, like home and away to Hungary only recently. They are kind of pushing the boundaries. The potential is there. All their squad play in other parts of the world. The likes of Borja, at Chelsea. He is the first kind of breakthrough in the Premier League. They have always been capable of producing these kinds of individual players but now they seem to be able to produce this kind of streetwise player. They came incredibly close to qualifying for Mexico 86. During the campaign, they drew with Poland and beat Belgium, so they were playing against teams who were, at that time, the best in the world. Historically they have had the players, but now they play abroad, which will make that bit of difference.

Where did the inspiration for your book come from?

Phil: I've always been interested in smaller nations and their football. When I saw Albania in the 80s, when they played England, it looked like an alien planet and that fascinated me a little bit and made it alluring to me. When the information for Albania came available, after communism, I just wanted to know more. It's years and years of obsession about Albania. In 1992, I went to Albania for the first time, on a day trip.

You have mentioned that you have an interest in smaller footballing nations as such: are there any other countries you have an interest in and are there plans for other books like the one you are writing?

Phil: Funnily enough, I am interested in and want to write a book on the Haitian journey to the 1974 World Cup and the background on how they got there, as it was very interesting. The regime there was very brutal. I would like to cover that. I would also like to cover a Turkish football book and their footballing history. So, yes, there are lots of interesting things from there, it's a vastly unexplored country, for an Englishman.

21.

Budapest VSC (Hungary)

BUDAPESTI VASUTAS Sport Club-Zuglo, as it is known currently, was founded in 1911, under the name MAVOSZ Budapesti VSC. It was a club that had various sports teams within its organisation, including table tennis, wrestling and water polo. But football is where we will keep our main concentration.

The early years were uneventful to say the least. The club played in the local leagues of Budapest, and in the lower Hungarian national leagues when the opportunity arose. But they are not on record for winning any major silverware, nor were they even in contention. In fact, the most interesting aspect of the club, up until the 1990s, was the many name changes they made. Here they are, in their entirety.

From 1911–45 the club was known as MAVOSZ Budapesti VSC. This name was changed when the club merged with Budapesti MAV Elore in 1945. Then, sometime in between 1945 and 1948 the club changed its name again to MAV Konzum Vasutas Elore. I can only imagine that during this time there was a lot of upheaval with football clubs in that part of Europe due to the Second World War, with Hungary being controlled by Germany at the time. But by 1948, the war was over and the club reverted to the more Russian-sounding Budapesti Lokomotiv SK, with a Soviet-allied government being put in place post-war, making Hungary part of what was known as the Eastern Bloc. In 1949, the People's Republic of Hungary was declared and 1954 saw the fourth name change occur, with the merger of Budapesti Lokomotiv SK, Budapesti Elore SK and Budapesti Postas SK to create Budapesti Torekves SE.

(Keeping up? There are still a few more name changes to come.)
This merger only lasted two years, with the demerger announced and all three clubs going their separate ways. Pre-merger Budapesti Lokomotiv SK became known as Budapesti VSC and remained so until the 1990s when the club changed name for the sixth time, now to BVSC-Mavtransped. The 1992 season saw the seventh name change, BVSC-Novep now the choice of title. But, for the third year in a row, the club opted for another change, and BVSC-Dreher was the new name. Throughout these three years, however, most football fans knew the club as simply BVSC, making the name changes a bit redundant.

It seems like the club's hierarchy just liked changing its name, as in 1996/97 the club was known as Budapesti VSC, then BVSC-Zuglo FC in 1997/98, with the following season seeing the club just drop the FC part of the name. They reverted back to Budapesti VSC for two years, from 1999 to 2001, before landing on the name BVSC-Zuglo FC once again. This lasted for ten years. However, the sports organisation didn't field a senior football team for the majority of this time, which would explain the lack of name changing in this period. When they did return to football, the name BVSC-Zuglo was the preferred choice, and that's the way it has remained since 2011.

Now that we have all that information out of the way, we can concentrate on the on-field antics. Through my research, I have found the club played in the top flight in the 1958/59 season, under the name BVSC Budapesti, and finished 12th out of 14 clubs. There was no relegation that year; however, the following season there was the threat of relegation, and BVSC finished bottom of the table, winning only three games all season, drawing ten and losing 13.

The club wouldn't be seen in the top division again until the 1991/92 season, which is when they really started to come to the attention of other Hungarian football fans, who in the following years started to recognise BVSC as a permanent fixture in the Nemzeti Bajnoksag I, the Hungarian top flight.

In 1991/92 they finished a respectable tenth out of 16 clubs, winning seven, drawing 12 and losing 11. The 1992/93 season was a bit more tense, with BVSC finishing 12th, one place and three points above the relegation zone. They actually won three games more than the previous season, winning ten, drawing six and losing 14, but it was a wake-up call, and they knew they needed to improve. The following season, they didn't see much improvement though, finishing 12th once again, and this time only two points clear of the relegation zone.

After two close calls in the previous seasons, the club made a big improvement on the pitch and finished a respectable sixth in the 1994/5 season. This was largely helped by the goalscoring exploits of Gyorgy Bognar and Zoltan Bukszegi, who between them scored 20 goals, almost half BVSC's total of 51 that season. It was a sign of the good times that were about to come, as the next season, 1995/96 was the best in the club's history. It saw them finish runners-up in the Nemzeti Bajnoksag I, five points behind the eventual champions, Ferencvaros. BVSC striker and former Hungarian international Ferenc Orosz notched up an impressive 15 goals, finishing only behind Ferencvaros's Ukrainian striker, Ihor Nichenko, who scored 18. The runners-up spot meant they qualified for the UEFA Cup qualifying round.

BVSC also made it to the Hungarian Cup Final that season. Going through the various rounds, they beat Szazhalombatta FC 6-2 over two legs in the round of 32, then beat Vasas SC Budapest 7-4 over two legs in the last 16. This set up a quarter-final meeting with Debrecen VC. The first leg ended 0-0 at home, with BVSC-Dreher Budapesti as they were known at this time, having to go away and get a result. A win or a score draw would be enough, as the away goals rule was active. And that is what BVSC achieved, drawing the game 2-2 and progressing to the semi-finals courtesy of the away goals rule. Their opponents in the semi-finals were city rivals, Ujpest TE Budapest. It was an easy win for the underdogs, BVSC, who won the first leg 2-0 and the second, away leg, 1-0. It set up a final with another Budapest club, Honved. The first leg was played at the Szonyl uti Stadion in front of 3,000 people. BVSC made home advantage count and won the game 1-0, with the only goal coming in the 35th minute, scored by Csabi.

The second leg was played nearly two weeks later, on 20 June 1996, at the Bozsik Jozsef Stadion, with a much bigger attendance of 8,000 people. The game was a cagey affair, with both teams desperate not to concede. It wasn't until the 84th minute that the deadlock was eventually broken, and it was by Honved. Piroska's goal brought the tie level and it looked like the final was heading to extra time. That was until the 86th minute when BVSC hearts were shattered by Honved's Argyelan. The home side held out to win the tie, 2-1 on aggregate, and lift the trophy. But it wouldn't be the last time BVSC would get to the final of the cup.

For the 1996/97 UEFA Cup campaign, the club faced Welsh opposition, Barry Town, in the first round. Both home and away legs ended 3-1 so it was decided on a penalty shoot-out. The Welsh side prevailed, winning 4-2 and thus ending the Hungarians' European adventure early. And so, BVSC's attention turned to domestic matters, with the club determined not to make the previous season a one-hit wonder. On the league front, they finished sixth, which wasn't as good as the previous season, but it was a respectable finish. But it was in the cup that they made the headlines again, reaching their second consecutive final, where they were desperate to overturn the previous season's result.

The first round took the form of 16 groups, with four clubs in each group. The top two of each group would progress to the knockout stages of the tournament. BVSC were placed in Group 14, alongside Velence FC, Balaotonfured FC and Vecsesi FC. They topped the group with ease, winning two and drawing one game. They faced Zalaegerszegi TE in the round of 32, winning the tie 4-3 on aggregate: after losing the first leg at home, 3-2, they came back in the second leg and won 2-0, thanks to two goals from Bukszegi, to progress to the last 16.

There they met Videoton FC Fehervar, and the first leg took place at the Stadion Sostoi in Szekesfehervar in front of only 500 people on 28 November 1996. BVSC won the game 1-0, thanks to a goal in the 54th minute by Bukszegi. The second leg, which took place on 5 December at the Stadion Szonyi Uti in Budapest, was only attended by around 100 fans. Those few saw BVSC progress from the tie with a 1-1 draw. The home side took the lead in the 23rd minute thanks to an own goal by Fehervar's Toth. The away side came back and equalised on the night in the 60th minute through Dveri, but with 30 minutes remaining, they couldn't find another goal to push the game into extra time.

The quarter-finals were much easier for BVSC, as they cruised past FC Sopron, 4-0 on aggregate. A 1-0 win in the first leg and a convincing 3-0 victory in the second leg was more than enough to see BVSC progress to the semi-finals, where they faced Szombathelyi Haladas. The tie was over after the first leg, when BVSC won 3-0 at home. The second leg was more of a formality and it ended 0-0, meaning the Budapest side went through to their second final in as many seasons. This time they would face city rivals MTK Budapest, who were overwhelming favourites.

The final took place on 21 May 1997. It was played at the Hidegkuti Nandor Stadion in front of 2,000 fans, who were treated to what can only be described as an onslaught. MTK were in no mood to provide the nation with a cup upset and started off quickly. It took them 12 minutes to break the deadlock, when Halmai made it 1-0. Just before the half-hour mark, it was 2-0, thanks to an own goal by BVSC's Eros. Illes added a third in the 33rd minute while Orosz finished the game before half-time, making it 4-0 in the 36th minute. Two more goals were added in the second half when Kenesei scored the fifth in the 66th minute and the rout was completed in the 80th when Lorincz slotted home a penalty. It was a tough day for BVSC, but they would see tougher in the next few years.

The cup defeat did come with a silver lining, with the club qualifying for the UEFA Cup Winners' Cup. They entered the qualifying round in the hope of going one better than the previous year. They were drawn against Liechtensteiner club, FC Balzer, who compete in the Swiss leagues but had qualified by winning the Liechtenstein Football Cup. The Hungarians were favourites to progress, and they didn't disappoint. The first leg of the tie took place on 14 August 1997 at the Sportplatz Rheinau, in front of over 600 fans. Despite going behind in the 38th minute due to a Wornhard goal, the Hungarian side bounced back and scored three, the first coming in the 50th minute from Telsers, then Fuzi (76th) and Csordas (84th) gave the away side a 3-1 win to bring into the second leg. With a much bigger crowd in attendance, just under 2,000, at the Szonyi Uti Stadion in Budapest, the home side built on their advantage. Komlosi settled the nerves early with a goal in the 12th minute while Bukszegi finished off the job in the 90th minute to win the tie 5-1. It was BVSC's first victory on aggregate in Europe and they had progressed to the first round to face Spanish side, Real Betis.

The first leg was played in Spain at the Ramon Sanchez Pizjuan Stadium in Seville, on 18 September. The hosts won 2-0 thanks to a brace scored by Alfonso Perez, a man who played for both Barcelona and Real Madrid in his career, while also making 38 appearances for the Spanish national team between 1992 and 2000. It was a huge step up in class for BVSC, but they knew they still had the smallest chance in the second leg back in Budapest. If they could get an early goal, they may make their bigger, more experienced counterparts nervous.

On 2 October they played the second leg and it took only seven minutes for the Spanish side to take the lead and effectively put the tie to bed. Alexis Trujillo scored the goal, a man who made 222 appearances for Betis and is regarded as a hero amongst the Seville club's fan base, captaining the side, as well as his hometown club, Las Palmas. If anybody was in doubt that the tie was over at this point, they were in no doubt in the 49th minute when that man again, Perez, popped up to make it 4-0 on aggregate and send the Spanish side through.

Back to domestic matters, and the 1997/98 season was a somewhat forgettable one. The club managed to finish tenth, winning 12, drawing ten and losing 12, while they were knocked out in the early rounds of the cup. Their decline continued into the 1998/99 season when they were relegated after finishing 17th out of the 18 clubs, winning only seven games all season. But the club did not compete in the second tier, and didn't appear in the Hungarian football league system until the 2002/03 season when they reappeared in the Nemzeti Bajnoksag III. That season, they finished seventh but found themselves getting promoted to the Nemzeti Bajnoksag II. They finished 15th in 2003/04, avoiding relegation. However, football within the sports club ceased its operations and BVSC were no longer present in Hungarian football. A club that had only a few years before competed in European competition, playing against Spanish giants Real Betis, were no more. Well, for at least a decade.

Fast forward ten years, to the year 2012, and on 18 July BVSC started a men's senior team once again, competing in the Budapest Labdarugo Szovetseg league, winning it in their first season and scoring an amazing 123 goals in 26 games. They went up to the MBIII (another amateur regional league) in 2013/14 and won that league too, gaining back-to-back promotions. In the MBII league the progress stopped for a few seasons, with the club finishing sixth in consecutive campaigns, then fourth in 2016/17, before going one better in 2017/18 by finishing third. It was only a matter of time before they would gain promotion to the MBI and in 2018/19, that is what they did, scoring 112 goals and only conceding 12 in the process. They were now one league away from the Hungarian professional leagues, and in May 2020 the club achieved promotion again and were back playing in the Nemzeti Bajnoksag III.

That season was unfortunately interrupted by the Covid-19 pandemic and was brought to a premature end. However, it didn't disrupt the club's ambition to try to climb the Hungarian football ladder and they just narrowly missed out on promotion to the NBII in the 2021 season when they finished second in the Keleti (Eastern section).

Unfortunately, only one club gets promoted from each section and Budapesti VSC (as they are now known) were beaten to that spot, comprehensively, by Tiszakecske. As I write this, the club's aim is still to get promoted to the NBII.

22.

IB Akureyri (Iceland)

THE CLUB Knattspyrnufelag Akureyrar, commonly known as KA, were founded in 1928. A football club from the north of Iceland based in Akureyri, they play their games at the Akureyrarvollur, a small multi-purpose stadium that only holds 1,645 spectators at most, with only 715 seats. The club itself is a multi-sports organisation, with volleyball, judo and handball teams. Their home colours are yellow while their away kit is blue.

KA competed in various football tournaments in Iceland, mainly down south in Reykjavik. They competed on three separate occasions in the Islandsmot tournament (the national championship), mainly against clubs from Reykjavik, including Fram, KR, Valur and Vikingur. Another club from Vestmannaeys also competed. KA weren't very successful in their first attempt to win the tournament, in 1928, getting knocked out after losing two of their three games and drawing the other 0-0. In fact, KA failed to score in any of their games and it resulted in the media giving them the unfortunate nickname of 'KA-Null'.

But not to be put off by their bad experience, the club travelled down south once again in 1929, this time better prepared and with more experience. They competed this time around, but it wasn't until 1932 that they finally broke the mould. After losing 1-0 to Val in their first game, played in particularly harsh conditions, KA went on to win their next two, beating Fram 2-0 and Viking 3-0. It meant they became Icelandic champions for the first time in their history. But it wouldn't be until a decade later that KA would compete in the Islandsmot again.

In 1941 the club decided to play in the Islandsmot for the fourth time in their history. Hoping to emulate their triumph of ten years previously, those hopes were quickly dashed when the club failed to win any of their four games in the competition, drawing one and losing three. KA went back up north, but were determined to prove themselves to be the best football club in Iceland. And so, they invited the then champions, KR, up to Akureyri to play in a best-of-three matches. KR won two while KA won one. Two players from another Akureyri club, Por, played for KA in the second match, and with that, the idea of merging the two clubs started to become realistic. It made sense that the two clubs should put together their resources and best players, so that they could compete against the bigger clubs from the south.

The first match that this happened in was in July 1942, when the two clubs, under the name Akureyri's Sports Council, played against the Icelandic champions, Vals. Two games were played with the teams winning one each. This solidified the idea that the two clubs were in much better shape if they stayed together, and so, in 1943, they entered the Islandsmot as Akureyri Sports Council for the first time, and thus, IB Akureyri were founded, officially in 1946.

Initially, the southern clubs from Reykjavik were not happy that Akureyri had merged its two clubs and thought it to be unfair. So much so, that they made a complaint to the IBA, Iceland's Football Association, but these complaints fell on deaf ears. However, despite all the drama, Akureyri failed to make an impression in their first Islandsmot as a new club, failing to win any of their five games, only drawing two and losing three. It wasn't until eight years later that the club would compete in the Islandsmot once again.

From then on, they continued to play in the Icelandic championships, with a different format being brought in for the 1958 season, having two divisions in place instead of just one. Akureyri were placed in the Second Division, and it took them two years to gain promotion, and then, in 1960, the first ever top flight match took place in Akureyri. It was a huge deal in Akureyri and for IB. The chairman at the time, Armann Dalmannsson, addressed the home crowd before the game, to explain to them what a huge moment this was in the club's history. Their opponents were Keflviking, a club from a town called Reykjanesbaer. IB won the game 3-1.

Despite their bright start, the club were back in the Second Division in 1964 but didn't stay long, and gained promotion to the First Division in 1965. After that, the club found themselves challenging for the Icelandic title, without winning it. In both 1965 and 1966, IBA were only two points short of bringing the title up north. There was another near miss for the club in 1968: despite starting off the season well, the second half saw their title challenge somewhat derail and it meant they finished up in third place. This was to be the height of their success for some years. While the club were never in danger of relegation, they never really challenged at the top either and so mediocrity crept in for almost a decade.

However, 1970 came and it was a disastrous year for the club as IBA were relegated to the Second Division. Talks began as to whether the sports organisation should continue to have a football section, or whether it would be better off putting its resources into other sports and areas of the organisation. Luckily, they decided to give it a little bit longer, and the football club reacted by gaining promotion after only one season in the Second Division. But once again, in 1974, the club was relegated and this time they would make changes. The merger ended and the two original clubs of KA and Por would revert back to what they were, two separate clubs in Akureyri. This was done at the request of Por, whose representatives made the decision only a few days before the new season started. On 27 January 1975, a meeting was held with all whom it concerned and Por decided that they would be sending their own team down to the KSI competition. IBA had already registered for the new season, so things became complicated for KA as they had not registered as themselves. In the end, KA were able to compete in the Third Division of the Islandsmot and from 1975, the two clubs were formally separated, meaning IBA were no more.

That was the story from KA's point of view. Por Akureyri, or Por as they are commonly known, have their own history. Founded in 1915, the club is also a sports organisation that has different sporting departments in it, like handball, judo and basketball to name a few. Their full official name in Iceland is Iprottafelagio Por and their nickname is Porsarar. Their home kit is white while their away jerseys are usually red. They play their games at the Porsvollur stadium, which has a capacity of only 984.

From reading the reports of the merger, it would seem KA were the dominant team in Akureyri or the bigger club of the two, with only a few Por players really representing the IBA club throughout its history. It is no surprise that it was them who ended the merger with KA, to go it alone and attempt to compete in the Islandsmot under their own name, as they feared they would be swallowed up completely in time by their rivals. And it seems like they made the right move, because as I am writing this, the small club from Akureyri is still in existence, despite only competing in Iceland's Second Division, the Inkasso-Deildin.

Their history as the club they are now is one of highs and lows, with the club winning the Second Division twice, in 2001 and more recently in 2012, only to be relegated many times. The 2011 season is probably one that sums up Þor as a club, with the side making it to the Icelandic Cup Final that year, only to lose out to KR in the final, 2-0. That season was a mixed one, as they saw their league form collapse and they were relegated from the top flight.

To really gain some insight into Icelandic football I spoke to the author of many books about the subject, including *Sixty Four Degrees North* and *Lava Bol*, Marc Boal. His knowledge was amazing, considering he isn't even from the country itself and is Scottish. However, this hasn't stopped him from becoming an influential figure when it comes to Icelandic football. So much so, that he was awarded the Silver Badge, an honorary medal presented to those who have promoted Icelandic football. He became the third Scotsman to be awarded it. While he has written many books on the subject, he also runs a Twitter account, Icelandic Football UK, and that is where I was directed to find him.

Marc, cheers for answering my questions on Icelandic football. You were one of the first people that I was directed to when searching for someone who was a bit of an expert on the subject. You run the Icelandic Football UK Twitter account. Can I ask, why Icelandic football? What is the connection?

Marc Boal: Plenty of information on the links below, regarding my association with Icelandic football.

He doesn't answer the question, but instead sends me a link to an article that pretty much tells me what I need to know.

I click on the link and read about how Marc was awarded the Silver Badge from the Icelandic FA and why he has dedicated so much of his life to promoting Icelandic football. It all started when he played amateur football himself and visited Iceland to play in a tournament back in 1986. After his return, he kept in close contact with those he had made friends with over there.

In the interview Marc says: 'I've spent most of my life at sea, but I always come back to football and my connections in Iceland gave me a chance to experience the game as it grew in a different country.'

The interview continues to tell us how Marc has written and edited his own Icelandic football magazine, and he tells us what he hopes to achieve from his dedicated work.

'In the future I am hopeful of encouraging even closer ties between the two nations through football ... There are some plans already in the pipeline regarding youth development and learning from the Icelandic grassroots concept.'

The club that I am writing about from Iceland, IB Akureyri, are one of the few Icelandic clubs that I could find that could be deemed a 'Forgotten Club'. In fact, on the list of defunct football clubs from Iceland, they are the only club there. Are Icelandic clubs that well run? Should the rest of the world be taking note?

Marc: There are actually a few clubs that went out of existence or have become defunct, many clubs from rural areas have now had to arrange mergers in the modern day. Leiftur were one of the biggest clubs in recent years to fold, but they ended up merging with KS Siglufjordur to form the now KF Fjallabyggd. Tyr from Vestmannaeyjar were also a reasonable size club.

What is the culture like with Icelandic football fans? We saw how they can create an atmosphere when following the national team, with the 'Thunderclap' as it was known here in Ireland, becoming rather famous during the Euro 2016 campaign. But what are they like at club level? Is everything very peaceful and respectful or are there fierce derbies played in Iceland and, to your knowledge, were IB Akureyri part of any of these derbies?

Marc: The domestic leagues' fans can be noisy at times, but whenever it is an important match, the fans can be very boisterous. You can expect to see drums, cowbells and even fans with trumpets at derby games. The crowds in Iceland are family orientated at domestic games, very different from the UK and central Europe. There has been a trend in recent years of supporters' clubs emerging in Iceland.

Icelandic clubs seem to be well run, but they don't feature very often when it comes to European competition. The newly created Europa Conference League may open the door to the rest of Europe to see more Icelandic clubs play. But beforehand, they really have underachieved in European competition. Is there a reason, in your opinion, as to why that is?

Marc: This is a major conundrum for Icelandic clubs, and there are a number of factors why they have struggled in Europe. Most teams are semi-pro, and the financial aspect is one of the issues; the league format has changed this season, so there will be more meaningful games which will also help with progression. The Conference League will help smaller clubs in the current money-driven market. Vikingur Reykjavik were very unlucky not to make the play-offs this year after losing out to Lech Poznan. Hopefully in the next two to three years we will see teams from Iceland in the Conference League group stages.

At the moment, who is the best player playing in the Icelandic league? And are there any up-and-coming youngsters that we should know about?

Marc: The best player in the Icelandic league is Kristall Mani Ingason, who played with Vikingur Reykjavik. A fantastic talent, he has signed for Norwegian giants Rosenborg BK.

Countries like Iceland, which have small populations, yet can still compete on the world stage of football, always fascinate me. Coming from a small island nation myself here in Ireland, Iceland has been a bit of an inspiration of late, especially when they beat England at Euro 2016. In your opinion, what have they got right over there recently and why is it all coming together now?

Marc: Youth development is a key factor along with competent coaching. Iceland had fallen behind in recent years; the national team was an aging squad, and there is a huge rebuild on at the moment. However, it could take another two to three years before we see them light up the international stage once again. The building blocks are all being pieced together, especially at under-18 and under-21 level.

A question I usually ask everyone I interview, and sometimes the toughest one to answer for some, but who has been the best player to ever play for Iceland, and who has been your favourite player to come from Iceland?

Marc: The best player to come out of Iceland was Siggi Jonsson in my opinion, but he was plagued with injuries after a horrendous tackle by Graeme Souness in a World Cup qualifier. Asgeir Sigurvinsson was also a formidable player who starred with VfB Stuttgart in the 1980s; he also had a spell at Bayern Munich.

23.

Juventus IF (Sweden)

JUVENTUS IDROTTSFORENING or Juventus Athletic Association were formed in 1948 by a group of Italians who had settled in Sweden in the 1940s. The club was to be modelled on the original Juventus of Torino back in Italy. They adopted the same crest and used the famous black and white stripes as their home colours. The club were based in the city of Vasteras, which is in central Sweden and played their home games at the Raby IP. Playing in the lower leagues, the club didn't cause too much of a stir in their early days and just played a part in keeping the locals occupied. In truth, there are little-to-no records of their fixtures, results or honours up until 1999, which would suggest they were an amateur club for most of their existence. So, it is in 1999 where we will start to look at how this club did.

The club were affiliated with the Vastmanlands Fotbollforbund, one of the 24 districts within the Swedish Football Association. They organise lower tier and youth football in the eastern half of the province Vastmanland County. This would include tiers from Division 4 to Division 8. In 1999, Juventus IF were in Tier 7 Division 6 in the Vastmanland Ostra section. They finished second but that wasn't enough to gain promotion as only the winners of the section were awarded that. In 2000 the club finished second from bottom, 11th out of 12 clubs and were relegated to Tier 8 Division 7. It would take the club two seasons to gain promotion again to Tier 7 Division 6. They did so by winning their league, after coming sixth in the 2002 season.

The 2004 campaign saw the club gain back-to-back promotions, coming fourth in their league but gaining promotion through the play-off system. They had now reached the dizzy heights of Tier 5 Division 4. But it didn't last long, as in 2005 the club came bottom of the pile, finishing 12th, winning none of their 22 games that season, drawing two and losing 20. The club only managed to score 18 goals and conceded a huge number, 150 in 22 matches. The 2006 season saw them compete in Tier 6 as there had been a new league created above them, pushing everyone down a tier. For three seasons, Juventus IF competed in this league, finishing tenth (2006) and fifth (2007) until finally getting promoted again in 2008 when they were runners-up. They also won the VLT Cup that season and the Futsal trophy to go with it. The club saw it as their very own 'Treble'.

It was back up to Tier 6 Division 4 and it was there they remained for three seasons. The 2009 campaign saw the club finish a respectable fifth place out of 12, winning eight of their games, drawing three and losing 11. They scored 40 goals that season and only conceded 42, showing a big improvement on the previous season. 2010 was much the same, as the club once again finished fifth out of 12, winning eight of their games, drawing five and losing nine. They even managed to have a positive goal difference of eight goals, scoring 53 and conceding 45.

The positive direction the club was going in continued into the 2011 season when they finally got promoted again. They finished second behind Kungsor BK, winning 15, drawing two and only losing five matches all season. They scored an incredible 76 goals in their 22 matches, making them the top scorers in the league that year and only conceded 34. They achieved promotion via the play-offs and found themselves playing in Tier 5 Division 3, the highest level the club had achieved in their history. The 2012 season saw the club compete in the Sodra Sveland and they finished a respectable sixth in their debut season, before 2013 saw them drop one place to seventh but 2014 saw an improvement as they achieved their highest ever finish, coming fourth. But that was to be that from Juventus IF as they dropped out of the league in 2015, and eventually merged into IFK Stocksund in 2016, a club who themselves no longer compete in elite football in Sweden.

24

Calais RUFC (France)

NICKNAMED '*LES Sangs et Ors*' – the Blood (Reds) and Golds – Calais Racing Union FC were founded in 1974 after two amateur clubs in the area, Racing Club de Calais and Union Sportive, merged. Racing Club Calais were somewhat cup specialists, featuring in the last 16 of the Coupe de France quite regularly in the 1920s. They even managed, as an amateur club, to reach the quarter-finals in 1922. Their biggest result was beating CASG Paris in the second round of the tournament, 3-2, in 1921. The club opted to go professional in 1933, but struggled financially and so they dropped out after only five years of professional football, in 1938. They remained in the amateur leagues until 1974 when the merger with Union Sportive happened.

Union Sportive were founded later than Racing Club de Calais, in 1947. They were a product of another merger of two amateur clubs before them. They had a less glamorous history, with the only notable success for them being to reach the last 32 of the Coupe de France.

It was 1974 when the two clubs decided to merge, incorporating both their names into the new club's moniker, Calais Racing Union FC. They also used both of their original club colours for the new outfit. The club remained an amateur side, playing in the lower leagues of the French football pyramid, having moderate success as well. They were crowned champions of Division Three (North) in the

1980/81 season and were champions of CFA Group A four times, in 1987/88, 1997/98, 2002/03 and 2009/10. They were title winners in CFA 2 Group B as well, in 2010/11. CFA, is the Championnat de France Amateur league in which 64 clubs compete in different groups. It is effectively the fourth tier of French football under Ligue 3.

It wasn't Calais Racing Union FC's league triumphs that interested me though, while researching them. It was their 1990/2000 Coupe de France campaign and the story that it told. I had been informed by French football experts that this cup run was like no other and that it could easily have been mistaken for a movie. When I investigated it, it really did come across as *Roy of the Rovers* stuff and it was just too unbelievable not to include in this book.

In 1999/2000, Calais entered the Coupe de France, not realising that they would be embarking on a surreal journey. The club would knock out professional clubs such as Racing Strasbourg and Bordeaux on their way to reaching the final at the Stade de France, where they would face Nantes on 7 May 2000 under the guidance of Spanish coach, Ladislas Lozano.

The round of 16 saw Calais narrowly get past Division 2 side AS Cannes on penalties, winning the shoot-out 4-3 after the match had been drawn 1-1. The quarter-finals saw Calais take an even bigger scalp, defeating Division 1 side Strasbourg 2-1 to set up a semi-final tie with French football giants Bordeaux. With the game being played at the Stade Felix Bollaert, Lens, not many gave the amateur side a chance, but like in previous rounds, they surprised everyone. With the game ending 0-0 in 90 minutes, it went to extra time. Many would have predicted the professional side, Bordeaux, would have too much for the amateurs in regards fitness levels. But their predictions were proved wrong as Calais took a surprise lead in the 99th minute with a goal from their midfielder, and local lad, Cedric Jandau. Bordeaux hit back though, with the French international forward Lilian Laslandes equalising in the 108th minute. Calais weren't shaken by Bordeaux and took the lead again when Milien struck in the 113th minute. They were now 15 minutes away from an unthinkable Coupe de France Final. The amateur side held on, and even improved the scoring by getting a third in the 119th minute, with Gerard getting the final goal of the game.

The final was played in front of 78,717 people, something that the Calais players would never have experienced before, with many of them still working their day jobs as dock workers, teachers and office clerks. Nobody would have blamed them for letting the occasion get the better of them, but that was not to be the case. Like the other rounds before, Calais went on the attack and showed no fear to their professional counterparts, and even took a surprise lead thanks to a 34th-minute goal from their number 11, Jerome Dutitre. Nobody could quite believe what was happening, with the amateur side looking like the professional one, with one hand on the cup as they took their lead into half-time.

Pundits and fans were awaiting the second half with huge anticipation, hoping to see something special happen. An amateur side winning a major honour in one of the top leagues in Europe is not something that anyone could envisage in today's game, not even 20 years ago. Unfortunately, five minutes into the second half, the fairy-tale ending started to disappear when former Manchester City, Newcastle United and Wigan striker, Antoine Sibierski, equalised. He, his team-mates and the Nantes fans were probably the only people to celebrate the goal as the desire of a whole nation to see the underdog win was obvious. Calais defended brilliantly for the rest of the game and had their own chances to take the lead. At 1-1, going into the 90th minute, Calais looked like they would get another 30 minutes in extra time to regroup and have another go, but then their dreams came crashing down when referee Claude Colombo awarded Nantes a penalty in the 90th minute. Up stepped that man again, Antoine Sibierski, to spoil the party and he did it with no hesitation, slotting away the penalty, giving Nantes a 2-1 lead and enabling them to win the Coupe de France for the third time in their history, and retaining the title from the previous season.

Calais RUFC never really progressed up through the leagues, but did win championships, albeit in the lower echelons of the French footballing pyramid. The club itself dissolved in September 2017, due to financial difficulties, but left a legacy of being one of the more popular underdog stories in French football history.

25.

CF Reus (Spain)

CLUB DE Futbol Reus Deportiu, SAD or just CF Reus for short as they were known, were founded on 23 November 1909, and were based in the Catalonia region of Spain. They played their home matches at the Estadio Municipal, which has a capacity of 4,700. The football club were in fact a product of the collapse of the sports organisation, Reus Sport Club. But, by 29 September 1917, they were back to being a part of a multi-sports organisation, when they merged with Club Velocipedista and SC Olympia. But once again, the football side went solo, in 1951, with CF Reus Deportiu dedicating itself to just football, while Reus Deportiu stuck to other sports that were involved in the organisation.

They were a club that spent most of their life playing in the lower leagues of Spanish football, with the highest league they reached being the Segunda Division B, Spanish football's second tier. The club didn't make much of an impression until the 1940s when they entered the fourth tier of Spanish football, where they finished second in Group 1 in the 1940/41 season. The following season they finished fifth in their group while 1942/43 saw the club finish third. The 1943/44 season saw the club compete in the third tier for the first time, or the Tercera Division as it was called. They were placed in Group 4, with nine other clubs. They finished a respectable third, winning nine, drawing four and losing nine that season, finishing four points behind the group winners, Mallorca.

The 1944/55 season was a bit of a bizarre one for CF Reus, who competed in Group 5 this time around. The group consisted of ten teams and Reus finished sixth, with the top two teams going through to the championship play-off. They were Gimnastic de Tarragona and Levante, but the rest of the teams had to take part in a relegation play-off. Even poor old Girona, who finished third, had to face the threat of relegation. Reus avoided relegation, finishing sixth once again. It has to be noted, the whole relegation-promotion play-off structure back then was very confusing and a little bit bizarre. When looking into it a bit more, I found that it wasn't really down to results most of the time. Instead, clubs would opt out of going up, or decide to get relegated based on financial or political reasons.

Unsurprisingly, the 1945/46 season was given a new format, which, albeit still confusing enough, made more sense than the previous version. Keep up with me here. The new format saw the division have 100 clubs, competing in ten geographical groups. The top three in each group would progress to the second phase. That meant 30 clubs would go to phase two, which was comprised of five groups of six. The winners of each of those groups would progress to the final phase, which was another group competition. The top two clubs from the final phase group would gain promotion to the Segunda Division, while the club that finished third would have to face the club that finished 12th in the Spanish Segunda that year, in a promotion/relegation play-off. Reus were placed in Group 5 in the first phase, or the regular season as it was called, and gained qualification to the second phase by virtue of goal difference. They had finished third, behind Badalona and Jupiter, and were just above Tortosa, by only seven goals.

And so, into Group 3 they went for the second phase of the season. But that was to be the end of their progression as they could only manage to finish third in the group, four points behind the winners, Arenas Zaragoza. That year saw Malaga, Levante and Baracaldo promoted to the Segunda Division.

If you thought that format was hard to get through, with 100 clubs vying for promotion, well, the Spanish FA didn't agree. They added another 20 clubs to the equation, and another two geographical locations into the mix. So now, 120 clubs competed in 12 different groups of ten. This time, only the top two teams progressed, leaving 24 teams to compete in the second phase. Three groups of eight clubs were made, with each club having to play each other home and away. The winners and runners-up of each of the three groups progressed to the final phase. Once again, each team played each other twice, home and away, with the top two gaining promotion to the Segunda Division, while third place had to play a promotion/relegation play-off against the team that came 12th in the Segunda Division that year. Reus didn't have to worry about much of that as they finished ninth in their first phase group, although, while that may sound bad, they did only finish six points behind second-placed Jupiter.

The 1947/48 season was a mixed one for the club. Once again, the format was changed, but this time the number of clubs was reduced to 112 instead of the previous 120. Eight geographical groups were formed with 14 clubs in each. However, only the champions of each group would progress to the Fase Intermedia (second phase) in which they would compete in two groups of four. The winners and runners-up of these two groups would progress to the Fase-Final (final phase), where the top two of the four clubs would gain promotion to the Segunda League. Reus were placed in Group 5 but they struggled. They were relegated to the fourth tier once again, losing out on a relegation play-off spot by goal difference. In fact, it was so close that the two clubs above them, who both occupied the relegation play-off spots, only edged Reus out by goal difference, Sans, by six goals and Espana Industrial by ten. However, as I said, it was a mixed bag for the club that year, and they did go on a bit of a cup run, reaching the fourth round. They were knocked out by fellow Catalonian club, Unio Esportiva Lleida, who themselves dissolved back in 2011.

It only took the club a year to come back up to the Tercera Division and they once again competed at that level in the 1949/50 season. By now, there were only 90 clubs competing to get into the Segunda Division, and Reus were one of them. Under the name Reus Deportivo, they finished 12th in Group 3, meaning they neither progressed to the next round, nor did they get relegated. You may think that was a waste of a year? Well, Reus would have taken it the following year, because in the 1950/51 season, they found themselves relegated once again, finishing rock bottom of Group 3, winning just eight games, drawing nine and losing 21. They had conceded a whopping total of 96 goals, which tells you where the problems lay.

It took two years for them to bounce back and that's what they did after finishing top of their group in tier four of the Spanish footballing pyramid. The 1953/54 season saw the club finish 13th in the first phase of the league format and therefore not progress to the latter stages. This was the theme of Reus's life as a football club, up until the 1957/58 season, when disaster struck again and the club were once again relegated. A further two seasons in the fourth tier occurred before they finally got back up to the third tier again. This time, they would make their stay a little bit more permanent. They had a decade of mid-table finishes and nothing spectacular happening at all. Some may say it was good to finally be stable, others would say it was boring and predictable.

But as predictable things go, Reus were just that and in the 1969/70 season they finally saw themselves getting relegated once again, down to the fourth tier and there was no immediate bounce-back either. The club spent six seasons down in the fourth tier, until 1975/76, when they finally gained promotion. But they were almost immediately relegated once more when they finished 19th in Group 4, meaning they had to play in a relegation play-off. In their two-legged tie with CD Pena Azagresa, the club lost 4-2 in the first leg away from home. A big performance was needed in the second leg in front of their home fans and that is what they gave them, winning 4-1 and 6-5 on aggregate to secure their third-tier status once again.

The club remained competitive in the years that followed, finishing in the top half of the table, but it was the 1980/81 season that saw the club achieve what they may not have thought possible a few seasons beforehand. Placed in Group 5, Reus topped the league table, winning 22 games, drawing nine and losing just seven. They won the league by one point, finishing ahead of Figueres and just two points ahead of third-placed Badalona. It meant they progressed to the second phase, a two-legged knockout match against Real Aranjuez, a club based in Madrid. The Catalonian side easily beat their opponents from the capital, winning 1-0 in the first leg and 2-0 in the second to secure a 3-0 aggregate win. It set up a final round match against Arosa. The winner would secure promotion to the Segunda Division. Arosa won the first leg 1-0, but Reus were confident they could overturn it in the second leg and that is exactly what they did, winning the match 3-0 and gaining promotion with a 3-1 aggregate win. It was the first time the club would be competing in the Segunda Division, and the highest they had ever been in terms of league status. The next few years would be fun for the club nicknamed '*la avellana mecanica*', which in English translates to 'the clockwork hazelnut'.

The season was 1981/82 and CF Reus Deportivo had finally arrived in the Segunda. They were placed in Group 2, alongside 19 other clubs. The main objective in their first season at this level was to avoid relegation straight away, and they accomplished that by finishing 14th, winning 11 games, drawing 13 and losing 14. However, the 1982/83 season turned out to be a disaster. Placed in Group 1 this time, alongside the other northern clubs, Reus finished 20th, rock bottom of the league, winning just five games all season, drawing seven and losing 26. It meant they were back in the Third Division once again. And that's where they remained until the 1984/85 season when they plummeted even further down the ladder, being relegated after finishing 19th out of 20 clubs in Group 5. And it wasn't even a close call, with the club finishing 12 points behind the side in 17th, Mollerussa.

The setback meant they were relegated to their regional league for the 1985/86 season, but they won that with ease, and took their place back in the Spanish Third Division. But five seasons later, after relative mediocrity, they were relegated once again in 1990/91. Yet again, in the Catalonian regional league, they gained promotion straight away, finishing second.

After a ninth-place finish in the 1992/93 season and a 13th finish in 1993/94, the club were relegated again, finishing bottom of their group once more. This time, they would have to wait a few seasons before getting promotion. They played three seasons in the Catalonian regional league before coming second in the 1997/98 season and gaining promotion back to the third level. And four seasons later the club gained promotion to the Segunda Division once again. In the 2001/02 season they finished third in their group, gaining qualification to the promotion play-offs, and through that eventually went up to the Segunda Division B. But that stay was short-lived and they finished 18th out of 20 clubs, just three points adrift of safety.

The next season saw the club qualify for the promotion play-offs but unlike their previous success in the play-offs, they failed to gain promotion. Instead, they had to wait for the following year to do that; after finishing fourth in Group 5 and just about qualifying for the play-offs, by a point ahead of CF Peralada, the club navigated their way through the knockout stages to once again gain promotion. But in true Reus style, they immediately got relegated, finishing 17th, winning just nine games all season.

Another five seasons followed in the Tercera Division, until another promotion (I've lost count of how many in their history by this stage) was gained. You would be forgiven for thinking that this promotion would end in the same way as previous ones, with the club almost immediately getting relegated again. But no, this time they held their own for five seasons before the unthinkable happened in the 2015/16 season. CF Reus won their group, Group 3, and qualified for the group championship play-offs. It was a season that was helped by the goal scoring exploits of Edgar Hernandez, who finished fourth in the scoring charts, only behind Villarreal trio, Fran Sol (16 goals), Carlos Martinez (15) and Carlitos Lopez (13). One would think that having the three top goal scorers in your team would win you the league, but they would have to settle for second place, one point behind CF Reus.

The group championship play-offs took place, with four clubs competing to gain promotion. It was a simple knockout situation. The four teams were drawn against each other to play a semi-final and the winners of each semi-final would then progress to the final but would have the comfort of knowing both finalists would be promoted regardless of the result. The final was merely to decide who would be crowned the Segunda B Division champions.

CF Reus were drawn against Racing Santander. The first leg was played away from home at the Sardinero, in front of a crowd of 17,000. The home crowd were silenced early on, however, when Reus took the lead in the 11th minute thanks to Vitor Silva. Their lead was doubled in the 29th minute by their centre-back, Dinis Almeida. Not content with their 2-0 lead, the visitors made it three, when David Haro slotted home in the 58th minute, all but promoting Reus to the second tier of Spanish football for the first time in their history. They, of course, had to complete the second leg of the semi-final tie against Racing Santander and they did so by winning the game 1-0, thanks to a fifth-minute goal from Haro.

The final would be a two-legged affair, and their opponents were UCAM Murcia, who had just knocked out Real Madrid Castilla. Both clubs seemed to be happy enough in the knowledge that they would be going up and you would have thought that would make for an exciting, open game of football, with neither side having anything to lose. Not so, as both the first and second legs ended in 0-0 draws. It took a penalty shoot-out to decide the champions of the Segunda Division B. In the end, the trophy went to UCAM Murcia, as they won the shoot-out 5-3. Haro was the unfortunate player to miss his penalty.

That year also saw CF Reus reach the round of 32 in the Copa del Rey. After beating Asco, Arandina and Lleida Esportiu in the early rounds, they arrived at the round of 32, only to be knocked out by the mighty Atletico Madrid. Despite taking the lead in the first leg, through Carbia's

30th-minute goal, Atletico hit back with goals from Vietto (36th minute) and Saul (63rd). The second leg was a close affair, but was won 1-0 by Atletico, thanks to Thomas Partey's goal in the 53rd minute. It was the furthest CF Reus would ever get in the competition.

And so, Reus took their place in the 2016/17 Segunda Division, playing against some of Spanish football's biggest clubs. But it did not faze them, as they finished a respectable 11th out of the 22 clubs that competed in the league. Levante and Girona gained automatic promotion that year, while UCAM Murcia, the team that gained promotion with Reus the previous year, were relegated, although it must be said, narrowly, by two points. However, while things were looking good on the field, the situation off was starting to worry the Reus fans.

They participated in the 2017/18 season, finishing a respectable 14th this time, but they were starting to build up a huge financial debt at this stage. Playing in the higher leagues and trying to compete with some of Spain's bigger clubs was becoming too much for the small Catalonian outfit, and it soon became apparent that they would no longer be able to compete at that level unless a major investment was injected into the club.

They started off the 2018/19 season as planned, but the team were struggling on the field. They had only won five times in the first half of the season, and things were about to get even worse. On 18 January 2019, one day before the second half of the season was due to start, the LFP [Spanish Professional League] informed CF Reus that they were to be expelled from the league due to their failure to pay their players. The club were effectively relegated and finished bottom of the league, having to forfeit the rest of their fixtures and thus giving everyone a 1-0 walkover. They weren't just relegated to the Segunda Division B, but even further down, to the regional league back in Catalonia. The club had been included in the Segunda Division B, but were expelled when they still had not paid their players' wages.

Subsequently, the club were also excluded from playing in the regional leagues, until they had paid their debt. But they were unable to do so, and therefore were left without a league to play in. However, in October 2019, the Court of Arbitration for Sport ordered that the club be reinstated to the Segunda Division. This never materialised and Reus were liquidated a year later, on 20 October 2020, with the club's owners failing to present a plan to pay off a debt that was now estimated to be around 9 million euros.

And so, the club CF Reus, in its original form, ceased to exist. I spoke with a man who has written plenty of articles about the club, especially around the time of their demise, who is also the lead Spanish football writer for OverTheBar.net. Many people pointed me in the direction of Paul McGarraghy when I asked who the best person to speak to was in regards CF Reus, and so I asked him some questions about the club and about the state of Spanish football in general. Here is what he had to say.

Hi Paul, first of all, thank you for taking the time to answer my questions. CF Reus are an interesting club to say the least. I know you have written about them in the past. Can you tell me what gained your interest in them at the time?

Paul McGarraghy: Hi Philip, thanks for getting in touch. So, CF Reus were a club I had sort of had on my radar for a while, as I've always had a keen interest in Spanish football and Reus reached the Segunda Division (second tier) arguably on the back of money put into the club by Joan Oliver and Joan Laporta – two names Barcelona fans will know. However, in late 2018 I had heard rumours that the club had not been as profitable as the owners wanted and there were staff becoming concerned about not being paid. So, I started keeping an eye on developments and trying to make sense of the information that was coming out of the small town. To me, as someone who lives just a few miles from Bury Football Club in England, there seemed to be a couple of similarities between what was happening under Stewart Day at Gigg Lane before he sold to Steve Dale, and what was happening at Reus.

At the time there was next to no coverage on the situation in English and considering this was a town with a large airport that so many English speakers would fly to/through on their way to Salou or Portaventura (Universal Studios Mediterranea, as it was once called) it seemed odd that nobody was picking up on the story, so I picked it up myself. The club were given a three-year ban from football and a €250,000 fine – for any club to receive such a harsh punishment was pretty much unheard of, let alone the damage that it would do to a club of Reus's stature. I did some digging and found out what information I could to put out the story in the first article. (Paul sent me a link to that first article, an interesting read titled: 'CF Reus and How the Spanish League Killed a Football Club', which can be found on the Over The Bar Football website.)

After the first article went out, there were further developments surrounding the club with demonstrations from staff and supporters, but again there wasn't much coverage being provided other than the local newspaper, seemingly because the people involved – Javier Tebas, Joan Oliver and Joan Laporta – didn't want it to be broadcast to a wider audience. But I could see this was a big story that really deserved more coverage so after some digging I was able to put out a second and then a third article. The articles pretty much speak for themselves and with hindsight it's pretty clear that the information I was being given was even more accurate than I perhaps appreciated at the time. I think the fact that I was the only English-speaking person covering it made people want to volunteer info to me presumably because they thought it would bring the situation a bigger audience, and I found quite a number of Reus fans following me on social media and getting in touch. (Paul sent me a second and third article, follow-ups from the first.)

After the third article took off, the club's new owner, Clifton Onalfo, got in touch with me and we had a number of chats and he agreed to an interview to tell his side of the story. I should point out that he is the brother of Curt Onalfo the former player and now coach and was assistant coach to Bruce Arena at New England Revs when they set their record a year or two ago. Clifton is an interesting guy and had previously owned a club in Connecticut in the 1990s; he and his brother and fellow real-estate tycoon Russell Platt had been looking to buy a club. There were a number of clubs in Europe that they looked at, but I'm unable to say more about this – other than what's in the articles – as I'd given Clifton my word on confidentiality. They heard Reus was on the market and were given the opportunity to buy it from Laporta and Oliver – again, the articles I've published and the interviews with Mr Onalfo on OTBFootball.net (Over The Bar) cover this accurately, so I'd refer you to them for the details. Essentially, the full details of the club's financial situation were not disclosed to the new owners and Javier Tebas was pressuring the two parties to come to a deal because he was threatening to expel the club from La Liga. The deal was concluded and afterwards the US owners found themselves being given a demand for payment from La Liga for money the previous owners hadn't fulfilled – this is in the articles and the emails included on OTB. As I described in the articles and as Mr Onalfo explains in the interview, Tebas went ahead and expelled the club anyway and things got messy. La Liga owed the club a significant amount, we're taking millions in TV money, but were claiming the club had debts of between €8 and €9 million. If La Liga had offset the TV money vs the debt and allowed the US owners more time to have their lawyers and accountants do more investigating then I think it would have played out differently.

They spent a lot of time in the lower leagues of Spain, never making it to the top flight. Do you think, with more of an investment, they could have made that step up or is that just me being naive?

Paul: I think the intention from the various owners was to establish the club within the Segunda Division for the medium term and consolidate that position, build up the business model and improve infrastructure in that time, with a long-term ambition of reaching the top flight. In terms of the size and location of the club, I'd say that the second tier was a good position to be in and perhaps their ceiling. It's very close to Barcelona, where you've obviously got FC Barcelona and Espanyol who are going to suck up the majority of fans in the region, plus Girona (owned by the City Football Group) is not far away so there's a limit to growth. However, one of the things that made Reus appealing and worked in its favour is – as I mentioned – that the city is one that tourists and holidaymakers pass through, so there was the opportunity to pick up some extra money from a growth point of view.

I read an article describing them as 'The club the Spanish FA killed'. Is that the truth? Or is that pushing the blame somewhere else?

Paul: Yeah, I'd say that on balance La Liga share a large portion of the blame. I think you're referring to my article which is similarly titled (a title chosen by the editor, but I stand by it). In fact, the more I learnt the more I was satisfied that I had called it correctly. La Liga, in particular Javier Tebas, should take a lot of the blame, but from what I've seen and heard, I think Joan Oliver and Joan Laporta are the chief culprits – the main villains of the story.

Quite a few clubs in Spain could have featured in my book. There was no shortage of contenders. What do you think is the main reason for so many football clubs becoming defunct?

Paul: In the past there has been a relatively poor and, it has to be said, politically motivated financial environment in Spanish football, driven from the top down by powerful men in suits, with efforts made to appease certain clubs and stakeholders rather than having tried to build something sustainable. There has been some reform, as we're seeing with the La Liga 'computer says no' model currently in place, which hampered Barcelona from registering players in 2022, but there's still a long way to go and there's too much 'political' weight behind certain clubs which means the smaller clubs are at risk. There's also too much of an imbalance between the coverage the top clubs receive and what the smaller clubs do and this all feeds into attention from fans (which are seen by clubs nowadays primarily as consumers) and from scrutiny too. It's also due to the fact that there's historically been a huge gulf between the way TV rights were shared in Spain, but the new economic controls should improve that, but the legacy issues are still taking their toll on clubs.

If you could pick another Spanish club that would feature in this book, who would it be and why? (Remember they have to be dissolved or merged with someone else.)

Paul: I'd probably say SD Compostela. They were essentially liquidated and reformed twice – first in 1962 and again in 2004.

I watch Spanish football, it's one of the most popular leagues in the world. But there does seem to be a big gap between those clubs with money and those who are working on a much smaller budget. This usually means that some clubs may suffer the same fate as CF Reus did. Is there anything that can be done or is being done in Spanish football to stop this happening and maybe close the gap? Or again, am I being quite naive in my thinking?

Paul: La Liga have made an effort in the last few years to change their economic controls and share out the TV rights, but it is still far from good enough in my opinion. There are also the financial controls in terms of player registrations which we've seen hamper Barcelona and Real Betis, which is an attempt to stop clubs struggling financially, but it's not the best model and as this summer has shown, it still needs work. The TV rights are a big one though and I am not confident that the CVC deal La Liga proposed is the right way of going about it, but it is very hard for the league to compete with the Premier League in terms of demanding money from sponsors and TV companies. The departures of Messi and Ronaldo have definitely played a part in this, but it would be ignorant and inaccurate to attribute issues to those two players. Atletico Madrid challenging the big two has helped, but La Liga need to work on improving their marketing as a whole. It's the second (almost the first, in my opinion) best league in the world to watch and has so many storylines and subplots as well as some of the most interesting and unique clubs in the world and yet it really is not marketed very well at all.

Who is your favourite Spanish player of all time and who in your opinion is the best Spanish player of all time? It can be the same player.

Paul: My favourite Spanish player of all time is David Silva. I had the privilege of watching him week in and week out for ten years while he was at Manchester City (I'm a season ticket holder and travelled all over Europe watching the Blues). He's a magician. However, it's hard for me to really say who is the best Spanish player of all time, as the country is spoiled with the likes of Xavi, Iniesta, Puyol, Ramos, Xabi Alonso, Paco Gento, Alfredo Di Stefano (although technically, he was Argentinian), David Villa, Raúl, Fabregas, Pique, Busquets, Guardiola, Luis Enrique, Txiki Bigiristain, Iker Casillas … too many to mention.

26

Al Nahda SC (Lebanon)

FOUNDED ON 3 February 1926, by three men, Elias
Nakhle Boutrous, Emile Raffoul Boutrous and Elias
Moubarak, Al Nahda SC became Lebanon's first football
club. In a country where religion was a huge part of people's
lives, it is no surprise that the football club got most of its
backing from the Orthodox community, within the Mar
Elias district of Beirut. The club adopted the colours black
and white, which led to their nickname being '*les Diables
Noirs*' or 'the Black Devils' when translated into English.
Their stadium was situated in Mar Elias and they played
in it from 1927 onwards, with various work done on it
throughout history.

Al Nahda played friendlies against neighbouring towns
who started to establish football clubs themselves. They
also ventured outside Lebanon a few times to play in other
countries, but again these were just friendly matches or
exhibition games. This all changed on 22 March 1933,
when the representatives of 13 football clubs met in the
Minet El Hosn district in Beirut to form the Lebanese
Football Association. In May 1934, the Lebanese Premier
League was formed. It was known as the Edmond Rubeiz
Cup, in honour of the Nahda player who had died a year
previously from typhoid. The competition, while known
as a 'league', was played in a knockout format. Nahda beat
ASDPHB 7-1 in the final.

The 1934/35 season was won by AUB, while DPHB won it the following year. AUB came back to win their second title in 1936/37 and then made it consecutive titles by retaining their crown in 1937/38. It was in this season that the Lebanese FA Cup was set up, and just like the first Lebanese Premier League, Al Nahda went on to win it, beating Hilmi-Sport in a two-legged final, drawing the first leg 1-1 whilst winning the second leg 3-2.

DPHB won their second title in the 1938/39 season, while the next year saw the Lebanese Premier League cancelled due to the Second World War. Despite the ongoing conflict, the league recommenced for the 1940/41 season and DPHB won their third title, and their second in a row. Al Nahda won their second Lebanese FA Cup that year but it wouldn't be until the 1941/42 season that Al Nahda would lift the Lebanese Premier League title again. They followed it up again in the 1942/43 season, winning the league for the third time in their history.

So, in the first decade of Lebanese football, it was quickly established that there were three clubs dominating the league. Between them, Al Nahda, AUB and DPHB had won the title in the first nine seasons. However, the monopoly was about to be broken when Homenetmen won the league in the 1943/44 season. A club with strong political beliefs, as shown when they refused to play Israeli club Hapoel Tel Aviv in the Asian Champions Club Tournament in 1970, would become only the fourth club to win the Lebanese Premier League. The fifth club, Homenmen, won it the next season in 1944/45, while Homenetmen won it for a second time in 1945/46. Al Nahda were to restore the norm of the first decade when they won their fourth title in 1946/47, while also securing a league and cup double that year, winning the Lebanese FA Cup by beating Pagramian, 2-1. That made it back-to-back cup wins as they had won it in the 1944/45 season after beating Racing Beirut, 5-4 on aggregate.

In what would be seen as a bit of power sharing, the title was shared by Homenetmen and Al Nahda over the next decade, with Homenmen popping in twice to shake things up (1944/45, 1953/54). Homenetmen won the Premier League in 1947/48, Nahda won it in the 1948/49 season but this would be the last time the Black Devils would lift the Lebanese Premier League title, and indeed, it would be the last major trophy the club would win.

In what can only be described as a difficult period for Lebanese football, the 1949/50 season was cancelled, but when football resumed, Homenetmen made sure that the season off didn't affect them, and they took the 1950/51 title. The Lebanese Premier League was not in operation for two years, from 1951–53 due to political unrest and other situations arising outside of football at the time, and while some seasons were fulfilled, it was a theme for the next two decades that the football season just did not take place for one reason or another. From 1957 to 1975 a total of nine seasons were cancelled, and then in 1975 the Lebanese Premier League stopped completely due to the civil war in the country, only to resume in 1985.

By this time, a new footballing power had come to the stage in Lebanon, a club named Ansar, who at one point won ten consecutive league titles from 1989/90 to 1998/99. They, alongside Ahed, are now the powerhouses of Lebanese football, while the likes of ASDPHB, Al Nahda and AUB are no longer around, and Homenmen and Homenetmen are now playing in the lower leagues of the Lebanese football pyramid.

What happened to Al Nahda? Well, they were relegated to the Lebanese Second Division in 1956 when they lost a relegation play-off to Second Division winners, Sagesse. It was a straightforward 10-0 victory for the Second Division champions, and Al Nahda never came back up. The club remained there until the 1990s, and after once being one of Lebanese football's powerhouse clubs, they were declared bankrupt and folded. Lebanon's first ever football club was no more.

To get an understanding of Lebanese football, I spoke to Lebanese FA administrator, Maroun Mahfoud, a man who was full of knowledge when it came to the subject. Here is what he had to say.

Hi Maroun, thank you for answering my questions on Al Nahda and Lebanese football. First, Al Nahda, what can you tell me about them and why did they go bankrupt? A club that was so successful in their early years, how did it end like that?

Maroun Mahfoud: That's the problem of amateur football. The sustainability of a certain club is relative to the support it gets from a wealthy individual or political party. Throughout the years, the caretakers of Nahda switched to other interests and left it to its destiny.

There isn't much to find when doing research on individual players who played for Al Nahda or indeed any of the big clubs that dominated in the early years of Lebanese football. Can you tell me about any player that would have stood out back then, and who is the big player in Lebanese football today?

Maroun: Oscar Dana (GK), Muhieddine Jaroudi, Georges Chaderavian, Joseph Abou Nader, Emile Nassar. There are always players who stood out, most of them played between Nahda and Homenetmen. Just some names off the top of my head: Joseph Nalbdandian, Camille Kordahi, Manuel, Vartivar and lots more. Today's best player is without hesitation Hassan Maatouk, 99 international caps and 21 goals (joint top-scorer since 1971).

Most people around the world would be unaware of Lebanese football. I know, through my research, that the big clubs would be Ansar, who won the league 11 years in a row and more recently, Ahed. In Lebanon, is football well supported? What are the fan bases and crowds like on a matchday?

Maroun: Football is the number one sport in Lebanon. The biggest fan base is for Nejmeh SC, the third-biggest club in Lebanon. Usually the games are the highlight of the week. When it's a game that includes those three teams, the stadiums are packed, not that the stadiums can host big numbers. A marching band is usually present and the cheering is non-stop, although opposing teams can take taunting to the next level.

A few Lebanese clubs have gone, like Al Nahda. Why is that? What is the problem in Lebanese football or is there an underlying problem?

Maroun: I think it's the same answer as question one. The game is at amateur level still, from an administrative point of view. Also, the 15-year civil war didn't help. There is a clear break between football in 1975 and the 1990s.

In your opinion, will we ever see Al Nahda return to the Lebanese football league in any way, shape or form?

Maroun: Sadly no, I think we've seen the latest of Al Nahda.

Lebanon as a football nation: can you ever envisage a time where they may qualify for a World Cup in the future? Are there plans in place to even compete at that level?

Maroun: How could a nation qualify for a World Cup without at least one proper stadium? With the financial situation in the country, I see it as a dream that grows farther and farther from reach. At the moment, the plan is to survive, not to evolve.

A question I ask everyone, but in your opinion, who is the best ever Lebanese player to play the game? And who is your favourite Lebanese player to ever play the game? It can be the same player.

Maroun: I don't like the 'GOAT' question, but I can name some players that are eligible for such status: Mardik Tchaparian, Levon Altonian, Joseph Abou Mrad, Vardan Ghazarian, Moussa Hojeij, Roda Antar, Youssef Mohammad, Hassan Maatouk.

27

FC Jokerit (Finland)

FC JOKERIT were a Finnish football club based in Helsinki. They were founded in 1999 and were owned by a man named Hjallis 'Harry' Harkimo, who is a colourful character to say the least. A Finnish businessman, sportsperson and YouTuber, he is also a member of the Finnish Parliament, running his own political party known as Movement Now. The club only lasted four seasons but did have a bit of success during that time.

In their first season they won the Finnish Cup, starting off in the seventh round, beating Rakuunat Lappeenranta 2-1 away from home. Rakuunat are another club that have since been dissolved. The quarter-finals saw Jokerit play at home, where they met FC Lahti, a club who themselves had only been founded in 1996. Jokerit won the game 2-1 and progressed to the semi-final where they met one of Finland's biggest and most successful football teams, HJK Helsinki. A local derby, it was seen by most as just a training match for HJK, who would surely steam-roll past their smaller local rivals, who had just begun their football journey. But that wasn't to be the case and nobody had sent the FC Jokerit players the script, as they beat their city rivals 1-0 to progress to the Finnish Cup Final. Surely, after beating HJK, they would go on and win the trophy? The team that stood in their way was FF Jaro, a club based in the Finnish town of Jakobstad. They were also known as

Jaro Pietarsaari. The final of the Suomen Cup, as it's known in Finland, was contested by the two clubs in front of an attendance of 3,217 and it was FC Jokerit who lifted the trophy at the end of the game, winning 2-1 and claiming the club's first bit of silverware. It also saw the club gain qualification for the next season's UEFA Cup.

In the league the club finished a respectable fourth of 12, winning nine, drawing six and losing seven. This qualified them for what was known as the championship group in which the top eight clubs would play each other again to compete for the title. Not much changed in position for FC Jokerit and they stayed in fourth place, with a record of 11 wins, seven draws and 11 losses.

The 2000/01 season saw the club compete in the UEFA Cup first round where they were drawn against Hungarian opposition, TK Hungaria. They lost the first leg 1-0 and the second leg 4-2, meaning they were knocked out 5-2 on aggregate. That wasn't the end of their European journey that season, with the club falling into the Intertoto Cup, a mini tournament, the winner of which could try to progress into the UEFA Cup. Unfortunately, FC Jokerit drew Premier League side West Ham United and while they drew the home leg 1-1, they lost at Upton Park, 1-0, courtesy of a Dave Kitson goal.

But that didn't stop Jokerit from doing well in their domestic form and the club finished second, behind Haka Valkeakoski. They finished with a record of 16 wins, 14 draws and just three losses, which qualified them once again for the UEFA Cup first round. But once again, they found European football to be a step too far as they were knocked out by Ukrainian side, CSKA Kyiv, beaten 2-0 in both the home and away legs.

The 2001/02 season saw the club dramatically fall down the table, finishing 11th out of 12 and facing a promotion/

relegation play-off after only recording seven wins, seven draws and losing 19 games. Their opponents for the play-off were the side they had beaten in the 1999 cup final, Jaro Pietarsaari. The first leg, away from home, ended in a 1-1 draw, setting up the second nicely, but it was the Second Division side who would cause the surprise this time, winning 4-3 and gaining promotion at the expense of FC Jokerit.

The club didn't spend much time in the Ykkonen, Finland's second tier, and finished second out of nine, just behind KooTeePee Kotka. Jokerit gained promotion after going through the various qualification stages, and saw themselves once again competing in the Veikkausliiga, Finland's top tier. In 2003/04 the club finished tenth out of 14, winning seven, drawing seven and losing 14. But that was it from the Helsinki-based side, who were sold to rivals HJK Helsinki in March 2004 and renamed Klubi-04 and placed in the Kakkonen, the third tier of Finnish football.

I mentioned that FC Jokerit had a bit of a wild following, and in respect to Finnish football fans, they made negative headlines more than once. Known as the 116% Boys, so-called because they stood in section 116 and gave 100 per cent support to their team, they were some of the first football hooligans to make a mark in Finnish football. There had been minor fights between other clubs' fans beforehand, most notably between supporters of Tampere United and FC Lahti, but the 116% Boys took it to another level.

The club had been warned about racist chanting at games before their trip to FC Haka, and there was a heavy security presence put in place for the game. This didn't stop the fans, around 50 of them, from invading the pitch when Haka scored a last-minute winner to secure a 2-1 victory. Reports show that two officers were injured during the fighting and reinforcements had to be called to usher the

116% Boys back on to their buses for their journey home. But the fans decided they didn't want to go home and caused even more disruption, heading towards local bars and causing damage to property in the area. Their buses were stopped on their way back to Helsinki but only one person was charged with any misconduct. It put Finnish football in a bad spotlight, with the media comparing FC Jokerit to Millwall. It resulted in the Finnish football authorities tightening up security at their football grounds, with away fans being searched.

I interviewed Finnish football expert, Rich Nelson, who runs the Escape To Suomi Twitter account, covering everything you need to know about Finnish football, and judging by his detailed answers to my questions, it is well worth a follow.

I have been told you are the man to talk to in regards everything Finnish football; what can you tell me about FC Jokerit?

Rich Nelson: Jokerit took over the place of PK-35 Vantaa in 1999 (Vantaa is a district within the Helsinki region), mainly as an attempt to engineer a big second Helsinki club to rival HJK, trading on the brand of the (far more successful and well known) ice hockey team. Finnish football in recent years has been fairly transient and a lot of clubs have folded and reformed. Some have merged and re-split while Jokerit is the highest-profile attempt at buying and rebranding: I suppose the closest equivalent would be MK Dons in England. PK-35 were in financial trouble, and on becoming Jokerit, PK-35 reformed lower down the pyramid.

To me, FC Jokerit seemed to be a sort of project within a bigger project. Is this the case? Was there another motive

for the foundation of the club in 1999, or do you know the reasons why?

Rich: The main reason for the club was an attempt to buy into the market without the tradition or history. Football and hockey do have some connections (such as TPS in Turku or Ilves in Tampere) where one club has multiple sports. That they put so much money into the Toolon stadium (currently the Bolt Arena) shows how much cash was behind them. There was ego there, Hjallis Harkimo went in with all guns blazing and was a very sheepish man at the press conference confirming the end. As he said then, 'We hoped that the people following Jokerit's hockey matches would also get excited about football, but those who arrived at the stadium could be counted with the fingers of one hand.' That they won the Finnish Cup so soon helped build momentum, they had a strong team with big names, but sponsors weren't too interested and they struggled to fund the side.

While doing my research on FC Jokerit, I found a few other clubs who they had played to have been dissolved as well. Is this a problem in Finnish football?

Rich: Clubs dissolving is pretty common – there isn't really a huge amount of money in Finnish football, and most clubs get a large source of income from junior teams rather than senior games. In the mid-2010s, both PK-35 (again) and former champions Honka had to reform, while Covid has been the main reason why RoPS (Rovaniemi) have essentially put everything and everyone up for sale and dropped a division. In the women's top flight Kansallinen Liiga, TiPS of Tikkurila came second and immediately withdrew from the league because of a lack of funding. Ice hockey is by far the most appealing spectator sport in Finland, and while the Finland national football team are doing well (see Euro 2020) and attracting a lot of money, the domestic game isn't doing too well below the biggest clubs.

Finnish football came to life in the 90s and early 00s with players like Jari Litmanen, Sami Hyypia and Mikael Forssell all becoming household names in the Premier League. Did this help promote the Finnish National League?

Rich: The strong performances of those players did very little for the league – most of the national team players did and still do play abroad. Litmanen and Forssell's returns to Finland did raise some interest, but they were both well past their best at that point. Most of the highest quality young players get taken to the academies of big clubs in Europe before they make much headway in Finland. The standard of the Veikkausliiga has improved immensely and it's a lot more visible than it was say ten years ago, but for all the good attendances, there are some woeful ones (a top-flight game in October had an attendance of 237).

How do you see the league progressing in the next few years? Can clubs like HJK make inroads in European competitions? And now with the UEFA Conference League, surely, we will be seeing more of the Finnish clubs in action?

Rich: There is proper competition at the top of Veikkausliiga: last season had a final-day decider between HJK and KuPS, the previous two winners, which attracted decent attention. Some of the other clubs such as Inter Turku and SJK are well backed too. But HJK's income dwarfs the others – they earned around 4 million Euros from playing in the group stage of the Conference League, which would cover their entire budget for two years. HJK's minimum expectation every season is to reach a group stage, but they didn't do great in 2021 and not drawing a big club such as Spurs or Roma didn't help. They have been investing in Finland internationals and decent foreigners so should do at least as well again next year. The Conference League is a great draw for Finnish clubs, but it's likely to just extend the financial divide between HJK and the rest.

Finally, can you tell me an interesting fact about FC Jokerit that the readers wouldn't know about? And can you see them ever making it back to the top tier of Finnish football?

Rich: Regarding the future of Jokerit, I definitely can't see anything big in their future – the club name is pretty toxic now (as a football club), meanwhile the hockey operation is also a bit of a laughing stock because of the move to the KHL (Russian hockey league). The rules have tightened up around buying into clubs now, and HIFK, another Helsinki club, almost went out of business because of ownership issues. It's also a bit of a closed shop as the Veikkausliiga is run by the clubs rather than the FA and they won't want a pretender. They'll remain a quirk in Finnish football history, unfortunately.

28.

Stord Sunnhordland FK (Norway)

FOUNDED ON 18 December 2002, the club were originally named Stord/Moster, as they were a merger of two clubs, Stord IL and Moster. Stord IL had been competing in the Third Division of the Norwegian football pyramid at the time, whilst Moster were playing in the Fourth Division. The project was initiated by football agent Terje Simonsen and professional footballer Kjetil Lovvik. It was a project that many from the outside looking in had deemed destined to fail, and never believed it would be sanctioned in the first place. However, in November 2002, Stord's football section approved the plans and let both men invest their money into the project. The goal was to reach the Second Division of Norwegian football within five years, and once they had done so, they would revise the plan.

Everything was set up and ready to go, with head coach Magnar Aaland appointed, while Kristian Innvaer was appointed chairman of the board. However, Magnar resigned during pre-season and that left assistants, Elvind Egeland and Oystein Djuve to take charge of the team. Another spanner in the works appeared when Egeland resigned, pursuing another career outside of football. Icelander Kristinn Atlason was appointed head coach. It seemed as though a bit of stability was in place, but that wasn't to be the case as more resignations started to

flow into the office. Oystein Djuve handed in his notice
while fitness coach Tore Hammer did the same. In April
2003, two youth coaches handed in their notices., leaving
Simonsen taking over the youth section by himself.

On the pitch, things looked slightly better, with owner
Lovvik even registering himself as one of the playing staff.
He helped them win the league that year, becoming the
club's top goalscorer that season, as they won 14 games out
of the 22 they played. However, they lost in the promotion
play-off to Norheimsund IL, 4-3 on aggregate. It meant
another season in the Third Division.

It became apparent in the early days of this project that
making a profit was not going to be easy. In their first year
they were in a deficit, which was somewhat a shock to co-
owner Simonsen, who had been accused of using the whole
operation to make a profit for himself. Nevertheless, the club
continued to be successful on the field and once again they
won their Third Division group, winning 18, drawing one
and losing three games all season. This was despite another
managerial change at the start of the season when previous
head coach, Kristinn Atlason, who had won the league the
season before, was sacked in favour of Vegard Hansen. This
time the club won their promotion play-off match, beating
Nest-Sotra 3-2 on aggregate. It was something of a surprise
as Nest-Sotra had already beaten Stord/Moster that season
in the early rounds of the Norwegian Cup.

The 2005 season was to begin in the Second Division,
and owner Simonsen had already outlined the plan for
the future of the club. He wanted to be challenging for
promotion by 2007. It was ambitious to say the least.
In their first season in the Second Division, the club
finished a respectable eighth out of 14 clubs in Group
3, finishing ten points above the relegation zone, while
never challenging to gain promotion. But off the field,

things were starting to unravel, and the club's financial position was starting to deteriorate, with both owners' investments being lost. Within three years of the club's formation, they were unable to pay players' wages and it emerged that the manager, Vegard Hansen was also not being paid. He left and with that Jonas Jonsson, took over as head coach.

The pre-season for 2006 was not ideal at all, with players effectively going on strike and not turning up to training because of, their wages not being paid. Jonas Jonsson was also not being paid and as a result he left the club to go and manage Mandalskameratens. By now it became public knowledge that Stord/Moster were in big trouble and when owner Simonsen's company ceased all financial commitments to the club, the writing was on the wall.

However, the club continued to prepare as best they could for the upcoming season, with Bengt Forland being hired as the new head coach. He was also put in charge of marketing as the general manager of the club and so his salary was 45 per cent coaching based, while 55 per cent was based on his marketing role. It was a plan that did not work out well, as in March of 2006, the club cut its budget by sacking all non-playing staff, meaning Bengt was now only working for 45 per cent of his salary, which he deemed not worth his time and so he left.

It was around this time the club were taken over by a new limited company called Sunnhordland Toppfotball AS and changed their name from Stord/Moster to Stord Sunnhordland FK. The new chairman of the board was Tjerand Espeland and one of his first jobs was to appoint a new head coach. Morten Tislevoli was hired and given one task, to try and stay in the Second Division while the new board tried to stabilise the club financially. However, Tislevoli couldn't prevent the demise of the club on the pitch and they were relegated after finishing 13th, second from bottom of Group 3 that year. They finished four points behind Askoy, who were placed just outside the relegation places. It is just as well it wasn't closer, as Stord were deducted two points for playing two ineligible players that season.

Despite the relegation, the club had plans to continue and even hired a new head coach, after Tislevoli left. Petter Fossmark was appointed, and his brief was to gain promotion that upcoming season. However, he never got the chance as in December 2006, it was decided to fold the club due to financial difficulties. As a result, their spot in the league system was given to Stord IL and most of the playing squad, or those deemed good enough, were transferred to them. Stord IL were a club founded in 1914 and still play their football in Division Three at the time of writing.

And so, with only one season under the name of Stord Sunnhordland, the club ceased to exist, bringing to an end a fruitless and failed project. The club itself left very little mark on Norwegian football, other than highlighting how not to run a football club, and that making a profit from a football club is harder than it looks. In fact, when I went to look for an interview about this club, from anybody in the know about Norwegian football, it became apparent that even experts on this league and football in this country couldn't tell me about Stord Sunnhordland, other than it was a mistake and one that was a bit of an embarrassment to Norwegian football.

29

North West Sydney Spirit FC (Australia)

NORTH WEST Sydney Spirit FC was founded in 1997, a club based in Sydney, Australia. A project that was inspired by the success of another Australian club, Perth Glory, they entered the National Soccer League in the 1998/99 season. The club colours were white, red and yellow, while they played their first home game at the North Sydney Oval. That match, against Sydney United, attracted a record attendance of over 18,000. The club then moved to the Brookvale Oval to accommodate a much bigger crowd. They were formed to represent the northern suburbs of Sydney in the footballing world, a part of Australia that had no football team, or at least not at that level before.

Their first season was a huge success, with the club finishing fifth out of the 15 clubs competing in the NSL. It meant they progressed to the semi-finals, after winning 14, drawing four and losing ten. They were drawn against fellow Sydney club, Marconi Stallions. After a 0-0 draw in the first leg at home, they were beaten 2-1 at the Marconi Stadium, meaning their season ended there and then. But it was a good start and a base that they could try and progress from. The club looked like they were going to be a huge success. That is how it looked at the start; however, things started to unravel early on, with financial problems creeping in.

The 1999/2000 season was not as successful for the club on the field, with Northern Spirit finishing a disappointing 13th, winning only 11 games, drawing three and losing 20. The 2000/01 season was very much the same, with the club finishing 13th, although this time they were in a league with 16 clubs competing in it, although Carlton, who finished bottom, withdrew after eight games and subsequently folded. Northern Spirit won just eight of their games that season, drawing eight and losing 14. But it was the stuff that was happening off the pitch that was making the headlines regarding Northern Spirit.

In fact, in the middle of their first season Crystal Palace owner Mark Goldberg bought a 31 per cent share in Northern Spirit. He had been given a chance to buy up to 35 per cent, but didn't opt to take more due to Crystal Palace's own financial troubles. Instead, he sold his share to a group of players and coaches including Graham Arnold, Ian Crook and Robbie Slater. In an even weirder twist, the club were then owned by Scottish club Rangers FC and even changed their shirt colour to royal blue, the same as the Glasgow club.

Back on the field, Northern Spirit were just finishing mid-table every season. With the 2001/02 season only having 13 clubs competing in it, Northern Spirit finished eighth, winning nine, drawing seven and losing eight. They finished only two points behind Melbourne Knights, who finished sixth, in the last qualification place for the Final Series. The 2002/03 season was a better one for the club, as they once again finished in the qualification spots, in sixth place, one point ahead of South Melbourne, to clinch their place in the Final Series. Unlike the last time they participated in this stage, it was now played in a league format, with the top six in the regular season playing each other twice. But Northern Spirit found themselves out of their depth, finishing fifth out of the six clubs, winning just two out of their ten games.

The 2003/04 season was one of near misses, as they failed to earn consecutive appearances in the Final Series. The club finished seventh, just two points behind sixth-placed Brisbane Strikers. It would turn out to be the last season in which Northern Spirit would compete in the NSL. In fact, it would be the last season of the National Soccer League in Australia, as it was to undergo a reform, and in its place the A-League would be created, with a different format. Northern Spirit would not, however, be around to take part in the A-League, and in the end the club dissolved due to financial problems that had been around since the club formed. However, that was not to be end of the club completely.

In 2004, after Northern Spirit had been dissolved, the club's youth teams were assembled into the newly created Gladesville-Hornsby Football Association. They eventually went on to merge with the Northwest Sydney Women's Football Association, with the men's team playing under the name North West Sydney Spirit FC. They have since had moderate success as a semi-professional club, winning the National Premier League NSW 2 in 2015. However, the club were not actually promoted as they did not meet the criteria set out by the New South Wales football association. The club still play in the NPL NSW Men's League. In 2021, the competition was called off after 16 games had been played due to the Covid-19 pandemic. NWS Spirit were placed sixth out of the 12 clubs at the time of cancellation.

The 2022 season went ahead, and NWS Spirit came fourth in their group, qualifying for the 2022 League One Finals. Unfortunately, they were beaten in the qualifying round by Northern Tigers, meaning that they will once again compete in the NSW Premier League next season.

30.

Grazer AK (Austria)

ORIGINALLY FOUNDED as Grazer Athletiksport Klub (GAK) in 1902, and from the Austrian city of Graz, the club was part of a franchise of sports clubs ranging from sports such as basketball, diving and tennis. But football, of course, was the most popular. The club itself was founded by a medical student from Prague named Georg August Wagner with help from other associates of his, and it was modelled on another Austrian club, Wiener AC. Wagner had organised the first public match in present day Austria eight years before GAK were formed, with the match taking place in the Graz municipal park in March 1894. Unfortunately, there is no official record of this game, no names of the clubs or even a final score, but it is known to be Austria's first real football match. One can only assume Wagner used the name GAK as one of the clubs who participated, especially as eight years later he helped form the club officially.

GAK flirted with mediocrity for the first 50 years of their existence and there was not much success to talk about until the 1960s when they saw minor success in coming second in the Austrian Bundesliga, the club's highest finish at that stage. They also reached their first Austrian Cup Final in 1961 but were beaten 4-1 by Austria Wien. From that season they then entered European competition with their first match coming against Odense BK in the

Cup Winners' Cup in 1962. They then made their second appearance in an Austrian Cup Final but again were beaten, this time 2-0 by Rapid Wien in the 1967/68 season.

The club made regular appearances in Europe from then on, without making any impression in any of the tournaments. It wasn't until 1981 that they won their first major trophy. At their third attempt, the club finally lifted the Austrian Cup, beating SV Austria Salzburg 2-1 on aggregate over two legs. After losing 1-0 in the first leg, GAK turned it around and won 2-0 in the return, albeit they needed extra time to do so.

Their next cup triumph didn't come until the 1999/00 season when they won it again, this time needing penalties to beat, yet again, SV Austria Salzburg. The game itself finished 2-2. Their third cup triumph was probably their sweetest as it came at the expense of their biggest rivals, Sturm Graz. They beat their city rivals 3-2 in a thriller of a cup final in the 2001/02 season in what proved to be the most successful decade in the club's history. They went on to become runners-up in the Austrian Bundesliga in the 2002/03 season. But the season after proved to be the most successful one in the club's history. They finally won the Austrian Bundesliga but also completed the league and cup double with a win in the Austrian Cup Final against Austria Wien. The game itself finished 2-2 in normal time with GAK's Kollmann scoring an equaliser in the 86th minute. GAK went behind again in extra time when Austria Wien's Gilwicz scored in the 99th minute only for GAK to hit back minutes later with a goal from Aufhauser. The game went to penalties and GAK won 5-4 after Wien's Dundee missed the decisive penalty.

As mentioned, the club regularly took part in European competition but never really made it out of the group stages, only once getting as far as the last 16, in the 2004/05 season, when they were eventually knocked out by English club Middlesbrough 4-3 on aggregate. But arguably their biggest and most famous result in European competition came against another English club in the Champions League third qualifying round in the 2004/05 season, against European giants Liverpool. Although knocked out 2-1 on aggregate, GAK beat them in Austria 1-0. This became an even bigger result for the club as Liverpool eventually went on to win the Champions League that year, famously beating AC Milan on that night in Istanbul.

But the golden years for GAK as they were known came to a crashing end and in the 2006/07 season the club went into administration and as a result were docked 28 points. The next season they were not allowed to participate in any of Austria's professional leagues and were relegated to the Austria Regional League Central. The bad news kept coming and the club declared bankruptcy again and although a settlement was made with the creditors in September 2008, four years later the club dissolved after their relegation to the Regionalliga Mitte.

This resulted in a phoenix club being set up by the fans in 2012, who refused to let Grazer AK disappear. The new club would be called Grazer AC and they originally competed in the bottom tier of Austrian football from the start of 2013/14. It was in 2014, though, that a meeting took place to consider who Graz AC were and the final conclusion was that they were a continuous version of GAK and so become GAK once again. Even more impressive has been the rise of the club since, winning back-to-back championships every year to regain their professional football status and to play in the second tier of Austrian football. They play at the same stadium as their local rivals Sturm Graz, the Liebernauer Stadium.

There was only ever one place I was going to go to get an insight into Austrian football. When I joined Twitter a few years ago, and started Forgotten Clubs, one of the first podcasts I came across on the platform was one about Austrian football. It was the brilliantly named The Other Bundesliga. Hosted by three lads from England, Tom, Lee and Simon, I was determined to have them contribute to this book, and of course they answered my questions. Extremely insightful as always, here is what they had to say when I posed my seven questions.

Cheers lads, for taking the time to answer my questions on Graz AK and Austrian football. First of all, your podcast The Other Bundesliga is brilliant and is one of the first ones I started listening to when I joined Twitter, but I have to ask, why Austrian football? What was the story behind that for yourselves?

The Other Bundesliga: Thanks for checking out the pod from the early days! It started out as the three of us were mates who had all happened to move to Vienna for our separate jobs. We met there and were regularly watching games, and we also all worked in one way or another in sport, so at some point, once Tom learned to record and edit audio properly when working for a radio station, we thought 'why not make a podcast in English?'

We all love local leagues and the football which is near to us as people who are living in Austria, so we figured if we're really going to get to know the game here, we should kind of go on a journey along with people on Twitter for example, who might want to learn about the league as we discover it! We also figured that nobody was really looking at the game here from an outsider's perspective, and a lot of good young players were starting to come through. Salzburg were always on the verge of the UCL [Champions League] but hadn't made it there yet ... it just seemed like it could be a good time to start covering a league which we hoped would be on an upward trajectory in the coming years, and as it has proven, that's exactly what ended up happening! Now suddenly there are loads of big European games and people are realising that they know nothing about the league here, and are therefore turning to us for some insight!

There were plenty of clubs to choose from when it came to selecting a 'Forgotten Club' from Austria. I landed on Grazer AK, but which other club from Austria would you say has an interesting story behind them?

The Other Bundesliga: Grazer AK is definitely a great choice, but sadly a lot of other Austrian clubs have had complex histories with financial problems or mergers into other clubs. Clubs like Hakoah Vienna, who were once a well-known name and now no longer exist. More recently, Bundesliga side Mattersburg SV simply folded after a bank scandal involving their chief financier, but we'd say Wacker Innsbruck would be a great shout. Under the guise of FC Tirol they had Jogi Löw as their coach, and were dominating the league as recently as 20 years ago, and as of today they're fighting for their lives in amateur football, despite being relatively well supported and respected as a big name in Austrian football.

Grazer AK seem like the 'little brother' of Graz football, but they still seem to have a strong following. So why in your opinion did it all fall apart for them?

The Other Bundesliga: GAK are definitely the 'little brother' of football in Austria's second city at the moment, but for much of the last century the histories of Sturm and GAK were fairly closely aligned, with peaks and troughs for each club over the years. Thanks to the regional basis of leagues in the past, a huge part of the history of the two clubs involves decisive derby games going one way or another, so it's no wonder that the two sides are part of one of the very biggest derbies in the country.

We weren't covering Austrian football back in 2007 when GAK declared the first of four bankruptcy proceedings which would eventually end the club in effect, but before that they were seemingly financially backed to a large extent by the building machinery company Liebherr, which is a relatively big name worldwide even today. Apparently at some point, the money ran out, and all of a sudden, this club which had recently been winning leagues, cups and playing in Europe, was wiped off the face of Austrian football. It was a major scandal and a big shame of course, but football simply doesn't make great amounts of cash in this country. If you're spending big to chase the titles, you need to succeed to keep the balancing act going. As soon as the success falls away, there's a hole in the finances. If you look at clubs in different Austrian states, Salzburg, Tyrol, Carinthia, there are very similar stories from other clubs around the same time, so whilst GAK's fate was a massive shame, it was definitely not an isolated case.

Of course, Graz AK are still going, under a different model I suppose, but do you think they will get back to the level they were at, playing European football, and once again playing with the elite or is the gap between the top clubs and everyone else just too much?

The Other Bundesliga: If we think about the GAK side who beat Liverpool in their famous UCL winning year, and the famous Graz reds who were winning silverware in Austria as recently as 2004, it's hard to imagine that happening again in our lifetimes. It's unfathomable that anyone can usurp Salzburg in their current guise: they're in a league of their own, so nobody can really imagine becoming a regular trophy winner here. The continuation club of GAK have bounced back through the leagues in some style, as well-loved phoenix clubs sometimes do, but they've found their level at the moment, and they're pretty much mid-table in the Austrian second tier. It's definitely possible that they can win the Second Division and get promotion to the Bundesliga in the near future though. Much like the English Championship, there seem to be new teams making up the top six every season in Liga Zwa as it's known over here. So, one day soon, GAK can certainly win that, and we can see them being a popular team in the Bundesliga, given that they have a fan base which would fit right in, and fans all over the state of Styria would be happy to see the Grazer derby come back more often. We just had one in the ÖFB Cup (Sturm won 1-0) which was the first derby in 15 years, and it was very much celebrated, so hopefully that can become a more regular fixture in the Austrian football scene.

Austrian football, at an international level, has always seemed to be stable, as in the national team always seem to be in with a shout of qualification, or actually qualifying for major tournaments. What do you think is the limit for them? Do you ever envisage the Austrian national team winning or even challenging for a major honour in the future?

The Other Bundesliga: The Austrian national team is a strange one to analyse. The most talented players such as [David] Alaba are often a complex problem for national team coaches, working out how to get the best out of a bunch of players who play in quite specific ways at their club sides. We saw Austria put up a decent effort but ultimately get relegated from Nations League A in 2022, so they've sort of hit their ceiling between the B and A level, but they're probably closer to the B group in reality. The current debate is basically that the players, the league quality and just the talent level in the national side is actually higher than the results are suggesting, so hopefully qualification will become more of a formality in the future, if they can make the most of their potential.

Winning a competition is not really a reality for Austria, but if you look at our smaller neighbours rather than comparing to Germany, there should be no reason why Austria couldn't emulate what a nation like Croatia have managed in the last decade or so. The league there is much weaker, and they don't exactly have a massive population or a hugely well-financed game there, so if Croatia can produce so many good national teams, then ideally Austria could too. That being said, football is a much bigger deal in Croatia than in Austria, where it plays second fiddle to skiing!

David Alaba is probably the best-known footballer in recent times to come from Austria. But who in your opinion is the best Austrian footballer to have played for the national team and who is the best player to have ever played in the Austrian league?

The Other Bundesliga: The best ever player to play for Austria might be Matthias Sindelar, 'the Paper Man'. Revered for his technical talents, he was pivotal for a few of the Vienna club sides in the early days of European football, and was a key part of the 'Wunderteam' of the 1930s, regarded perhaps as Austria's greatest ever national team. He also died in suspicious circumstances after humiliating the Nazis during Austria's annexation in World War Two, so he's a figure that attracts a lot of interest.

The best player ever to play in the Bundesliga? Recency bias may be affecting things somewhat, but we'd have to go with Erling Haaland. We're quite happy and a bit proud that he made his breakthrough here, and then when people said 'but it's only Austria', he managed to go even better in the Champions League, the German Bundesliga, and now the Premier League. He's a once-in-a-generation striker, and we got to see him emerge here first hand, which was really special. There's a little-known fact that may be of interest as we're talking about GAK here, and that's also that Sergej Milinkovic-Savic, now valued at over 100 million Euros, started out at GAK as a kid, as his father won the league here with the Graz side. He didn't go on to play as an adult here, but nonetheless, his start in football was in the red half of Graz!

Finally, with the creation of the Europa Conference League, can you ever see an Austrian club winning a European trophy in the near future? Red Bull Salzburg and Sturm Graz are just two clubs that come to mind that may do it at some level or is there another club you fancy to make the breakthrough?

The Other Bundesliga: The Europa Conference League should be a real boost to Austria's chances of success in Europe, in theory. If you look at the last few seasons, Salzburg have gone beyond the UCL [Champions League] groups, WAC and LASK have gone beyond the UEL [Europa League] groups, and LASK again went past the UECL [Europa Conference League] group stages with a very good group campaign last season. These are tiny teams in the grander scheme of things though, and if you look at the European map as a whole, the new competition structure has really just allowed the underperforming 'big names' to get to the latter stages of a lesser competition. Sides with former Champions League stature make up most of the UEL knockouts, and huge clubs even end up near the business end of the UECL, so while in theory it helps Austrian teams to go further, they're not likely to be beating the likes of Roma or Marseille, the ilk of teams who are in the latter stages. Salzburg should have a genuine chance of winning one of the lower two, but they're unlikely to see any UECL action soon, and they haven't really done as well as expected when they've dropped into the UEL recently. Oh well, we can still hope!

31.

Aldershot AFC (England)

FOUNDED BY a local sports journalist, Jack White, in 1926, Aldershot Town FC joined the Southern League in the 1927 season. White's determination to have a football club represent the town paid off as he persuaded the local council to get behind them. And their faith was paid back straight away with their first ever game ending in a 4-0 victory against Grays Athletic. The game was played at their home ground, the Recreation Ground and attracted a reported 3,500. The Shots, as they are known, ended their first season in a respectable seventh place and continued to stabilise until 1932 when they won their first league title in the form of the Southern League. This promoted them to apply for membership to the Football League and they were accepted at the expense of Thames FC. The 1932/33 season was their first in the Football League and saw the club change their name to just Aldershot.

The first few years for the Shots were forgettable to say the least, with the club finishing 17th in the Third Division South in their first season. They rose three places the season after, finishing 14th and in 1935/36 the club went another three places up the table by finishing 11th. That was to be a false dawn for Aldershot, who finished bottom of the league a year later and had to re-apply that year. Luckily, they were accepted, and the following years brought progress, seeing them finishing tenth in the 1938 season, their highest finish to date. Mediocrity followed until the club finished 18th in 1958 and were relegated to the newly formed Fourth Division. Aldershot were one of the first clubs to compete in this division, after the restructuring of the Football League, but also have the unwanted record of being the first club to finish bottom of the division, which they did in 1958/59 (22nd). Once again, the club were forced to reapply to join the Football League and once again they were successful.

The 1960s passed without much happening of note, but that didn't stop the club attracting big crowds. In 1970 the club recorded their biggest ever attendance in an FA Cup tie against Carlisle. The reported attendance was 19,138, which was impressive for a Fourth Division club. Three years later the club gained their first promotion in the Football League, 41 years after they were formed, and it was only by goal average. They came fourth and just pipped Newport County to gain promotion to the Third Division.

Things looked like they were on the up for the Shots, as they finished eighth in their first season in the Third Division, but they struggled to find that form in seasons after, flirting with relegation in 1975 and just avoiding the drop by a single point. The inevitable happened the following year in 1976, when they were relegated back to the Fourth Division. They almost made an immediate return but were just beaten to promotion by Brentford, Watford and Swansea. The season after played out the same scenario as the club just missed out on promotion by a single point, this time to Wimbledon. Even though the club failed to gain promotion, coming close on numerous occasions, they were still punching above their weight, finishing higher than such prestigious clubs as Portsmouth and Huddersfield Town.

Season after season saw Aldershot jump around the places in the Fourth Division, finishing 16th in 1981/82 but then fifth in the 1983/84 season. But it was the 1986/87 season when Aldershot made a little piece of history, being one of the first clubs to gain promotion via the play-off system. Firstly, they beat Bolton Wanderers in the semi-final, to set up a play-off final against a strongly fancied Wolverhampton Wanderers. Aldershot had clearly not read the script and defeated the four-time FA Cup winners 3-0 on aggregate over two legs to take the place in Division Three. Tipped to go straight back down again, Aldershot defied the odds and avoided relegation by three points. However, the 1988/89 season saw them relegated as they finished bottom of the pile, 17 points off safety.

At the start of the 1990s, financial problems became apparent for the club and their main aim was just to stay alive. This affected the playing side and the club finished 22nd in the Fourth Division. The summer of 1990 saw the club wound up with debts of £495,000, until 19-year-old property developer Spencer Trethewy came up with £200,000 to save them from going bust. This, however, turned out to be a false hope and it soon emerged Trethewy's dealings were not what they seemed and he was kicked off the board in 1990. He was subsequently found guilty of fraud and jailed for two years in 1994.

Aldershot continued to struggle and on 25 March 1992 they finally went out of existence and had to resign their position from the Football League midway through the season. All their results were dismissed and they became only the second club to undergo that process, after Accrington Stanley before them. The club's final league game came at Cardiff's Ninian Park and ended in a 2-0 loss. Their last home game was a defeat to Lincoln City, losing 3-0. To put into context the on-field struggle of the club, they lost their last 16 games, their last win coming against an also struggling Maidstone, on 28 December 1991.

But like most clubs like Aldershot, who fell victim to poor financial planning, their followers would not let them completely die and a phoenix club was set up by the fans a year later. The club, named Aldershot Town, were placed in the Isthmian League Division Three, five levels below where Aldershot FC had once played. The club managed to reach the dizzy heights of the Football League again, playing League Two football in 2008 but were relegated in 2013. They are currently playing just below League Two, in the National Conference League.

The size of the club and the following they have at present meant it wasn't hard to find a fan to share their memories about the club, old and new, but I was repeatedly pointed in the direction of one person. One look at his social media accounts and you can see he is Aldershot through and through. Tim Cowden aka TimShots gave me an insight to what it was like to support the Shots through thick and thin.

First of all, what is your favourite memory from supporting Aldershot?

Tim Cowden: From the old club, it would probably be the trip to Wolves, May Bank Holiday 1987 – intimidating atmosphere, especially after the final whistle walking to the car! New club: toss-up between winning promotion back to the Football League on 15 April 2008 with a 1-1 draw at Exeter. Or the Hampshire Cup Final at The Dell, 1999.

What was your favourite away day?

Tim: Old club – many a football special with 40–50 of us going on inter-city away days when we were young! These days any jolly to London, two or three times a season is about as good as it gets, more about the social side of the day out than the match itself!

I have done a bit of research on Aldershot FC and Aldershot Town as they are known nowadays. In your own words, what is it like supporting the club?

Tim: Following the old club from age ten to 30, when we went out of business, was a journey … We never really had any glory in those years; two promotions, I was too young for the first in 1973 but certainly the 1987 one is a lifelong memory. But generally, mediocrity was the order of the day.

The reformation sparked life into the club, we were suddenly winning every match. Promotions and championships followed along with cups and the holy grail of a return to the Football League achieved after 16 seasons. It all turned sour in 2013 with the club relegated and nearly folding again. We had a couple of play-off attempts to get back into the FL, should have gone up in 2016/17. Lost our way in 2017/18 after a great start – since then it's been dire.

I know Aldershot are in the Conference Premier (at the time of writing). How far up the leagues do you see your club going, especially in the next few years?

Tim: Our spiritual level is Division 4/League 2 – [I] like to fool myself one day we could be in the Championship but not sure there's ever going to be a time we can get above Division 3/League 1. The dream for most of us is to see the club play at Wembley – we've been so close several times, plus on occasion, we've reached a play-off final, it was when it was home and away (1987) or Wembley was being redeveloped (2004).

Who do you believe is the best player to have put on the Aldershot jersey?

Tim: I'm going to go with club legend Ian McDonald – joined in 1980, stayed all through to the bitter end in 1992 as player and manager – a real gentleman and the best penalty taker the club ever had!

Finally, any special mention you would like to give to anybody involved with Aldershot Town FC?
Tim: These days ATFC owe so much to Mark Butler – goalscorer turned marketing manager – bleeds red and blue. Was a fan of the old club as a boy and a member of the class of 1992 that saw football return to the town after the club went **** up. I'll never forget the work put in by Ian Reade in the 1980s, organising the away-day travel. Really got me hooked on the whole ground-hopping aspect.

32.

Racing Club Luxembourg
(Luxembourg)

ONE OF the first clubs in the country, Racing was founded in 1907, meaning that they could compete in the first-ever National Division in 1909/10, which was held in a knockout rounds structure because there weren't enough clubs to play a league at the time. Racing Club did well, moreover, they won the whole thing, beating Hollerich 3-2 in the final. The next year they didn't enter the league, but they tried again in 1911/12 when they even had several players in the national team for their first-ever match (1-4 versus France). In the league, though, they finished a disappointing third out of four, with seven points in six matches. Then – for still unknown reasons – the league wasn't held in 1912/13. In the next season though, there were more clubs involved and relative success came for both the team and the country. While Luxembourg finally got their first win in a friendly, a 5-4 thriller against France, Racing Club Luxembourg finished in third place behind Hollerich and Sporting Club Luxembourg.

However, in 1914 World War One started. That forced the FLF [Luxembourg federation] to organise the league with a tournament structure (groups and knockout), with groups of two/three. Racing were put into the only three-team group after the regional allocation and finished second behind Sporting Club (still four points higher than Hollerich), meaning that the competition ended for them after just two matches. It was a big disappointment because they simply couldn't have been nearer to first place. In their match against SCL, they lost 6-5. If that one had been a draw, they would have gone through on better goal difference.

The following year, the league had time to plan the structure so the six teams were able to play against each other twice, just like before the war. Every supporter of Racing was waiting for a resurrection of the team. Instead, it happened to be Hollerich's resurgence as, after the disappointing 1914/15 season, the navy blue team managed to win the title with seven wins out of ten, including an 11-1 record victory over Jeunesse Esch. Racing finished a disappointing fourth, missing out on the podium by goal difference only.

In 1916, Stade Dudelange got relegated from the league and were replaced by a new club, Young Boys Diekirch, who still exist as I write this, which is a rarity among these teams. The league table didn't change significantly though – Hollerich now won the league by winning every single match. Racing only managed to collect eight points in ten matches, but surprisingly that was enough to secure them third place. Furthermore, they could finally finish above city rivals Sporting Club. The contest between Racing and SCL was tight again, with one of their matches resulting in a 4-6 Racing win. In 1917/18, Jeunesse Esch's place was taken by CS Pétange, who clearly weren't ready for the First Division, finishing last and forfeiting a match, even suffering one 0-13 defeat. Unfortunately, this wasn't Racing's year, again. They could finish only one place above relegated Pétange in fifth place.

In the first post-war season, Racing fans and players were optimistic about their chances, despite the club just drifting down the places every year since foundation. Sadly, that year wasn't an exception, and Racing only survived because of Young Boys going winless for the whole campaign, even forfeiting the last couple of matches. Moreover, Sporting won the title, which was an even bigger problem for RCL supporters than their own team's form. In the tenth season of Luxembourgish football, Racing suffered the biggest defeat of their history, an 8-1 loss against Stade Dudelange. With two wins and eight losses, they came in last. And if it hadn't been for rule changes from the federation, they would have been relegated and maybe even dissolved. But with the league being expanded to eight teams, that meant no one was going to be relegated. One of the promoted teams, Rumelange, hold the worst league campaign record. They ended the season with 14 losses out of 14, and a minus-75 goal difference, and several two-digit defeats. The other side to be relegated was Racing, and this time even the Luxembourgish FA couldn't help them.

The second tier proved to be no challenge for the team, who won every game and scored 75 goals in 14 matches. And the good performances gave a motivation boost to the team, who even got to the cup final from the Second Division. In the final they successfully beat Jeunesse 2-0, to become the first-ever team to lift the newly created Luxembourgish Cup. The fans did not know that this cup was going to be their last trophy. And they couldn't even have guessed the reason.

After another unsuccessful campaign (seventh place, 11 points) Racing found themselves in the bottom two come the end of the 1922/23 season, facing the prospect of fighting their way back up from the Second Division again. Racing fans were pessimistic. With the number of clubs rapidly growing in the country, the Second Division title was nowhere near guaranteed. But in the summer of 1923, something happened in the minnows' capital. Something which wasn't expected by a single fan at the time. Something which helped Racing stay in the league, but had a huge drawback.

There were no rule changes or receding teams, but the solution which kept Racing in the top flight was a merger. The club merged with the outfit the supporters wanted the least: their biggest enemies, Sporting. With this solution, the merger team CA Spora Luxembourg (CASL) became financially stable, got a decent little ground (Racing's former pitch) and of course Racing didn't have to go down because of that. We now see that it was truly a blessing in disguise.

The new team's name Spora came from the first three letters of 'Sporting' and the first two of 'Racing'. Similarly, the club colours came from Racing's blue and Sporting's yellow kits. They started off with a second place in 1924 behind Fola, and that was the beginning of the club's best era, whole decades of success, and even a historical European Cup match – but don't rush forward, go back to 1925.

Spora finished in second place in their first three seasons – with three different champions (Fola Esch, US Dudelange and Red Boys Differdange). In 1925 they only lost the league by goal difference as Dudelange scored one more goal than Spora. CASL even played a cup final in 1925, forfeiting the second match against Red Boys after a 1-1 draw. After being used to finishing second, Spora were finally able to break the curse in 1927 – but unfortunately they didn't move in the desired direction, finishing on the bottom of the podium this time, with Union Luxembourg winning the league. Union Luxembourg: does this name sound familiar? I guess not. That's because Union were also a merger team, arising from two successful clubs of the previous decade, Hollerich and Jeunesse SV.

The next year, Spora also had to accept third place, and such honourable placings in the first years of a club's history are definitely an exceptional start, but because of the history of both clubs, fans weren't that patient and obviously they wanted the highest feats in the least time possible. Well, they only had to wait a year and the first title of CA Spora Luxembourg arrived; furthermore, they scooped it up with an eight-point lead. The '*Blo-a-Giel*' (Blue-and-Yellows) also won the cup, in their second rematch after two draws against Dudelange.

In the next five years, they always finished in the top three in the league, even winning it once, while in the domestic cup they lost three finals within half a decade. Three consecutive National Division titles then were enough proof for even the most sceptical fans that long-term consistent success was written in the club's DNA. Even their sixth-place finish coming as a bolt from the blue in 1937 wasn't enough to upset their apple cart. The next time they failed to appear on the podium was in 1940 – the last year before the league stopped during World War Two.

After the war, Spora enjoyed some less fruitful decades, with several extraordinary results but no consistent dominance. Despite winning the National Division in 1948/49, the club were relegated just five years later. Then came the miraculous years: back-to-back titles which meant a place in the 1956/57 European Cup (the first one was held in 1955/56, but with Luxembourgish teams not invited to take part). In the preliminary round, Spora were drawn against a massive team: Borussia Dortmund from Germany. Although the Luxembourgish side couldn't get through, nobody can say they didn't try everything: after a narrow 3-4 defeat, the Blue-and-Yellows managed to somehow beat the *Schwarzgelben* 2-1. The 5-5 aggregate score meant that the teams had to play a third fixture to decide a winner, and

Dortmund pulled off an easy 7-0 victory there. (Under the current away-goal rule, Spora

would have gone through without playing the third match.) That second-leg win is still considered as one of, if not the best single result a team from the Grand Duchy have ever achieved in Europe.

A narrow defeat against a much bigger ranked team can hardly be considered a turning point in the club's life, but in some respects, it was. They only won the league twice in the 1956-2005 period and, although in the 60s the club were still able to finish in a UEFA Cup place several times, similar successes didn't follow.

Their next European Cup appearance was in 1961/62, after winning the 1960/61 domestic championship. Even with the most famous manager the club ever had (András Béres, who went on to manage Belgian powerhouses Club Brugge and Anderlecht), Spora were sent home with a disastrous 2-15 aggregate defeat by Danish side Boldklubben. It is important to note that it was Boldklubben's only season in the European Cup, and in their following tie they were knocked out 0-12.

In that decade Spora became a strong mid-table side in the 12-team league, finishing in the fifth-to-seventh positions except for one or two standout results (second or third places). Even in the cup, they could only triumph twice in the ten years. After the cup wins, they obviously always got the opportunity of playing in the European Cup Winners' Cup (for the sake of younger followers, this was a tournament in which most of Europe's domestic cup-winning teams could compete, but it ceased to exist in 1999). However, defeats against Magdeburg and Shamrock Rovers cut both their cup runs short.

If that wasn't enough, their big rival Union came back from hell's deepest pit (after a title drought of more than

20 years), and became hugely dominant in both the league and the cup (in fact, they went unbeaten for the whole 1970/71 campaign). The boot was on the other foot: Union fought back to the very top and were capable of staying there consistently, while for Spora, even a third place meant a surprisingly good finish from the 70s onwards. There was another remarkable fairy-tale story in the 1960s: the one of Aris de Bonnevoie. Another club from the capital, the team won the league and played in the cup final of the 1963/64 season – in their fifth season in the top tier! Unfortunately, Aris were unable to repeat these successes and, apart from a cup win in 1967, didn't win another piece of silverware in the rest of their history.

The next time Spora played in Europe was in 1980 (except the Fairs Cup tie versus Leeds in 1967) but a lot of things happened before that. First, there was a relegation and two years spent in the Division of Honor [second division]; then relegation again, this time followed up by instant promotion. The first year back turned into a great campaign, which ended in a cup victory: Spora beat Progrés Niedercorn 3-2 after extra time. They didn't really have a chance the next year in the European Cup Winners' Cup, though: they suffered a pair of 0-6 defeats against then-Czechoslovakian Sparta Prague.

Things still looked good in the capital of Luxembourg, until they realised that their previous seventh-place league finish didn't represent an average feat: it was the biggest this squad could achieve. In the season following their cup win, they only managed to gain 15 points in 22 matches, thus only staying up by a single point. The team wasn't that lucky in 1981/82. It was a disastrous season, bringing only two wins, a minus-31 goal difference and several big-margin losses (such as a 0-4, a 1-6, and a 0-5), which meant another season down in the second tier.

However, we could still say the 1980s was a superb decade for the club. After achieving the expected promotion, Spora finished fifth on two occasions before stepping on the podium several times to crown the decade with a league title. After finishing in fourth place, they progressed to the play-off round between the top six teams (similar to that of the Belgian Pro League now). Incredibly they managed a ten-match undefeated streak against the other five biggest teams in the country! They got the title of course by overcoming their 2.5 points handicap. For that accolade, they got an amazing prize: the opportunity to play Real Madrid, as they were drawn as Spora's European Cup opponents. Unfortunately, that ended in a 0-9 aggregate defeat but avoiding a two-digit aggregated scoreline was still something Spora could be proud of (after losing 2-11 to Feyenoord the year before, and a few years later they were also beaten by Sheffield Wednesday and Frankfurt, both by two-digit margins).

But things started to go wrong when Spora came bottom of the league, with only eight points collected in 22 matches. Remember, in 1998/99, a win meant three points, which makes it look even worse. But the cherry on the top was the 0-5 defeat at home to Union. Spora got relegated and then decided they had no other option but to merge with Union and Alliance to create one bigger club. Many clubs in the country had been living beyond their means for years so they had to reduce costs and focus on making a profit instead of pulling off dream transfers. Indeed, Spora had a smart plan: they were one of the first teams to go through that major change and they did it relatively quickly – while other clubs, despite staying in the division, struggled with the process for long years and had to settle for mid-table, even if they could have been capable of a bronze medal or better. The changes were not exactly welcomed by the players, but it had to be done to help the club progress.

In all, the 11 under-21 players who were in the first team went to eight different clubs; two of them got an offer from abroad, but they couldn't make it to the senior sides in Portugal and Germany, respectively. So, what we see there is a big sliding doors moment. Only God knows what could have happened, were the best youth players of the country not scattered to the four winds. What I can say with certainty though, is that it was a huge blow for Luxembourgish football. Two of the biggest historical clubs of the country – Spora and Union (plus the smaller Alliance) – disappeared from one day to the next, while the most talented group of players didn't get the chance to play together anymore.

33.

Cesena FC (Italy)

CESENA HAVE an exceptionally long history to be proud of. Cesena Calcio were founded in 1940, although there had been some footballing life in the city in the 1920s and 30s. The most important team then was US Renato Serra Cesena, who already played their matches in black and white shirts. The club played in various divisions from 1921 to 1936 but the Italian league revealed in 1939 that RSC lost their licence for the top two leagues. Then came the historical moment, from when our story starts, with Marzio.

Marzio is one of the biggest supporters the club has had, following the Seahorses from 1968. His story with the club started in a beautiful and unique way when he first visited a home match, on his own. He was a child and his parents had no interest in going to football matches. Guards were checking at the gates that no child could get in the stadium alone, so Marzio looked for men who were alone and stood by one of them. He got in successfully and the atmosphere of the stadium made Marzio a supporter of the black-and-whites for a lifetime.

The official date of the foundation was 21 April 1940. The club were named AC Cesena 1940 and were formed by three people: Conte Rognoni, Renato Piraccini and Arnaldo Pantani. A former player of US Renate then manager and technical director at AC Cesena, Conte Rognoni became president and Piraccini took the role of the sporting director.

The club took the colours of Renato Serra and the city itself, while the story of the seahorse on their badge is unknown even by Marzio.

He says, 'It's sure that the animal already was in the first logos of Renato Serra but we don't know why did they choose a seahorse.'

The team, however, found success in no time. They played in Serie C in their first year which was a shorter season because of the war situation in the whole of Europe. In that year, Bologna were in the third league as well, even though they had a handful of national team players. Nonetheless, Cesena defeated them 2-0 and 5-0. Marzio adds, 'This 5-0 was like a miracle at the time. So unbelievable of a miracle that newspapers and radios said 0-5 to Bologna instead as they thought they were misinformed.'

When the war was over, the club found themselves in Serie B (it was both B and C because the two leagues formed one big 96-team championship) but they struggled to survive. They got through their first season but their second one saw them being relegated and they spent the next two seasons in Serie C. They played the next three seasons in the C league and surprisingly were in the bottom half of the table, then finished in last place in the spring of 1951. In the last season they played with András Kuttik as their manager and he brought in the Chinese-born Hungarian striker, Lajos Kovács. Kovács became the first foreign player at the club, and the fans liked him as well, although he didn't stay for long. Both Hungarians (Kuttik and Kovács) were released after a few months because the club didn't appreciate their passion for regularly looking at the bottom of a glass. But there is something that even Marzio doesn't know.

'We don't have information about Kovács's career's latter stages. If you have or find information about him since he left Cesena, please inform us. The people in Cesena would be very grateful.'

After the relegation, dark times came for the club. They played only in amateur divisions in that decade and had to play their home matches at the summer trotting racecourse. All they could be pleased about is that they finally got a new stadium, La Fiorita, in 1957. This is where Cesena FC (the rebranded club) currently play.

It has a capacity of 23,860 and this was amongst the possible venues for Euro 2016 (as we know, France's bid was chosen instead).

The team successfully recovered in their new stadium and got promoted to Serie C. There was a huge turnaround in Cesena's fate: a turnaround that saw them emerging into a stable Serie A team! But that all started with Dino Manuzzi's arrival. We asked Marzio who that was, and he shared all the details with us about the man behind the success.

'Cesena's turning point was Manuzzi, who arrived in the 1964/65 season. He worked so hard; he was a president who didn't have much money. He was just a modest entrepreneur in fruit and vegetables. He only had one warehouse for his business, but he was very intelligent and astute. He built a great youth academy and was very careful about spending the money. Our Serie A team at the time featured at least five academy graduates every match.'

Manuzzi was an unbelievable man who brought the team to its well-deserved place in Serie A, without big investments or coaching team. He was such a favourite among the fans and in the club that La Fiorita was renamed after him following his death in 1982.

In those years the club played their biggest matches, including exciting ones against Sivori's Juventus or Rivera's Milan who were arguably considered the greatest team at the time. The 1970s was Marzio's favourite decade in the club's history.

'It was wonderful. A small team from a small city in Serie A. Serie A itself was smaller as well, it only contained 16 teams, so it was slightly easier to stay up unlike nowadays when it's impossible for such a small team.' Let us admit it, he's right. Today's game focuses on the bigger and wealthier teams. However, I think there are lots of people who'd be interested in seeing traditional teams like Cesena finding their way to the top tier.

'In those years,' remembers Marzio, 'Cesena was a strong defensive team. And our midfield had similarities with the Netherlands' national team.' One thing is for sure, a lot of analysts and tacticians would love a team like this nowadays.

Cesena's last match of the 1975/76 season was extremely crucial: they played against Juventus, and if Juve won, they'd have won the Scudetto but Cesena also needed a win to be involved in the following year's UEFA Cup. Cesena won the match, Torino won the title, and the Seahorses qualified for Europe for the first (and last) time in their history. But as we can see now, they weren't ready for that number of matches, losing 4-3 on aggregate against Magdeburg in the first round of the UEFA Cup, and being relegated from Serie A the same season.

But do not forget, they were a fairly big club with a lot of supporters by the time they got relegated, and they had beaten Juventus, Milan (three times) and both Rome clubs during the previous four years. The record attendance in La Fiorita was in the 1974/75 season when Cesena beat Milan in front of 36,000 supporters. The other thing the club could start to build on was the impressive youth system. The decade saw them winning two National Primavera (youth) Championships and the famous Viareggio International Youth Cup on one occasion in 1980 (besides playing six seasons in the top division and winning two Serie Bs with the senior team).

In 1981, one of the greatest players the club ever had arrived. Walter Schachner was born in Austria and took part in the World Cups in 1978 and 1982 with Austria, the latter while playing for the Seahorses. He had so big an influence among the fans that the core ultras group renamed themselves '*Weisschwarzbrigaden*' ('Black-and-white Brigade' in Schachner's language, German). However, as Marzio noted, 'There are some who think the renaming wasn't because of Schachner's arrival, but I think it really was.'

In 1981/82 the club experienced some smaller successes, such as the defeats of AS Roma. But that year was not just about great results: the big owner of the club, Dino Manuzzi, passed away in 1982. He had been involved in a car crash in 1980 and passed the business to his nephew Edmeo Lugaresi. After Dino's death, Cesena instantly renamed their stadium Stadio Dino Manuzzi. And despite the great victories, the club fell back to Serie B the season after.

In the 'two-points-for-a-win' era, contests for positions in the league tables were much tighter and Cesena eventually found themselves involved in the relegation battle year after year – that was a big disappointment, even if they survived safely every time. They had to wait until spring 1987 for a promotion.

'The next epic wins since the Roman one came in that season,' adds Marzio, 'in the play-offs where we had a chance to get promoted if we were the best out of us, Lecce and Cremonese.'

The results were Cesena 0-0 Lecce, Lecce 4-1 Cremonese and Cesena 1-0 Cremonese. 'The last match was Lecce v Cesena to decide who goes up,' says Marzio. 'There were about 15,000 Lecce supporters against only

5–6,000 of us, but we won 2-1 at the neutral venue in San Benedetto del Tronto.'

It was a very strange season in Serie B, with Cagliari getting relegated and Lazio only surviving the drop in a relegation tiebreaker. But Cesena got to Serie A and that is what counts. The 1987/88 Serie A season started badly for them, going winless through seven matches (three draws and four losses). But they found their way to success and won four out of four matches after that, against Fiorentina, Juventus, Como and Hellas Verona.

At the end of the season, they were in a calm mid-table place and that is probably what they wanted for the following year. Unfortunately, their next season got much more exciting, and it was the bad kind of exciting. Before the last match, Cesena stood on 26 points, Verona – their opponents – were only one point behind, and some relegation places were not decided. Udinese (with 25) and Lecce (28) were also involved in the battle. Udinese won their last match while Lecce lost, but the yellow-reds were nevertheless safe. The Cesena v Verona match decided everything. The loser would go down with Udinese, the winner would stay up. It seemed like it would be a draw (which would be good for Cesena) but a goal ended the excitement: it was scored by Agostini from Cesena, one of the favourite players of the fans at the time.

So, the *Bianconeri* maintained their place in the top league and signed two Brazilians too: Amarildo and Silas. Amarildo was the better of them, scoring a sum of 13 goals while with the team, even in the tougher times.

'Amarildo was so religious and he had a strange habit. Before every match he gave a Bible to the defender who marked him,' says Marzio, who emphasises, 'He did this even against the biggest teams.'

They were prepared to jump a level – they had quite a good squad, with Amarildo, their stadium was expanded to a capacity of 23,860 and fans were also behind the club, and do not forget their manager was Marcello Lippi (yes, the man who won the World Cup in 2006 with Italy). But the two Brazilians weren't enough as the team gained only 19 points which was only enough to finish in the 17th position from 18. The club remained in Serie B for years – the closest they got to a promotion was in 1994, the first season of Marzio's new job. He loved the team, so he worked at the stadium for ten years.

'In my first four years I was like a guard at an expensive sector. I had to make sure that nobody with cheaper tickets would get there. Then I worked for one year as a steward but I didn't like it so I switched. In my last five years, I worked in the private parking – but I only had a task until the match started, so from then, I could watch the whole match. It's a fantastic stadium, one of the most beautiful in the country. Excellent visibility, all covered, only seats.'

In the 1993/94 season, the club finished in fifth place, which meant they had to fight for promotion in a tiebreaker against Padova. However, the match ended in a 2-1 loss, so the black-and-whites had to stay at least one more year in the second tier. They pushed for the podium every year, but it wasn't enough. In these years, the next true legend played at the club after Schachner. Dario 'Bison' Hübner became the top goalscorer in Serie B in 1995/96 but was part of the shock coming the next year.

Cesena came 18th in Serie B in 1997 which meant another relegation, this time to Serie C – the first time in 30 years. The club's darkest times started, with four consecutive years spent in Serie C, and when they finally got promoted, they couldn't remain in Serie B (losing in the play-off against Pistoiese). They then stayed in Serie C for three years, were promoted in 2003 after two incredible play-off ties against Rimini and Lumezzane and the next season they did what nobody expected, achieving another play-off place – now for promotion out of Serie B. However, they failed to climb two leagues in two years but it was still a great overachievement by a newly promoted team.

Obviously, everyone knew that after such a season the performance would drop but they hoped they would not ride a roller coaster again to Serie C. They survived in the first year in 15th place but were not able to repeat it. Next time they were bottom of the table after the 42 matches, which meant they took the step back one more time.

Then came the man who quickly became extremely popular among black-and-white fans. His name was Pierpaolo Bisoli and he did what even the biggest fans could not dream of at that time: he brought them back to Serie A in two years. Yes, that was two consecutive promotions, an achievement that the club hadn't done before (or since). It was an unbelievable feat, even if we consider that Giaccherini, Schelotto, Volta, Antonioli, Bucchi and Do Prado were all part of the team then. On the last day of the championship, Lecce were in a comfortable position, but the final automatic promotion place between Brescia and Cesena had to be decided. Both teams faced opponents who were fighting for survival, especially Padova (Brescia's opponent). Padova secured themselves a place in the relegation play-offs with a win over Brescia while Cesena's win came from a goal by Marco Parolo which helped them take second place. (By the way, Brescia won the four-team play-offs, and joined Lecce and Cesena in Serie A.)

Everything looked good, but then things started going wrong. Igor Campedelli became the new owner (the last owner of the club), and Bisoli agreed a contract with his former club Cagliari, who could not properly replace Massimiliano Allegri. Massimo Ficcadenti was announced as the new head coach as the club started their first Serie A season since 1991. Things started well with a 0-0 draw with Roma, a 2-0 win against Milan and a 1-0 win against Lecce: that is seven points and top spot. The club quickly had three consecutive defeats after that (maybe former president Edmeo Lugaresi's death had its effect on the performances). Cesena struggled in the autumn but started winning games in winter. However, defeats followed, against Chievo and Bologna (Cesena's biggest rivals, according to Marzio). The club managed to win against Lazio, and later also against Brescia (in the first game of the year, in heavy snow). Cesena kept working hard and were successful: Bari collapsed significantly, earning just 24 points in the whole season, meanwhile, Cesena put on some decent performances, clinching a win in extra time against Chievo, scoring the equaliser against Juventus, and beating Sampdoria, Bologna, Cagliari and Brescia while still managing to gain a draw against Parma and Fiorentina. Brescia started losing the plot like Bari, while Sampdoria still failed to have a real chance of staying up, so Cesena eventually did remain in the top league.

At the end of the season, Ficcadenti and the club parted ways. A talented young manager, Marco Giampaolo, arrived, with a great desire to win. The owner supported him in everything and purchased Adrian Mutu and signed other talented players like Eder (later at Inter, now in China), Martínez (on loan from Juventus), Candreva (on loan, later at Lazio, now at Inter), Guana, Rodríguez (later at Torino and Hellas) and Ghezzal (played in the 2010 World Cup with Algeria). Everything seemed to be good, but they only got three points from nine matches and Giampaolo's time had gone. The new coach Arrigoni lost against Lecce in his first match, which clearly showed the club's direction. Heavy 4-1 defeats against Atalanta and Udinese held Cesena back and at the end of the season, Mario Beretta was the new manager, but he could not perform miracles, and Borriello's goal in a match against Juve sent the Seahorses to Serie B.

The club wanted to bounce straight back after the relegation and president Campedelli hired his brother Nicola as head coach. The start was a total disaster, which resulted in the sack for Nicola after ten matches and the whole Italian media laughing at the grotesque situation around the club. Bisoli was hired back to save things and he started sorting everything out, but the club's financial situation was also worrying, to the extent that the president was asking the fans and the city to donate, without much success. At the start of the 2013/14 season the club's only objective was to financially survive. But the club were surprisingly successful and while sitting in a play-off place during the winter, they bought three additional players (one of them was a certain Gagliardini). At the end of the season, Cesena received their first penalty: a not so significant one-point deduction for late payments.

The club performed slightly inconsistently but reached the top eight, which meant they needed two wins to get promoted. They defeated both Modena and Latina and got back up to Serie A.

Bisoli had achieved the unexpected for the second time but started stumbling in Serie A so he was sacked after a loss against Atalanta away from home. Di Carlo, the new trainer, had a great youth section to work with: Kessié (now Milan), Caldara (Atalanta), Sensi (Inter) and Gomis (Torino) all came up through the club's youth ranks. However, a 2-3 loss against Sassuolo meant that Cesena were once again relegated and thus spent only one year in the top flight. The next season saw a lot of opportunities to get themselves in good positions but a defeat at home against Spezia was costly.

The club were now financially poor, and Drago, who had replaced Bisoli as manager, only lasted for 12 matches. Camplone, his successor, really brought some great memories to the club: promotion was still a dream, but a cup run took them to the quarter-finals (where they lost against Juve 1-2) for the first time since 1971.

The next summer saw another change of leader, now-former manager Castori arriving from unstable Carpi. The club's goal was once again not to go bankrupt, but probably a promotion would not be enough to achieve this. The season ended in 13th place meaning staying up, but everyone knew that in a month the club's story would end. On 16 July 2018 the board announced they club wouldn't play in Serie B the next year and just eight days later the FIGC [the financial regulators] officially dissolved the club.

After all that, Romagna Centro (the other club in the region, founded as Polisportiva Martorano in 1973), who participated in Serie D in 2018, underwent a takeover by local businessmen and proposed renaming themselves as Cesena FC. The club became AC Cesena 1940's phoenix club, with most of the previous club's fans also supporting the new one. They were promoted from Serie D in their first season as Cesena FC (or RC Cesena).

I had a few more questions for Marzio.

Who was your favourite player in the Cesena shirt?
Marzio: I have four, all of them are attackers. [Dario] Hübner, [Massimo] Agostini and [Ruggiero] Rizzitelli from Italy, and [Walter] Schachner from Austria.

Who do you consider the best player ever to wear the Bianconeri shirt?

Marzio: It's hard to decide. Rizzitelli is one of our own, he grew up in the city, then later played at Roma and Bayern, then went back to his beloved Cesena, married and still lives there. Pierluigi Cera was also class, he gained a silver medal in the 1970 World Cup and wore the captain's armband at the club for five years. Contrarily, the best foreigner at the club was arguably Schachner who played at two World Cups.

What were the reasons for going bankrupt?
Marzio: I don't really know what to say. What I want to say possibly wouldn't be printable.

How important was having a great academy to getting promotion to Serie A again?
Marzio: Cesena has a large academy system which collects all the players from the Romagna region, and a lot of academy products were later used in the first team.

Who do you think is the best player from the youth academy in the last 15 years?
Marzio: We bought Luis Jiménez when he was young and he was with the club in the toughest times but if we strictly think about our academy players, I have to say [Emmanuele] Giaccherini, who played in the national team and Juventus since leaving us.

34.

Jewish Guild (South Africa)

THE JEWISH Guild was a social and sports society that was founded in 1897 and its organisation included a football team, the Old Arcs. The club colours were blue and white, blue being the colour of their home kit, with white being their away colour. In 1960 the name of the football team was changed to Jewish Guild.

Only four years after the name change, Jewish Guild reached the final of the Castle Cup. This was the domestic cup competition run by the Football Association in South Africa during the apartheid era, between the years of 1959 and 1977. The competition was only open to teams made up of white South Africans. It was known as the Castle Cup because of the sponsorship of Castle Breweries. Jewish Guild won it that year in Durban City, while still playing their football in their provincial league. It was the first time the club had won a major trophy, and it seemed to set them up for a future in the higher leagues of South African football.

In 1969, when South Africa's National Football League voted to create a Second Division in their football pyramid, Jewish Guid were one of ten football clubs to join. Their first season ended in a respectable mid-table finish of fifth. The club were determined to build on that success and did so the following season when they were runaway winners of the league by nine points in 1970, ahead of second-placed

Durban Celtic. That saw Jewish Guild promoted to the top flight of South African football, albeit in apartheid South Africa where only white players were permitted to play in the league.

The club competed in the top division for the next five years, finishing mid-table most of the time, with their best finish coming in their final season, in 1975, when they were fifth out of the 15 clubs that competed. But that was to be the end of Jewish Guild, as after that season they decided to merge with another football club, Johannesburg Corinthians, who seem to have been forgotten about. The only information I could find about them was a small snippet about how they were a consistent side in the Second Division, gaining promotion and nearly winning the league one season while also reaching the semi-finals of the NFL Cup in the 1960s.

The newly formed club was known as Guid Apollo and was then renamed again in 1977 as Roodepoort Guild, who competed in the last NFL season. Then, a non-racial league was created as the NFL (the whites-only league) and the NPSL (the black players' league) merged to create the new common NPSL [National Premier Soccer League].

The most famous player to play for Jewish Guild was none other than George Best, who has played for other 'Forgotten Clubs' like Cork Celtic from Ireland, LA Aztecs (two spells), Fort Lauderdale Strikers and San Jose Earthquakes from the United States, and Sea Bee from Hong Kong. Jewish Guild, who he played for five times and scored once for, were the first club he joined after he left Manchester United in 1974. All five games were competitive matches and not exhibition matches like he would participate in for other clubs. While he attracted thousands of spectators to the matches, he also drew criticism from club officials who were not happy with the fact he kept missing training sessions in favour of going out and partying. He didn't last long in South Africa and was put out on loan back to England, where he played for Dunstable Town and then Stockport Town.

Best, while being the most high-profile player to play for Jewish Guild, was not the only British player to do so. It was common practice for South African clubs to sign British players to raise their profile and try to attract a few extra supporters to the matches. Among them was Tommy Henderson, a Scottish footballer, who played right-wing. He joined Jewish Guild in 1974, having played for Leeds United, Hearts and 'Forgotten Club', Cork Hibernians. Another foreign import and one that was probably more known in South African football for his part played in the quadruple-winning Kaizer Chiefs side of 1981, was Portuguese-born South African midfielder, Frank Pereira, also known as 'Jingles' Pereira, a nickname he got when he was ten years old for having kept two pennies in his short pockets while playing football matches. He made 29 appearances for Jewish Guild from 1972 until 1973, scoring 23 goals in that time. Former Liverpool goalkeeper, Doug Rudham, also played for Jewish Guild. Rudham played for Liverpool in the 1950s, and was a South African, who made one appearance for the national team.

35.

Club Atletico Corrales (Paraguay)

FOUNDED IN 1919, Club Atletico Corrales, also known as Atletico Corrales, or CALT, were a football club based in Ascuncion, Paraguay. The club colours were red and navy and they played their home matches at the Estadio Atletico Corrales. Like many football clubs created in the early 20th century, they were formed by a group of workers from a company, in this case Compañia Americana de Luz y Tracción (CALT), a private company that oversaw the electricity and tramlines in Paraguay. The club started off in the lower divisions of the Paraguayan football pyramid, finally gaining promotion to the top tier after winning the Paraguayan Second Division, or the Division Intermedia as it was known in 1929. The club competed in the top tier in 1930, but things weren't exactly organised in Paraguay with regards football. Due to the World Cup being hosted in 1930, and the extension of the league to 14 clubs, only half of the league started in September. CALT would eventually finish 11th that year.

The 1931 season was one that went on for over a year. A huge break during the season due to disagreements and misunderstandings within Paraguayan football meant the season which started on 3 May 1931 didn't end until 26 June 1932. The whole thing was a huge mess, with two factions threatening to separate and create their own football leagues. It posed questions as to whether it was a good decision for

Paraguayan football's top tier to go professional that year. In the end the football continued, and a split never happened. CALT finished a respectable ninth in the league, which was eventually won by Olympia.

It wasn't until 1935 that the Paraguay football league would return after being cancelled due to civil unrest in the country. That would be the first season that the Paraguay Premier Division would officially be seen as fully professional, and therefore Cerro Porteno are considered to be the first ever professional winners of the Paraguay Premier Division. CALT finished sixth that season, but it would be the last time they would be named CALT. The Paraguayan Football Association made a rule that clubs could no longer have the name of a company for a football club, so from then on they were known as Atletico Corrales.

The 1936 season saw Atletico Corrales finish second from bottom, tenth out of 11 clubs, but the 1937 campaign saw a huge improvement with the club finishing fourth. A drop down of two places in the 1938 season saw the club finish sixth. But it wasn't Atletico Corrales's domestic form that made them stand out from the other Paraguayan football clubs. In 1939 the club were given permission to miss the 1939 season so that they could embark on a tour of Latin America to face clubs from various countries. This would be the equivalent of Crystal Palace asking the FA if they could take a season off to travel around Europe to play different teams from different European countries. But the club were given permission to do so and off they went, playing against clubs from 11 different countries: Argentina, Chile, Cuba, Mexico, El Salvador, Costa Rica, Colombia, Dutch Antilles, Suriname, Venezuela and Ecuador. The tour began on 4 April 1939, and finished on 19 April 1940. It was financed by the board of directors of CALT and they made eye-catching signings, not least the Mexican-born player, Luis de le Fuente, nicknamed 'the Pirate'.

Da le Fuente is known as one of the all-time greats of Mexican football, being the first Mexican-born player to play in four different countries: Argentina, Mexico, Spain and Paraguay. He started his professional career at the age of 15, when he made his debut for Mexican club Aurrera in 1929. The Pirate was known for his dazzling footballing skills and was a real entertainer for the fans. He had an eye for a pass but also an eye for goals, which he could score in any way possible. Strong in the air and two-footed, he was a handful to deal with for many opposition defences. He helped CD Veracruz to two Primera Division de Mexico championships between 1945 and 1949, cementing his status as one of the all-time greats of Mexican football. In 2021 he was named in the IFFHS CONCACAF men's team of all time.

In Argentina, Corrales played two games against Mendoza, winning the first 4-3 on 15 April, but losing the second game the next day 6-2. They then played three games in Chile against a Chile XI in Santiago, winning two and losing one. A total of seven games were played in Mexico, where they only won twice, drew one and lost four. It was one of the more eventful sections of their tour. The sides they faced were: Club America on 4 June, losing 4-2; Espana-Asturias (two clubs combined) on 11 June, losing 4-1; Euskadi on 18 June, drawing 4-4; Necaxa on 25 June, winning 3-1; Asturias FC on 2 July, losing 5-2; Atlante on 9 July, winning 3-1; and Espana on 16 July, losing 10-3.

Next up was a trip to El Salvador, where they played a combined XI three times, winning two and losing one. Costa Rica proved to be an easier task for the Paraguayan side, as they played five games there, winning four and losing just one. They started off on 20 August, playing against Orion FC and winning 4-1. Next up was a game against CS La Libertad, which they won easily, 6-1. They had a few days off until they played their third game in San Jose, this time on 3 September, against CS Herediano and once again they won, 3-1. It wasn't until their fourth game on 10 September that they fell to defeat, to SG Espanola, 3-1. But Corrales recovered for their final game in Costa Rica to beat LD Alajuelense 4-2 on 17 September.

And so, it was on to Panama where Corrales played one game against a Panama XI and easily beat them 9-3. Colombia was the next destination, featuring a total of seven games, winning just three, drawing two and losing two. The only known result was against Boca Juniors de Cali, which was recorded as a 3-2 defeat. November and December of 1939 ended with a trip to Curacao, Suriname and Venezuela. Their results in Curacao saw them play five, winning four and drawing one. All of their four wins came against a Curacao XI with the one draw coming against a Suriname XI that were based in Curacao at the time (3-3). They then travelled to Suriname to play but there is no record to be found of the individual matches there. They finished the year off in Venezuela, playing four games and winning all four, beating Venezuela three times (2-1, 2-0 and 5-2) while also beating club side Dos Caminos, on 31 January, 2-0. Ecuador was another country they visited just before they revisited Colombia again, playing CA Atlanta twice, drawing 4-4 in one of those games. The other was played against Millonarios in which they lost 5-3.

In total, the tour consisted of 53 games, with Corrales winning 30, drawing nine and losing 14, scoring 159 goals and conceding 121. It was seen as a money-making project by the CALT board, who had already lost naming rights to the club and were looking to cash in by playing these exhibition matches.

The club returned to domestic business for the 1940 season, finishing seventh in the league that year. 1941 saw the club finish bottom of the league, 11th out of 11, relegating them to the Second Division. That's where they remained until 1949 when the Paraguayan government decided to nationalise the electricity services which meant the private company CALT was no longer functional and therefore Atletico Corrales ceased to exist as they had nobody backing them financially anymore.

36.

Dukla Prague (Czechoslovakia)

BACK INTO Europe we go, but this time we are taking a trip back to a time when certain countries hadn't been formed and football clubs belonged to nations that aren't even around anymore. I am not going to give you a lesson here on the geography of Europe or the wars that took place in these parts of the world. No, if you wanted to read about that, well that's a different book you are looking for. But football did continue to be played in these countries and football clubs continued to operate, with fans of course. But unfortunately, like in stable countries, some football clubs didn't last the test of time.

This next football club played in the Czechoslovakian league, a country that is now two separate nations, Czech Republic and Slovakia. This club came from the Czech Republic, and the city of Prague. When I approached fans of this former club, they were quick to tell me it was not a 'Forgotten Club' and that they still play their football under a new name. Of course, I knew all of this, as it is the case with most clubs that I have covered, that they return as a phoenix club, sometimes run by the fans themselves. But this club did unfortunately dissolve back in 1996 and therefore qualify as a 'Forgotten Club'.

They are a club with a decent history. In fact, they can boast that they had seven players represented in a World Cup Final at one point, whilst also reaching a European semi-final themselves once upon a time. Like their history, their present is also a complicated one, with the club still being represented in name: however, that is not the club that is the actual descendant of the original. That is FK Viagem Pribram. If you know who they are, then you should know the club I am about to tell you about is Dukla Prague. No fan interviews for this one as they refused to accept that they are a 'Forgotten Club'.

Founded in 1948 as Armadni Telovychivny Klub, or ATK Praha, they started their existence in the top flight of Czechoslovakian football. The club were part of a wider sports organisation and was run by the Czechoslovak Army. They wore the colours of brown and yellow, while playing their games at the Stadion Juliska.

It didn't take long for their first name change, however, and in 1953, they changed their name to Ustredni Dum Armady (UAD) Praha. In that same season, they won their first league title. In a 14-team league, each club only played each other once, meaning there was a total of 13 games per club. UAD Praha came out on top, winning ten, drawing two and losing only one. They finished three points ahead of their nearest rivals, Spartak Prague Sokolovo, or AC Sparta Prague as they are known today. UAD's top scorer that season was Otto Hemele, with nine goals in the 13 games. He went on to make ten appearances for the Czechoslovakian national team, scoring four goals in total. With no European competition to play in until 1955, the club would have to wait before they would get to test themselves against the best around the continent.

The 1954 season was a little underwhelming, as the club finished fourth, in what was now a 12-team league, with clubs playing each other both home and away. They finished five points behind eventual winners Slavia Prague Sokolovo. In the 1955 season, they just missed out on their second title and a place in the European Cup, when they finished second, two points behind eventual winners Slovan Bratislava. Ladislav Prada scored 17 goals that season, just behind the eventual golden boot winner, Emil Pazicky, who had scored 19, with both Slovan Bratislava and Slovena Zilina.

Not to be discouraged, the club went into the 1956 season with high hopes, and with a new name. It was this season that they became known as Dukla Prague, in memory of those who passed at the Battle of Dukla Pass in 1944, during the Second World War. Who knows if the name change was what spurred them on that season, but the club went one better than the previous year and won their second title, beating Slovan Bratislava to the trophy by five points. It also meant they had qualified for the European Cup first round. It would become even better for the club when they drew English side Manchester United. They were subsequently knocked out, 3-1 on aggregate, but they had gotten a taste for success and it wasn't long before they were lifting their third title.

In fact, they did this in the 1957 season, winning it by the slimmest of margins, on goal difference over rivals Sparta Prague Sokolovo. A third title and another chance to play in the European Cup. This time the draw was regionalised, and so they played Croatian side NK Dinamo Zagreb. The first leg ended in a 2-2 draw away from home, but the Czechoslovakian side edged it in the second leg, winning 2-1 and progressing to the next round. It was here where they met Austrian side Wiener Sport Club and were knocked out, 3-2 on aggregate. But Dukla were starting to establish themselves as one of the biggest clubs in Czechoslovakia.

The 1958/59 season saw the club finish runners-up to Slovan Bratislava, who won the league convincingly, by a five-point margin. But that was to be the catalyst for a dominant run for Dukla on the domestic front. The club went on to win four league titles in a row, from the 1960/61 season to the 1963/64 season. They also won the Czechoslovakian Cup once in that time, in the 1960/61 season. During all of this domestic success came European adventures, and in 1961/62, the club recorded their second success in the European Cup, beating Bulgarian side, CDNA Sofia, 6-5 on aggregate. They then beat Swiss club Servette, 5-4 on aggregate in the next round, progressing to the quarter-finals, where they met English side Tottenham Hotspur. After a historic 1-0 win at the Stadion Dr Vaclava Vacka, in front of over 32,000 people, with a goal in the 59th minute from Kucera, they travelled to England, hoping to cause an upset and progress to the semi-final. Unfortunately, it wasn't to be, and Spurs took an early lead in the 11th minute thanks to a goal from Bobby Smith. That lead was doubled soon after when Dave Mackay scored in the 15th minute to give Spurs the advantage on aggregate. Although Dukla pulled a goal back to level the tie just before half-time through Jelinek (44th minute), the tie was settled in the second half with two quickfire goals. The first came from Smith once again in the 54th minute while Mackay also got his second of the game in the 56th minute. The tie ended 4-2 on aggregate to Spurs.

The next season, after winning the title once again, their European adventure started off brightly, with a 4-0 aggregate win over German side Vorwarts Berlin. The next round was even more convincingly won, when they dispatched Norwegian side, Esbjerg, 5-0 on aggregate. It meant they had once again managed to progress as far as the quarter-finals, but once again this was as far as they would reach, as they lost out to Portuguese giants, Benfica, 2-1 on aggregate. It was a Benfica side that included Eusebio, and one that went all the way to the final, only to lose to AC Milan, 2-1, with Eusebio scoring for Benfica.

By now, it was a routine that Dukla Prague would be playing in European competition, such was their dominance in their domestic league. In the 1963/64 edition, they started off with an 8-0 demolition of Maltese side, Valletta, winning 6-0 in the home leg, while winning the away leg 2-0. Harder tests were to come, but the next round saw them pass one of those tests, when they beat Polish side, Gornik Zabrze, 4-3 on aggregate. The quarter-finals beckoned again, but once more, they found themselves becoming stuck at this stage. Their opponents, German giants Borussia Dortmund, proved too strong for them over the two legs and knocked them out, 5-3 on aggregate. For the third consecutive year, Dukla had been knocked out at the quarter-final stage of the European Cup. The next season they would have another go, after winning their domestic league for the fourth time in a row.

Unlike their previous preliminary round matches, the 1964/65 edition of the European Cup started off a little bit more difficult for Dukla Prague. It was only by the flip of a coin that they progressed to the next round. No, really, that is actually how they progressed. After drawing 4-4 on aggregate with Gornik Zabrze, a coin was flipped to determine who would progress. Dukla won and they were to face the mighty Real Madrid in the next round. The game at the Santigo Bernabeu was a one-sided affair, with the Spanish side winning 4-0 on the night, with Amancio scoring a hat-trick. It meant the second leg was a bit of a formality. However, that didn't stop the Dukla players from putting in a shift, although they must have been deflated when in the 14th minute, Felo made it 5-0 on aggregate to Madrid. Dukla did pull one back in the 60th minute thanks to Geleta, who then put Dukla in front on the night in the

75th minute. They nearly hung on to a famous win until that man again, Amancio, popped up in the 89th minute to draw the sides level on the night and finish the tie 6-2 on aggregate to Real Madrid.

While Dukla didn't win the league in the 1964/65 season, they did win the cup and therefore qualified for the Cup Winners' Cup. While it was seen as the second tier of European football, there were still strong clubs competing in it. Dukla drew French side Rennes in the first round and knocked them out, 2-0 on aggregate. It set up a tie in the next round with Hungarian side, Budapest Honved. In what was a tightly contested two-legged tie, the Hungarians came out on top, thanks to the away goals rule. On aggregate, the tie finished 4-4 but Honved had scored three away goals to Dukla's one.

The next season, 1965/66, saw the club win the double, and return to European football's premier competition. They had only won the league on goal difference, beating Slavia Prague to the title. In a weird twist, the club met Norwegian side Esbjerg once again, and once again they dispatched them with ease, winning 6-0 on aggregate. It set up a tie with Belgium's Anderlecht, who they also dispatched with ease, winning that tie 6-2 on aggregate. Once again, the club found themselves at the quarter-final stage. On the three previous attempts they had failed to get past this round, but they were about to re-write history. They were up against Dutch side, Ajax. The first leg, played in front of a crowd of over 55,000, was drawn 1-1. Swart had scored for Ajax (50th minute) while Mraz equalised for Dukla (61st minute). The tie was finely poised going into the second leg. In front of just over 18,000 people, Dukla took on Ajax on 8 March 1967. The Dutch side took the lead in the 65th minute thanks to Swart once again. It looked like another quarter-final defeat for Dukla, until

Strunc levelled from the spot in the 72nd. It was 2-2 on aggregate and both teams were going for the win. Then, in the 89th minute, Ajax's Soetekouw put the ball into his own net and made it 3-2 to Dukla on aggregate and that's the way it ended, meaning for the first time in their history, Dukla Prague had made it to the semi-final of the European Cup. There they met Celtic and that was where the European adventure ended, as the Scottish champions knocked out Dukla, 3-1 on aggregate, after a 3-1 win at Celtic Park and a 0-0 draw in Czechoslovakia.

After that season, Dukla seemed to decline on the pitch, only picking up one trophy, the Czechoslovakian Cup in the 1968/69 season. They did not win the league again until the 1976/77 season, when they beat Inter Bratislava to the title by four points. It meant a return to European football as well, but this was cut short when they were knocked out in the first round by French side, Nantes. It was by the away goals rule, as Nantes had drawn and scored in Czechoslovakia, 1-1 and Dukla had only managed to get a 0-0 draw in France.

Dukla seemed to be starting some kind of revival, as they finished runners-up the next season and then won their tenth title in 1978/79. Their final league title triumph came in the 1981/82 season, when they beat Banik Ostrava to the title by four points. After that, however, they were reduced to winning just three more Czechoslovakian cups, in the seasons 1982/83, 1984/85 and 1989/90, with the latter being the last major trophy they won in their original form.

The 90s proved to be one of the worst decades in the club's history, as they were relegated in the 1993/94 season, finishing rock bottom of the league. But the club didn't play in the second tier that next season, instead playing in the third tier, and still not being able to gain promotion. In the end, in 1996, the club merged with Second Division side FC Portal Pribram. The new club became known as 1.FK Pribram.

For years the name Dukla Prague was lost and not used, bar an amateur team who played under that name, loosely. But in 2006 it was announced that Jakubcovice were to be taken over and renamed and rebranded as Dukla Prague, and so the name has continued. The club have been back in the top division of Czech football since 2011.

37.

Excelsior AC Roubaix (France)

FOUNDED IN 1928, from a merger between Football Club de Roubaix and Excelsior de Tourcoing, Excelsior Athletic Club de Roubaix adopted the colours black and white, while playing their home games at the Stade Amedee Prouvost, in the city of Roubaix. The club didn't turn professional until the 1932/33 season, in which they finished sixth out of ten clubs in Group A of the French Division 1. But it wasn't their league form that caught the eye that season. It was their run in the 1933 edition of the Coupe de France that gained the club recognition.

They were under the guidance of their English manager, Charles Griffiths, a man who had coached in Belgium, France, the Netherlands and Germany during his career. He even managed Bayern Munich in 1911/12, and managed the Belgium national team in 1920. Excelsior's opponents in the final were city rivals RC Roubaix, and so the intensity of the game was heightened. On 7 May 1933, 38,000 people paid to enter the Stade Olympique Yves-du-Manoir to watch the two sides compete for the chance to lift the Coupe de France. It only took three minutes for the deadlock to be broken when Excelsior's Marcel Langiller scored. He was the captain of Excelsior that day, a man who made 30 appearances for the French national team from 1927–37.

Their lead was doubled in the 23rd minute by Buge and then the trophy seemed to be won in only the 26th minute when Van Caeneghem scored the third to put Excelsior three up and in the driving seat before half-time. RC did pull one back in the second half thanks to a goal from Van Vooren in the 72nd minute but the damage had been done and Excelsior went on to win their first major trophy. In only their first season as a professional club, they could have been forgiven for thinking that football was an easy sport and that they would enjoy more success in the future. How wrong they were.

The club were brought back down to earth in the next season, finishing fifth in a now 14-club league. It was one place better than the year before, but they failed to lift the Coupe de France that season. The club remained in the First Division until after World War Two, when they decided to merge with two other clubs, US Tourcoing and RC Roubaix. The new club were to be known as CO Roubaix Tourcoing. They struggled to make any impression in French football and reverted back to their old name of Excelsior Athletic Club de Roubaix in 1970.

It was then that the club decided to go back to amateur status and played in the lower leagues, but they still seemed to struggle on and off the pitch. In 1977 they decided to merge with another club, again in an effort to drum up support and try to reach the top flight of French football. This time they joined forces with Sporting Club de Roubaix. The new name of the football club was Roubaix Football. They did have a very brief revival, competing in the 1983/84 Division 2, but they were never able to get back to the dizzy heights of Division 1.

The struggles continued and the football club went looking for another merger to fix their problems, this time turning to Stade Roubaix, formerly known as RC Roubaix and in 1990 they merged to form a new club, named Stade Club Olympique de Roubaix. Sadly, this merger didn't last either and the club dissolved in 1995 due to financial problems. And so, the end of Excelsior AC Roubaix was complete, although one could argue that happened back in 1977.

38

FC Ameri Tbilisi

FOUNDED IN 2002, based in the district of Gldani in Tbilisi, FC Ameri started life in the third tier of Georgian football, but they quickly gained promotion to the second tier in their first season. They struggled at this level and finished 12th out of 16 teams that season, which meant they were to be relegated but were given a reprieve when two sides dropped out, Lokomotiv Samtredia and Luka Batuni. Interestingly, that season, despite only winning 12, drawing seven and losing 13, they finished with a plus-ten goal difference, scoring 34 and only conceding 24 goals.

The next season saw a huge improvement in form, In 2004/05, FC Ameri Tbilisi jumped from relegation fodder to champions of the Pirveli Liga, the Second Division of Georgian football. It meant they had reached the top flight in only three seasons since their formation, by winning 23 of their games, drawing three and only losing four. They also scored 98 goals in total and only conceded 18 all season.

Their first season in the Umaglesi Liga in 2005/06 was a decent one, with the club finishing seventh out of the 16 teams in the league, winning 15, drawing four and losing 11 games. Once again, they finished the season with a positive goal difference, scoring 32 and only conceding 26. But that wasn't the highlight for the club that wore yellow and white stripes. That season they went on to win their first major trophy when they lifted the Georgian Cup. Games in the cup were played over two legs and in the round of 32, FC Ameri beat Meshakre Agara 6-1 in the first leg and 2-1 in the second. This set up a tie with Gagra in the round of 16, and once again FC Ameri won the first leg comfortably, 4-1. The second leg finished 0-0 but the damage had been done and Ameri went through to the quarter-finals. This time they faced much tougher opponent in Kolkheti-1912 Poti. They played out a nervy 0-0 draw in the first leg but FC Ameri managed to pull off a narrow 1-0 win in the second leg and progressed to the semi-final stage. Once again, the two-legged affair was decided by just one goal and it was scored in the second leg by Ameri Tbilisi. They had managed to get to their first ever major final and in their first year of playing top-flight football. The club were on the up. Only one team could stop them from lifting their first major trophy and that team was FC Zestafoni, a club who themselves had only formed in 2004, and so were even younger than Ameri Tbilisi.

The final was played on 13 May 2006, at the Mikheil Meskhi Stadium in Tbilisi in front of a crowd of 10,000. Ameri Tbilisi took the lead in the tenth minute through a goal scored by Davitashvili. Zestafoni soon equalised in the 29th minute with a goal from Georgian international forward, Ionanidze. It was all square at the break, but it didn't take long for FC Ameri to regain the lead in the second half with a goal from Rati Tsinamdzgvrishvili (try pronouncing that) in the 50th minute. It seemed as though Ameri were about to lift their first major trophy until Zestafoni equalised in the 90th minute when Ghonghadze hit the back of the net to send the game into extra time. Neither side could find a winner in the added period and so the game went to penalties. Ameri missed their first penalty (Dekanosidze), while Zestafoni put away their first two (Ganugrava, Imedadze). Ameri scored their following two (Bolkvadze, Tatanashvili) before Zestafoni missed their third (Pipia) to draw the sides level. FC Ameri scored their next two with Davitnidze and Khvadagiani slotting home both their penalties. Zestafoni could only manage to score one of their last two (Ionanisze) while Chanturia missed his, meaning FC Ameri Tbilisi won the penalty shoot-out 4-3 and lifted their first major trophy. Not only did they get silverware, but it meant they qualified for the next season's UEFA Cup.

In their first game in European competition, they faced Armenian side Banants (known officially as FC Urartu since 2019). They lost the home leg 1-0 but managed to win the away leg 2-1 and qualified for the second round through the away goals rule. This set up a tie against German side Hertha Berlin, with not many people giving the Georgian club a chance. But they remained competitive against the Germans drawing 2-2 in the home leg and only losing 1-0 in Berlin, meaning their European adventure came to an end. They also lifted the Georgian Super Cup in 2006, beating league winners FC Sioni Bolnisi 1-0.

The 2006/07 season saw FC Ameri finish in an impressive third place, only six points behind the champions that season, Olimpi Rustavi. It gained them qualification to the UEFA Cup the following year once again, but their league position wouldn't have mattered as they regained the Georgian Cup.

They started off their defence against Kakheti Telavi, losing to them 3-1 in the first leg at home but beating them 5-3 in return, meaning that FC Ameri went through on the away goals rule after a 6-6 aggregate score. With the cup format being changed, a group stage then followed and FC Ameri were drawn in Group A, alongside FC

Zestafoni, Spartaki Tbilisi and interestingly the side they had beaten in the first round, Kakheti Telavi, who, along with four other clubs, progressed in the cup to make up the 16 clubs and four groups. FC Ameri qualified from the group in second place, behind their rivals FC Zestafoni, with both clubs finishing on 13 points. Zestafoni topped the group on goal difference, beating FC Ameri 4-1 on 22 November. Ameri faced city rivals Dinamo Tbilisi in the quarter-finals, beating them 2-1 in the first leg and drawing 0-0 in the second. They progressed to the semi-finals to face Sioni Bolnisi, losing 3-0 in the first leg at home and seemingly leaving their defence of the cup in tatters. But the second leg was not a forgone conclusion and FC Ameri were not to give up without a fight. Amazingly they won the away game 4-1, meaning that although the two-legged tie finished all square at 4-4, FC Ameri Tbilisi went through on away goals.

It set up a final against FC Zestafoni, a repeat of the final the year before. The sides had met in the group stages as well. There was a rivalry forming between two of the newest clubs in the Georgian football league and it showed with 25,000 attending the final between the two sides on 26 May 2007 at the Boris Palchadze Stadium in Tbilisi. The game was refereed by a Turkish official, Cuneyt Cakir. Unlike the previous final, the game was a cagey affair with the sides going in at half-time all square, 0-0. It wasn't until the 61st minute that the deadlock was broken by FC Ameri. Georgian international forward, Dimitri Tatanashvili scored the goal. It proved to be the only goal of the game and FC Ameri once again lifted the Georgian Cup and at the expense of FC Zestafoni.

Their second stint in Europe ended in the first round that year as well, with the club drawing Polish opponents GKS Belchatow. Winning the home leg 2-0 put the

Georgians in a strong position. However, the Polish side made home advantage count and won the second leg 2-0, sending the tie to penalties. The Poles won the penalty shoot-out, leaving FC Ameri to concentrate on domestic matters. The 2007/08 season saw the club finish fifth, just outside the European qualifying places, winning 15, drawing three and losing eight. It would mean that they would have to win the Georgian Cup for a third year in a row if they were to enter the UEFA Cup for the next year. It was a challenge that FC Ameri relished, and they continued to be a force in the Georgian Cup.

FC Ameri had to navigate their way through a group stage first. They were drawn in Group A alongside Spartak Tshinvali, Meskheti Akhaltsikhe and Torpedo Kutaisi. They topped the group, winning five out of their six games, only losing to Spartak Tshinvali, 2-1 away. The quarter-finals proved to be an easy event for the Tbilisi side also, as they beat Magharoeli Chiatura 6-1 on aggregate (2-1 first leg, 4-0 second leg). They finished off the semi-final as a competition in the first leg when they beat Borijomi 4-1. The second leg ended 1-1, meaning they advanced to back-to-back finals with a 5-2 aggregate score. Not only was it to be another final, their third in three years, but it was to be another final against FC Zestafoni. the third consecutive final between these two clubs, and FC Zestafoni were due a victory having been denied in the previous two years. The final was once again played at the Boris Paichadze Stadium in front of 25,000 fans, but this time they would be seeing a different side lifting the trophy. FC Zestafoni took the lead in the 57th minute through Oniani, then doubled their lead five minutes later when Gotsindze scored. It looked as though they would finally get the better of FC Ameri until the 88th minute when Tatanashvili scored to make it a nervous ending for Zestafoni. Despite the late scare, they held on to win the Georgian Cup and deny FC Ameri a third consecutive triumph.

The 2008/09 season came, but FC Ameri Tbilisi weren't to participate in it. Just before the season started, the club voluntarily withdrew and dissolved, citing financial reasons for their decision. And so, FC Ameri Tbilisi, the side who had competed in the last three Georgian Cup Finals, winning two of them, had disappeared from the Georgian Football League.

One man who can tell us more about this extraordinary club is Georgian football expert, Luka, who runs a Georgian football account on Twitter. Here is what he had to say when I asked him about FC Ameri Tbilisi and Georgian football.

First, thank you for taking time out to answer my questions on Georgian football and FC Ameri Tbilisi. The first question I have to ask is, how did you get involved in Georgian football and where did your passion come from?

Luka: Me being born and raised in Georgia, as well as coming from a family that loves sports and football in particular, really got me into football from my early years, attending matches with my father and uncles, and it basically being one of the discussion topics in everyday life as well.

What can you tell me about Ameri? How did they come about and who ran the club?

Luka: As you might know, Ameri were officially established in 2002. It was run by local businessman Zviad Potskhveria, who had all the ambitions and decent financial leverage to make Ameri one of the better clubs competing in the top flight. He brought in some promising young guys with other relatively experienced players present at the club.

They were only around for seven years, but they won more than some clubs have done in 100 years. They must have attracted a bit of a following and built up a fan base in that time, or were they looked upon as a 'franchise' with no history by the other clubs in Georgia and their fans?

Luka: In terms of the amount of fans, they were based in a district of Gldani (Tbilisi) which, to this date, is the largest one in the capital, with more than a third of Tbilisi's population living there. Hence it really helped the club to gain lots of interest from locals, and had a solid attendance during league matches after their promotion to the top flight in 2005 and a somewhat successful European adventure in 2006. (They were a goal away from knocking out Hertha BSC from the UEFA Cup second round qualifiers.)

I can't ask you questions and not mention the club FC Zestafoni. After doing my research on FC Ameri I went and had a read about them as well. They made it to the 2014/15 season but withdrew from the league or as it says, they were expelled. What happened to them? I know they play in the Fourth Division now.

Luka: Zestafoni were one of the most promising teams in the late 2000s and early 2010s, but unfortunately due to disobedience to the league rules and some financial issues, they were expected to be expelled to the third tier, but due to unknown reasons, the club decided to go further down to the Regional League (fifth tier) and begin their journey from there. They got promoted to the third division in 2021 and are hoping to go even higher up, but unfortunately, the owner of the club Ilia Kokaia tragically died in a hiking accident in November 2021. A real shame for a guy who really loved the club and was the main reason for their success.

Who is your favourite Georgian player and who was the best Georgian player? It can be the same player.

Luka: As far as my favourite player goes, from the players I saw playing, I have to go with Guram Kashia (current) and Shota Arveladze (past) and in terms of the best ever Georgian (let's say after the Soviet era) it's either Kaladze, who had the most successful career out of any other Georgians abroad, winning the UCL twice and multiple Serie A titles, or Giorgi Kinkladze, who never fulfilled his potential and is deemed as one of the biggest 'what ifs' in our footballing history.

Georgian football isn't something that most people in Europe will watch or have any knowledge about. Can you give our readers some interesting facts about some of the clubs and the league?

Luka: Probably the most well-known club from Georgia has to be Dinamo Tbilisi, with them being one of the better Soviet sides in the 70s and 80s, winning the UEFA Cup Winners' Cup in 1981, and beating teams like West Ham, Liverpool, Napoli, Feyenoord and Inter at the time. The club has the best academy in the country, with current young Georgian internationals – Khvicha Kvaratskhelia, Giorgi Chakvetadze, Zuriko Davitashvili and Giorgi Mamardashvili coming in from the academy system of the club. Plenty of guys with decent potential are expected to be assigned to the first team in future as well and that's why I think they're the most interesting and scouting-worthy club in the country. I have to mention Dinamo Batumi as well, with them being the current title holders, and having the best fan base in the league (I would recommend looking them up).

Finally, FC Ameri Tbilisi, will they ever re-emerge, maybe as a phoenix club, or is the club gone for good?

Luka: As far as Ameri's existence goes, they tried to form an academy in 2011/12, but that didn't last for long. The only way the club can re-emerge, is if an enthusiastic businessman emerges from somewhere and tries to re-establish the club once again.

39.

Dick, Kerr Ladies (England)

THE CLUB Dick, Kerr Ladies was founded in 1917, in Lancashire in the north of England, after a group of women workers from Dick, Kerr & Co beat a group of men in an informal football match. The club, managed by office worker Alfred Frankland, gained even more attention when they beat another factory team, Arundel Coulthard Factory, 4-0 in front of a bumper crowd of 10,000 on Christmas Day 1917 at Deepdale, Preston North End's current home ground. The team were encouraged to play competitively by the factory as it was seen to boost morale during World War One amongst the women, who were left behind in England to produce ammunition for men who went to mainland Europe to fight.

They became a popular team and something of a money-spinner, but they used their new-found fame to raise money for charities that helped injured servicemen and continued to play various charity matches after the war, travelling all over the country. But they weren't just turning up and playing in these games, they were competing and winning them, beating men's teams with ease. Dick, Kerr & Co had so much faith in the women that they paid each team member 10 shillings to cover expenses for each game they played. Some people said that their early wins were down to stage fright from the men in the opposition teams, who couldn't believe that these women were matching or in some cases outplaying them in every department on the pitch, but of course this would seem like an easy excuse for the men to use to avoid their embarrassment.

There was no women's league at the time Dick, Kerr Ladies were playing and the Football Association were not keen on the idea of women's football at all. However, this didn't stop Dick, Kerr Ladies from playing and in 1920 a match was organised against a French women's team from Paris. This was to be the first women's international football match in the history of the sport. The French team was led by Alice Milliat, a pioneer for women's sport, and someone who made it possible for women to compete in more sports, including ones that featured in the Olympic Games.

Dick, Kerr Ladies continued to play matches in England, four in total that year, winning three and drawing one. In their first game, at Deepdale, they beat another local team 2-0. They then went on to beat a team from Stockport 2-1 and draw with a team from Manchester, 1-1. Their final game was a trip to London, where they played at Chelsea's home ground, Stamford Bridge, and beat a London team 2-1. The team went on a tour of France to play clubs from Paris, Roubaix, Le Havre and Rouen, drawing three and winning one.

The team caught the imagination of a nation, and this showed when they played a friendly against St Helen's Ladies from Liverpool. The game was played in front of a huge crowd of 53,000 at Everton's home ground, Goodison Park. This was a world record attendance at a women's football match, which was only broken 98 years later. (A match between Barcelona Women and Atletico Madrid Women had 60,739 spectators at the Wanda Metropolitano Stadium in Madrid, in March 2019.)

While the match caught the imagination of the people, it caused annoyance amongst the hierarchy of the Football

Association and on 5 December 1921, the FA effectively banned women from playing football, stating that, 'The game of football is not sustainable for females and it ought not be encouraged.' They claimed the move was to 'protect women', but many saw it as a way to defend the men's game, as the FA grew uneasy at the popularity of Dick, Kerr Ladies and the crowds they were attracting. More often than not they were out-doing the men's teams in attendances, and this led the FA to believe that it could harm the men's game. Only a year after 53,000 football fans had packed into Goodison Park to see two women's teams play, all women's football clubs, including Dick, Kerr Ladies, were stripped of official recognition by the FA.

Amazingly the ban on women's football lasted 50 years and wasn't lifted until July 1971. During the time of the ban, the women's game in England failed to progress as they were not allowed to play in any stadium that was under FA regulations, meaning they were restricted to smaller stadia or even just simply fields, which drastically reduced their potential for attracting support. Even after the ban ended, it took a further 22 years for the FA to recognise women's football, ignoring it until 1993, when the FA finally took over the administration and funding of it.

The ban on playing didn't stop Dick, Kerr Ladies from playing, with their manager Alfred Frankland stating, 'The team will continue to play, if the organisers of charity matches will provide grounds, even if we have to play on ploughed fields.' And so, they did, playing matches in smaller stadia that were not controlled by the FA, and fields.

But it wasn't only in England where the women's game or indeed Dick, Kerr Ladies faced discrimination and obstacles. The team decided to tour Canada and the US, deeming it to be a more competitive challenge than they were facing in the UK. But when they arrived in Canada in

1922, they were told that the Canadian Dominion Football Association had banned all women from playing competitive football matches. It was a disappointment to the team, but they headed down south straight away to play in the US. Their first game took place in Patterson, New Jersey on 24 September. They continued to play against nine US-based men's teams, creating a buzz over in the US, but once again they weren't just there to compete or to be looked at: Dick, Kerr Ladies held their own. Of the nine games, they won three, drew three and lost three.

They continued to play back in the UK, most notably against Scottish side Rutherglen Ladies in September 1923. Dick, Kerr Ladies were expected to win but surprisingly they fell to a 2-0 defeat. Subsequently, Rutherglen's manager James Kelly declared his team 'world champions' as Dick, Kerr Ladies had declared themselves that from 1917 to 1925.

In 1926 the team changed their name, to Preston Ladies FC, after Frankland had an argument with Dick, Kerr's ownership. They continued to gain widespread recognition, attracting up to 5,000 spectators at some of their games. The 'world champions' tag came back into the picture when the club played a match against then Scottish women's champions, Edinburgh Ladies. Preston Ladies won the match 5-1 and were once again declared the unofficial women's 'world champions'.

Among the players to play for Dick, Kerr Ladies was Lily Parr, who made 700 appearances for the club, spanning 1920–1951. Playing for 30 years is an amazing achievement but what is even more amazing is the fact she is recorded to have scored over 900 goals for the club in that time, starting her playing career at the age of 14. In her first season alone, she scored 48 goals and scored a total of 108 in that whole year. It was said that her childhood was the reason for her huge success in football, as she used to play football and rugby with her brothers, making her well capable of playing against other men.

I interviewed Charlotte Patterson, who writes about women's football, specifically Asian women's football, as well as writing for Roker Report, a Sunderland fan site, and being an assistant researcher for Football Manager. She answered my questions on Dick, Kerr Ladies and the state of women's football today.

Hi, Charlotte, thank you for taking time out to help with this book. What can you tell me about how Dick, Kerr Ladies started, and finished?

Charlotte Patterson: When World War One started, women took to the jobs that the men had left while they were at war, mainly in factories. One such factory was Dick, Kerr & Co, a train and tram-car manufacturer. However, during the war most factories began to produce resources and ammunition for the war. Despite women being discouraged from playing football, the company decided that it would be good for morale for them to play. During lunch and tea breaks, the women would go out into the factory yard to play an informal game of football with the apprentices. The factory took notice that the women kept beating the men during these games and decided to start a football team named Dick, Kerr Ladies.

The team started playing matches against different factories, winning many of the games they played. People began to take notice and soon afternoons and days were spent watching this factory team beat all that stood in their way.

The Dick, Kerr Ladies were flying. They played 833 games in their history, winning 759, drawing 46 and losing

28. However, their achievements could have been so much more. In 1921, the FA decided to ban women's football. This ban stayed in place for 50 years. Women were forced to play in small grounds, given no financial aid, no resources, support or backing. During those 50 years of being banned, Dick, Kerr Ladies continued to play on non-FA grounds, usually relying on charity-organised matches to play.

But in the end, despite a rename to Preston Ladies from 1926–65, the ladies' team finally folded. Without the resources and funding, they could not continue on as a team. A great tragedy for what was a great team which pioneered women's football.

As a woman who is very much involved in football, were Dick, Kerr Ladies an inspiration and if not, who is an inspiration in the footballing world to you?
Charlotte: Absolutely, I think they were pioneers for women and women's football. They proved to so many people in that time period that they could play and that they could be bloody good at it too and bring in thousands of people in attendance. Of course, it wasn't solely Dick, Kerr Ladies who paved the way. But their story and their achievements serve as an inspiration to every aspiring female footballer and women's football fan.

It sounds so corny and clichéd, but so many elements of women's football are an inspiration to me. Whether it's specific players, clubs or how in women's football there is a greater sense of community, safety, and acceptance. I was having a conversation the other day with someone, in that being gay in women's football is not a big deal at all. You never hear of any issues with homophobia or racism. We know what it is like being discriminated against for being a woman and being a woman who enjoys football. So, I think women's football has naturally always been inclusive.

It was never forced. It just was. I played football growing up and half of my team-mates were gay and that was just how it was. It was accepted, as it should be. So, whilst we still might have a way to go in terms of the physical development of women's football, I think socially we are the best.

Quite clearly there was a huge gender inequality problem in football back in the 1920s up until the 70s and probably in society in general, but in regards football, do you think it has got better for women nowadays to play the game or even participate in any way in the sport?

Charlotte: The ban on women's football stopped growth, stopped belief of young girls, stopped ambition and stopped possibilities. Who knows where the women's game would be now were it not banned for 50 years? The game ceased to exist for women during those years. Even now, the women's game is still trying to build itself up again. It took until a few years ago, in 2018, for the Women's Super League to be fully professional with all 12 top-flight teams strictly full-time. Yes, the women's game isn't perfect, it might be 'boring', it might not be up to your standard, but it's trying. If you don't like it, that's fine. But the constant and unwarranted sexist comments which come with it help no one. In time, hopefully the standard will improve. While slowly, I have noticed improvement each year. But it will take time to recuperate from the ban which stunted its growth and development for 50 years. But it doesn't matter what I say anyway, because at the end of the day some people won't change. Sexist comments and remarks will always be made. But if being a woman has taught me anything, it's that we are resilient, strong and never back down.

The ban that was put in place, what are your thoughts about that? If you had been alive back then, how would

you have reacted to being told that football wasn't safe for women and that women should be discouraged from participating in it?

Charlotte: It makes me really angry, so I can't imagine how women would have felt back then. Funnily enough, I just went to watch a play recently called *Wor Bella* which was about a woman called Bella Reay who worked in an ammunition factory during the war and played for the company team, Blyth Spartans Women. It was a really funny and compelling story and I'm not one for plays! But towards the end, she spoke about something I didn't even consider. During the war, when all the men were away, women had freedom that they had never had before. They had jobs, they could play football, they could go for walks unattended, go out to pubs and other simple activities that we would take for granted right now. She explained the sadness that women felt when the men returned from war, because them coming back and the war ending meant that all of those freedoms were gone. Women lost their jobs, their fathers or husbands went back to controlling what they did, they went back to the housewife role and then they lost their ability to play football. The woman explained the guilt she felt about being sad and angry that the men were returning, especially as they had been at war and so many died. But she couldn't help the emotions, as she may not have lost her life, but she lost something too.

I think had I been living back then, I would have certainly been rebellious and fought against the restrictions. Even when I was younger, I had to do the same. Not to the extent they did back then, of course. But when I was at school, I had to fight to get a girls' football team, I had to fight for the boys to let me play with them during break time and I had to fight against girls too, who told me to stop being a 'tomboy', called me 'gay' or a 'boy' just for playing and enjoying football.

I always question where women's football would have been today if not for that ban. Given the success and audience it had just when it was company teams, it would have likely grown into what the Premier League was when it was first created. But who is to say? The ban was an awful and abhorrent thing to do and there still hasn't really been a formal apology for it. Not that many people even know about it!

You have an interest in Asian women's football. That is quite a niche thing to be interested in, even in football terms. Can I ask what got you interested in that part of the world and its football culture?

Charlotte: Ha, it is a bit of a weird one, but it actually started off with a video game. When I was younger, I used to obsessively play these games called Dynasty Warriors and Samurai Warriors; the games both loosely cover elements of Chinese history and Japanese history respectively. The more I played the games, the more I learned about Asian history and then it eventually led me to researching and learning more about Asian countries, history and culture. Before I went to university and did my degree in nursing, I was actually considering doing a degree in East Asian Studies. So, with the huge love of football which I already had and my love for Asia, the two just meshed together and I found myself reading more about Asian football, trying to find where I could watch it and listening to podcasts on specific Asian countries or leagues.

I still listen to lots of podcasts now and try to find one from every Asian league or country where possible. I think recently I have fallen out of love with modern football in some regards and I find much more interest in watching these niche and developing leagues. Players play for their love of the game and that is what football is all about.

Have you faced any discrimination while working within the football industry and how do you react to it if it happens?

Charlotte: Yes and no. I'm quite thankful that my experiences at football games have always been great, with no issues of sexism. In recent years, my dad, who I used to go to games with, can't attend much, so I tend to go to games by myself. Again, nothing has happened that is significant, but I felt very uncomfortable at times when on my own and had some inappropriate sexual comments shouted at me.

In terms of in the industry as such, I have always received so much support from my peers. There are no issues around sexism and everyone is here for the same common goal – to talk about the sport we love. The problem I do have is with social media. I have received quite frankly some disgusting and repulsive comments over the years, mainly when I'm trying to talk about women's football. You'll get your standard 'get back in the kitchen', 'do you know the offside rule', 'make me a sandwich', 'you only go to attract men', 'blonde bitch' etc. But I have also had messages from people telling me to go kill myself, and that they hope I get raped at a game. It's comments like that, that make you forget all the nice things that have been said and how supportive everyone else is. I think the feeling is made worse by knowing that they will get away with saying these things because of the fact they create fake accounts and social media companies don't do anything about it.

Finally, how do you see the women's game progressing from now on? It seems to have caught the imagination of football fans, men and women, with record attendances

appearing in different women's leagues all over the world in the last few years. And what do you think can be done to keep it progressing?

Charlotte: Each year women's football continues to make strides, whether big or small, they all count towards progression. Women's football is so freely available now to people across the world, we have people commentating on the games, we have fan groups, websites, analysts, scouts, podcasters, people from all different kinds of fields starting to get involved or become part of women's football, which is so fantastic to see. Because again, I want to reinforce the message that no one is forcing anybody to watch or like women's football if they don't want to, but there just isn't any need to put it down and make sexist comments. As I mentioned earlier, women's football continues to grow regardless of the noisy opposition and those with fragile egos and caveman-like mentalities.

After each World Cup or big football tournament, we always see a big boom of interest and uptake in women's football. England's games at the Euros all sold out and we've also seen the likes of Barcelona Women break records with sell-out crowds at Camp Nou. Things are definitely improving, and I've seen more change in the last two to three years than I ever have in my life. It's an exciting time. But we still have to manage our expectations and reality.

Improving grassroots football, improving coaching, access to facilities and creating an environment of acceptance for kids at a young age, can only allow those children to reach heights I never thought possible when I was younger. My goal growing up was to be a footballer, but not only was there not a clear pathway, but the benefits, finances and appreciation just wasn't there when I was young. That's why I'm so happy and proud now, as I see so many young girls achieving things I could never do. And that is what will always keep me going.

When I put it out there that I was looking to speak to women in football for this chapter, I got a lot of mentions and tags, and that's how I came across Jenn Ramczyk, an American who loves her soccer. She is also one of the women who started the #HerGameToo campaign over in the United States, after it was launched in the UK by a group of women who wanted to make a stand against sexism in football. Jenn has carried on their good work, promoting the game for women and young girls across the water. Here is what she had to say.

Hi Jenn, my first question I have to ask you is how did you get involved with football? What influenced your passion for the game or who influenced it?
Jenn Ramczyk: I was introduced to football in high school. I didn't like going to American football games so I was looking for other sports. My sister knew a player on the boys' football team. So, we went to watch their game. It was very entertaining. We had an older lady explaining the rules of the game to help us understand. I was hooked from that point on. The World Cup came to the US in 1994, which was incredible to see football styles from around the world. This only grew my passion and love for the sport.

You are from America, a country that is known for the popularity of women's football, and one that has such a good standard; some might even say the women's game over there is more popular than the men's. What's your take on that?
Jenn: The women's game is more popular than the men's when it comes to World Cup years. Overall, it has lower

attendance at the club level. I would say compared to other countries, more people know there is a women's league. We need to get better at marketing the games and getting higher attendance at the local level. This in turn will help grow the game even more. I think it is getting better and we need to build on the progress.

The US women's team are seen as the best in the world, with some unbelievably talented players over the years. What is the reason that the US is able to produce such quality women footballers?

Jenn: It is due to young girls being given the opportunity to play the game at a young age. The average age to start playing is five or six years old. This lets them hone their skills and perfect their game. In my opinion, other countries didn't award this opportunity to young girls in the past, and this set the game back. In the US, this young development helped the future of the game here. As our ladies do great things, more young girls get into the game.

The women's game here in Europe is starting to take off quite a bit. Countries like England have the Women's Super League played on Sky Sports, while here in Ireland, the most recent Women's FAI Cup Final had its biggest attendance ever and just recently Real Madrid and Barcelona women's teams broke the world record for a match attendance at a women's football match. Looking from the outside, where do you think women's football can go from now? What would be progress in your eyes?

Jenn: I think women's football can continue to grow by encouraging young girls to play the game and developing their skills. There needs to be a continual progress of moving the game forward in terms of attendance, marketing and player development. Progress to me is to see the momentum continue with having players come into the game. It is great to see little girls with a passion for the game and wearing their team colours. Showing young girls it is okay to be a part of the sport, it isn't just for boys.

Dick, Kerr Ladies are seen as the pioneers of women's football in the UK and throughout most of the world. Who were the pioneers of women's football in the United States?
Jenn: The 1950–51 Craig Club Girls Bobby Soccers team. It grew from there to having what we have today.

On your Twitter account you have #HerGameTooUSA in your bio. It is a movement I am familiar with and one that, although quite new, has made a huge positive impact on promoting women's football in the UK and Ireland. What has that movement done in the US and are you actively a part of it?
Jenn: I initiated the start in the US and am actively a part of the campaign. We started at the end of March 2022 and have three teams that have partnered with us. We are still in the building phase and plan to have an MLS team join the campaign.

Thank you for answering all of these questions. I just have one more and it's a simple one, but one that may have a few answers. Who is your favourite player to ever play the game?
Jenn: My favourite players are Steven Gerrard, Kenny Dalglish and Jesse Marsch.

FC Amsterdam take on Ajax

FC Amsterdam take on MVV in October 1974

Sporting Fingal FC crest

*Sporting
Fingal v
Shamrock
Rovers*

*Amkar Perm
fans v Fulham
in the Europa
League*

Fans of Palermo FC show their colours on game day

Palermo FC celebrate promotion in 2022

CF Reus fans on tour

Chivas USA fans letting off flares

The Mighty Shots

Deva Stadium, home of Chester City

Cesena fans

Kayserispor crest

Calais fans

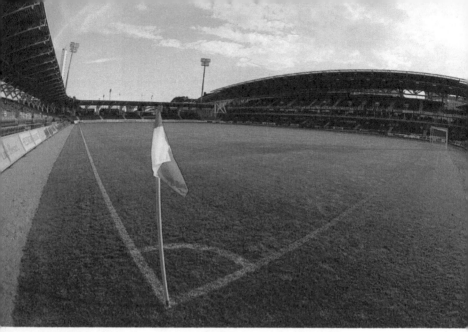

FinnAir Stadium, home to FC Jokerit

KSK Beveren fan enjoying the sun

Graz in action in Europe back in 1968 v Dutch club, ADO

APOP Kinyras FC crest

Dukla Prague v Manchester United

HFC Haarlem in action back on New Year's Day, 1959

Sportivo Palermo team picture

40.
Lechia-Polonia Gdansk (Poland)

THE MERGER of two Polish clubs, Lechia Gdansk and Polonia Gdansk, led to the founding of Lechia-Polonia Gdansk in 1998. Lechia had originally been founded in 1945 and played most of their football in the lower leagues in Poland. They did have a successful 1953 season in which they finished third in the top tier but this success was short-lived, and they found themselves meandering between the top two divisions. Their only noted success was the Polish Cup win in 1983 and the Polish Super Cup win in the same season. They had a run of seasons in the top flight after that but again found themselves dropping back into the second tier. In 1993 the club first merged with another club in Olympia Poznan to form Olympia-Lechia Gdansk, but this merger only lasted a season before the two clubs split. Three seasons later, in 1998, the club merged with Polonia Gdansk to form Lechia-Polonia Gdansk.

Polonia Gdansk had a more moderate history than that of Lechia. Founded in 1945 as NS Nt Gdansk and undergoing various name changes while playing in the lower divisions (they were also known as Stal Gdansk and RKS Stoczniowiec Gdansk), they finally landed on the name Polonia Gdansk. Yo-yoing up and down the leagues, mainly from the third tier to the second, the club never really threatened to break into the top echelons of Polish football. Only once did they come close, when they finished third in the Second Division, just narrowly missing out on promotion. Other than that, it was always either promotion or runners-up spots in the third tier, and when they did manage to get promoted to the Second Division they would either find themselves fighting against relegation or being relegated. The most stable era in the club's history came in the 1970s when they stayed in the Second Division for nine consecutive seasons, only to be relegated in 1983. As previously stated, in 1998, the club finally decided to merge with Lechia Gdansk, but Polonia fans were not happy with this merger. This was not going to be a straightforward process.

The newly formed club, Lechia-Polonia Gdansk, took their place in the Second Division West. They finished seventh out of the 14 clubs competing and made it to the round of 16 in the Polish Cup. It was seen as a successful first season, with the new club still trying to fix issues on and off the field. The following season, 1999/2000, proved to be a bit more turbulent, especially off the field. Polonia had decided to pull out of the merger and go back to their original form, but Lechia-Polonia Gdansk retained the same name. Fans of Polonia Gdansk refused to recognise the merged club as anything to do with their original club, and Polonia Gdansk started again in the sixth tier of the Polish football league. Lechia-Polonia finished 14th in their second season, which was a bit of a disappointment for the club, who thought they would be competing at the top end of the table. However, things were about to get even worse for them, as in their third season, 2000/01, they found themselves being relegated after finishing 19th of 20 clubs, and dropping down to the Third Division.

What had started out as a great idea, two clubs coming together and creating one super-club in the region, was starting to become a disaster, and it got even worse when

Lechia decided to create a separate club, going back to their old entity and starting in the sixth tier just like Polonia had the season before. Lechia-Polonia were still around for one more season, in the third tier, where they finished 15th of 19. But that was to be it from the club. They cited that they were experiencing financial difficulties and could not continue to operate and so ceased to exist.

Lechia Gdansk, since their reformation in 2001, have climbed the Polish footballing pyramid to finally reach the top tier, the Ekstraklasa, in 2019 and in the 2021/22 campaign they finished fourth. They also won the Polish Cup in 2018/19, beating Jagiellonia Bialystok, 1-0. They reached the final again in 2019/20 but were beaten by Cracovia 3-2 after extra time. Lechia have proven that on their own they were better off and probably look back at the merger and wonder what they were thinking.

In contrast to Lechia, Polonia Gdansk have not had the best of times since reforming back into their original entity. Now known as SKS Stoczniowiec Gdansk, they play their football in the lower, regional divisions. The highest position they have achieved since their reformation was two seasons in the Third Division, where they finished 14th and 16th. They then suffered back-to-back relegations, meaning they were playing in the fifth tier.

41.

HFC Haarlem (Netherlands)

FOUNDED IN 1889 and based in the city of Haarlem, HFC Haarlem adopted the colours of blue and red, usually wearing the red on their shorts, thus giving them the nickname '*Roodbroeken*' which in English translates to 'Red Shorts'. The club played their matches at the Haarlem Stadium, which had a small capacity of just under 3,500. Their first big success was winning the Dutch Cup Final in 1902. They beat HBS Craeyenhout 2-1 to claim what is now known as the KNVB Cup. It wasn't until the 1910/11 season that they would reach the final again, only to be beaten by Wuick den Haag, 1-0. The following season saw the club make it two finals in a row: this time they won, beating Vitesse 2-0 to lift the trophy for the second time in ten years. They would continue to do well in the cup competition, reaching the final once again in the 1913/14 season, only to lose 3-2 to FC Dordrecht.

Their first league success came in the 1946/47 season when they won their only top-flight title. The league format back then was very different to what it is now. The Netherlands Football League Championship as it was known, consisted of 66 clubs, split into six divisions across the country. HFC Haarlem were in the Eerste Klasse West-II Division. It was not an easy division by any means, with Dutch giants Feyenoord competing in it, although they would only finish sixth out of the 11 clubs. Haarlem finished top of the division, two points above a club we already know a little bit about, Blau-Wit Amsterdam (it's funny how stories like this can be connected). This qualified them for the Championship play-off with the winners of all six divisions competing in one final group to see who would be crowned overall champion. Of course, AFC Ajax were one of the clubs competing after they had won their division, the Eerste Klasse West-I, by a single point. NEC Nijmegen won the Eerste Klasse East title, SC Heerenveen won the Eerste Klasse North title, and NAC qualified for the Championship play-off after beating BVV Den Bosch 1-0 in a one-off tie after both clubs finished on 33 points in the Eerste Klasse South-I. Limburgia completed the group after they won the Eerste Klasse South-II title. After ten games, each club playing each other home and away, Haarlem ran out easy winners, finishing on 21 points, five points above second-placed AFC Ajax. They won seven, drew two and lost only one of their Championship games and so were crowned Dutch top-flight champions for the first and only time in their history.

With World War Two disrupting football all over Europe, the Dutch league didn't resume until the 1946/47 season. Haarlem were once again in the Eerste Klasse West-II Division but could only finish third, four points behind Blauw-Wit Amsterdam. The club saw themselves transferred to the Eerste West-I Division for the next season. It proved to be a good move for Haarlem, who won it in 1947/48, but they finished a disappointing fifth out of six teams in the Championship play-off. The disappointment continued into the 1948/49 season when they finished sixth out of 11 teams, winning eight, drawing two and losing ten games that season. The next season, 1949/50, saw the club make a return to the Dutch Cup Final for the first time in decades. They faced a strong PSV side and lost their third final, 4-3.

Mediocrity really was all that Haarlem had to offer for the next few decades, the Dutch league changing formats over the coming years, decreasing the number of teams contesting and therefore decreasing the number of divisions involved. The 1951/52 season saw Haarlem win the Eerste Klasse A Division, but in the four-team play-off division, they could only manage to finish third. The club then saw themselves being relegated in the mid-50s and with a change of format again making it harder to reach the top flight, they remained in the lower divisions until they gained promotion in the 1968/69 season to what was now known as the Eredivisie. The club finished 13th in the 1969/70 season, winning six, drawing 15 and losing 13 in their return to the top flight. But that respectable finish was to be forgotten about in the following campaign when the club finished 18th and bottom of the Eredivisie, winning only one game. It wasn't long until they were back up to the top flight, and they won the Second Division the following season to ensure they would be competing against the likes of Ajax and Feyenoord in 1972/3. Finishing 11th that season, winning ten, drawing nine and losing 15, it was a respectable return to the top flight. The next season was much of the same with the club only dropping one place, finishing 12th, winning ten, drawing six and losing 18.

However, the 1974/75 season saw the club relegated once again, finishing second from bottom (17th) winning only seven games all season, drawing ten and losing 17. They finished only a point behind 16th-placed NAC. Their stay in the Eerste Division didn't last long and they gained promotion at the first time of asking, finishing top, winning 23 games, drawing nine and only losing four all season. They scored an impressive 78 goals conceding 36. The

1976/77 season saw the club finish 12th, then in 1977/78 they finished 13th. The 1978/79 season saw Haarlem flirt with relegation, finishing 16th, just three points and one place above the relegation zone. But their stay of execution only lasted a season as they were once again resigned to relegation in 1979/80, finishing rock bottom (18th), winning just seven games, drawing ten and losing 17. But just like the last time the club were relegated, they won the Eerste Division at the first time of asking and won it with ease, finishing eight points ahead of second-placed SC Heerenveen.

But unlike previous seasons, where they would get promoted and just finish mid-table the next season, HFC Haarlem provided one of the shocks of the 1981/82 season in finishing fourth and gaining qualification for the 1982/83 UEFA Cup. In the first round they met Belgian side Gent, beating them 2-1 in the home leg. The away leg proved to be an exciting affair, finishing 3-3 which saw the Dutch side progress to the second round where they met Soviet Union side Spartak Moscow. This proved to be a bridge too far for Haarlem, who lost 2-0 in the first leg and 3-1 in the second, knocking them out 5-1 on aggregate.

Their European adventure didn't affect their domestic form and in the 1982/83 season they finished seventh, only two points outside of the UEFA Cup qualification places. They finished fourth in 1983/84 but were ten points off a European place, with the big three clubs, Ajax, PSV and Feyenoord, finishing above them by some distance. (Feyenoord were the league champions that season.) Mediocrity was the name of the game for HFC for years after that, finishing ninth (1984/5), 11th (1985/6), 12th (1986/77), ninth (1987/88), and tenth (1988/9). It wasn't until the 1989/90 season that they were finally relegated once again, finishing bottom of the pile, winning just four games all season, drawing seven and losing 23, scoring only 24 goals and conceding a huge amount, 74 in total.

Unlike previous relegations, HFC Haarlem didn't gain promotion straight away. In fact, they weren't even close, finishing a disappointing 14th out of 20. The 1991/92 season saw a little improvement with the club finishing tenth, but they were still nowhere near the promotion places. (That same year FC Wageningen went bankrupt.) The 1992/93 season was another mediocre year, in which the club finished mid-table in tenth place. With the promotion play-off system changed, giving the top seven a chance to gain promotion, one would think HFC Haarlem would have been at least challenging for one of those places, but the 1993/94 season saw the club drop down to 15th place, followed by 16th the next season, with the club seemingly stuck in a rut and struggling to find a way out of the Eerste Division.

In 1995/96 they were tenth, 12 points behind Cambuur who finished in sixth place and inside the promotion play-off places. And it got worse for HFC Haarlem the following season, as they finished bottom of the Eerste Division (18th). They were 15th in the 1997/98 and 1998/99 seasons as the club headed into the new millennium. But the new century didn't bring any new luck to Haarlem, as they finished 16th in the 1999/2000 season, 17th in 2000/01 and 12th in 2001/02, which saw the club playing in the Eerste Division for more than a decade. In the 2002/03 season they finished 14th and they were 13th in 2003/04.

The club continued to finish at the wrong end of the table and never gained promotion again to the top flight of Dutch football. In 2010, halfway through the season, the club were excluded from the professional football league due to them being bankrupt. HFC Haarlem played their last ever professional match on 10 January 2011, in a 3-0 away loss to Excelsior. Three months later, HFC Haarlem completed a merger with amateur side, HFC Kennemerland, forming the new club Haarlem Kennemerland. They play in the amateur leagues.

42.

ESV Ingolstadt (Germany)

THE ORIGINS of ESV Ingolstadt go way back to 1912, which is when one of the five clubs that merged to create Turnverein Ringsee as they were first known, was founded. That club was Sangerverein Ringsee, along with Gluckliche Heimkehr (founded in 1919), Frohliche Stunden (founded in 1919), FC Freiheit Ringsee (founded in 1919) and Spielvereinigung Ringsee (founded in 1920). It was in 1930 that the first name change took place, as TVR turned to RTSV Ingolstadt Ringsee. This then became RSG Ingolstadt in 1940, before finally settling on the name TSV Ingolstadt Ringsee in 1945.

On the other side, ESV had a less complicated foundation, although they were the result of a merger as well, between the clubs known as FC Viktoria Ingolstadt, who were founded in 1919, and another sports club, VfR Ingolstadt, who were formed in 1921. They merged to form VfB Ingolstadt Ringsee in 1925.

These two clubs, who had been created by mergers, then decided to merge in 1946 to form VfB Ingolstadt-Ringsee. This lasted until 1951, when a name change was made and ESV Ingolstadt Ringsee were established. But that was not the end of the name changing as in 1953, the 'E' part of ESV, which stood for Erster, meaning 'first', was then changed to Eisenbahner, which means 'railway', a reference to the club's connection to the German railways.

While VfB Ingolstadt-Ringsee competed in the two-tier Landesliga Bayern in 1945, another club, MTV Ingolstadt were also around and in the 1946/47 season, the league was expanded, and Northern and Southern divisions were set up. After the war, fierce derbies were a frequent occurrence, with no love lost. VfB competed at the upper end of the table, but never gained promotion to the next level, Oberliga Sud.

The 1953/54 season saw ESV finish second, and on the same number of points as SpVgg Weiden. It meant the two clubs had to go head-to-head in a one-off match to determine who would be promoted. Ingolstadt lost the game 4-1 and had to endure another season in the Amateurliga Bayern. The next season saw the club finish second once again, but like the previous year, they lost the promotion play-off match, this time to Kickers Wurzburg. The 1956/57 season saw the club drop one place to third, but that wasn't enough to even claim a play-off place. But it would be a long time until ESV would challenge again. In fact, their decline continued down the league table, until eventually, in 1960, the club finished bottom of the league and were relegated.

It wasn't long before ESV were back in the 1. Amateurliga Bayern Division, after they won the 2. Amateurliga Oberbayern along with the Upper Bavaria Championship. These few years would prove to be some of ESV's most successful, as after returning to their old league, they gained promotion straight away to the 2. Oberliga Sud. But they didn't stop there and finished runners-up in their first season. Usually this would have meant promotion to the next tier, however, German football was going through a restructure of its leagues, and the Bundesliga was formed. This meant there was no promotion or relegation that year and so ESV missed out, despite their efforts.

After the changes in 1963, ESV were placed in the Regionalliga, and as they were located in the south of Germany, were placed in the Regionalliga Sud, formerly known as the Oberliga Sud. It was a competition that had some household names competing in it, not least German giants FC Bayern Munich. But ESV competed relatively well and finished 12th in their first two seasons. However, in their third season, the club were relegated after finishing second to last. It meant a return to the Amateurliga.

A second-place finish occurred in 1967, while the following season, in 1968, they won the league and gained promotion back to the Regionalliga. The club spent a longer term there this time, four years to be exact, until they were relegated once again in 1972. In true ESV style, they almost bounced back straight away, only finishing second to FC Augsburg, a club who now play in the Bundesliga. ESV did have a second chance that season, through the German amateur championship, but lost out in the semi-finals of the competition to SpVgg Bad Homburg. The following season saw the club finish third, but it wouldn't have mattered had they won the league that year, as promotion was not on offer due to the German league once again changing its format, from the five Regionalligas to the two Bundesligas.

Arguably one of the club's best seasons came in 1978/9 when they eventually gained promotion to the 2. Bundesliga by virtue of winning the Amateur Oberliga Bayern. It also saw the club win more silverware, when they went all the way to the final of the German Amateur Championship, beating Hertha Zehlendorf there. The 1979/80 season would prove to be historic as well, but for different reasons.

This was the only season in their histories that both ESV Ingolstadt and MTV Ingolstadt would compete in the same professional league as each other. They played each other twice, with MTV getting the better of the results, with a 2-2 draw and a 2-1 win. However, it would be ESV who would have the last laugh as MTV were relegated that season, while ESV survived, finishing 17th, two spots ahead of their bitter rivals, who placed 19th. Five points separated the two clubs, but it would be the last time they would play each other in a professional league. This rivalry would be put aside in the future.

ESV were set to escape relegation, but then came another restructure of the German league system. Because of this the club ended up in the Amateurliga once again. Things didn't get any better for them when, in 1982, they were relegated once more to the Landesliga Bayern-Sud when they finished bottom of the 20 clubs competing in the Amateurliga. It didn't take long for the club to pick themselves up and gain promotion again and in 1984 that is what they did. Despite finishing in the top half of the table in the 1984/85 season, it was all downhill from there, as the club were relegated the following year, and after four seasons in the Landesliga, they found themselves being relegated once again, this time to the Bezirksoberliga Oberbayern, the fifth tier of German football, although after more changes to the German football pyramid it would become the seventh tier in the future.

ESV never really recovered from their fall from grace, just finishing mid-table most seasons at this level. In 1994 their decline finally hit rock bottom and the club were once again relegated, losing a play-off match to TSV Ampfing on penalties, 6-4. It would be the last the club would ever see of Landesliga football, as they dropped even further down the German football pyramid. In 1995, they finished bottom of the Bezirksoberliga and ended up playing in the Bezirksliga Oberbayern-Nord, the seventh tier at the time. They steadied the ship in this league, until 2000, when they won the championship and returned to the Berzirksoberliga.

While they competed at the top end of this league, they failed to gain promotion and financial difficulties started to become a huge burden on the club. In the end, in 2004, the club were forced to merge with rivals MTV to form FC Ingolstadt 04, which caused fans and players alike to leave the club completely to form their own club.

ESV still have a senior club playing in the lower leagues of German football, while MTV only have a youth team playing in their name. Ingolstadt 04 play in the 3. Liga at the time of writing, after being relegated in the 2021/22 season. They have suffered a bit of a fall, as the club did manage to gain promotion to the German top tier, the Bundesliga, for the 2015/16 season, where they finished in a respectable 11th place. Unfortunately, second season syndrome hit and the club were relegated in 2016/17, finishing 17th. Since then, they have been jumping between 2. Bundesliga and 3. Liga.

43.

Chivas USA (USA)

FOUNDED BY Mexican businessman Jorges Vergara and formed from the Mexican club Chivas de Guadalajara, a club that Vergara had taken over in 2002, Chivas USA were admitted into the MLS on 2 August 2004, when Vergara decided to expand the club. They played at the Home Depot Center along with fellow Los Angeles soccer club LA Galaxy. They, along with ten other clubs, would compete in the MLS of 2005. The club adopted the colours of red and white, from which they gained their nickname, '*Los Rojiblancos*', which is exactly what that meant. They were also known as 'the Goats'.

The club's first MLS game was on 2 April 2005, a home match against DC United, who had won the MLS Cup the season before. Chivas lost the game 2-0, which was no surprise. Not many had envisaged the club making any impact in their debut season. Chivas had appointed Thomas Rongen as head coach, a Dutch-American football manager who wanted to bring a certain style of play to the club. But they failed to produce on the field, winning just one game in their first ten in the MLS, and that solitary win came against fellow newcomers, Real Salt Lake.

Chivas decided to shake up their coaching department, with Rongen becoming the new sporting director. After a small stint of having interim manager Javier Ledesma, the club appointed Hans Westerhof as the head coach on 3

June 2005. Westerhof didn't last long, and he was relieved of his duties on 22 November 2005, after what was seen as a disappointing second season, in which the club finished bottom of the Western Conference, winning just four of their 32 matches, drawing six and losing 22. Despite their horrendous season, the club still managed to average an attendance of just over 17,000 per match. However, this was still much less than their city rivals LA Galaxy who were averaging just over 24,000 spectators per match.

With Westerhof's departure, the club knew they had to make the right appointment for the following season. It had to be one that would both bring results on the field and also capture the imagination of those fans in the stands. And so, on 23 November, the club appointed former MLS Coach of the Year, Bob Bradley. It was an inspired move as the club turned it around on the pitch during the 2006 season. They managed to qualify for the MLS play-offs by winning ten, losing nine and drawing 13 to finish third in the Western Conference, and finished sixth overall out of the 12 competing in both conferences. The other big achievement that year was finishing above city rivals, LA Galaxy, who failed to qualify for the play-offs. This was Chivas's chance to make their mark and gain the upper hand with regards soccer superiority in LA.

In the play-offs they were drawn against Texan club Houston Dynamo, and played the first leg on 22 October 2006, at Home Depot Center, Carson, in front of over 15,000 fans. The Californian side won the first leg 2-1, thanks to goals from Razov and Palencia, while Ching scored Houston's goal. It set up the second leg nicely. That took place on 29 October at the Robertson Stadium in Houston. The tie was still in Chivas's favour until Houston were awarded a penalty in the 64th minute. Bradley Davis put it away, meaning the score was now 2-2 on aggregate.

But the deadlock in the tie was broken in the 93rd minute when Ching scored again, meaning Houston Dynamo progressed to the next round.

It was still seen as great progression by Chivas under Bradley, who had just become the first man to win the MLS Coach of the Year award twice. The club felt like they were on an upward spiral and were looking forward to the 2007 season. However, success came with a price and Bradley was soon gone, picked to be interim manager of the USA's men's national team, and he went on to manage the USA men's soccer team at the Olympics. Once again, the club were on the lookout for a head coach, and that position was filled by Predrag Radosavljevic, a Serbian-American who went by the nickname 'Preki'. He had represented the USA at the 1998 World Cup and had been an assistant coach at Chivas the season before.

While most saw the appointment of Preki as a step backwards from Bradley and didn't see the club emulating what they had done in 2006, they were in for a surprise. In fact, 2007 would be the club's most successful season in their short history. They won their only piece of silverware, the Western Conference title, just pipping Houston Dynamo by one point. The club recorded 15 wins, eight draws and seven losses that season and qualified for the MLS play-offs while also qualifying for the 2008 US Open Cup. One of the main reasons for their success was the goalscoring exploits of Cuban forward Maykel Galindo who scored 12 goals, while American, Ante Razov scored 11. However, it would only be as good as that. The club would play Kansas City Wizards and would lose a closely fought two-legged tie, 1-0 on aggregate.

For the 2008 season, Chivas took part in their first intercontinental tournament. They lost 2-1 to Mexican side Pachuca in their first game and would not progress from their group, winning just one game, drawing one and losing one. It was a group that consisted of fellow MLS side New England Revolution and Mexican sides Pachuca and Santos Laguna. The competition had been founded in 2007, but was abolished in 2010, due to lack of interest.

The club would finish runners-up to Houston Dynamo that season in the Western Conference, winning 12, drawing seven and losing 11 games. For the third consecutive season they qualified for the MLS play-offs, but it would be deja vu for the Californian club, as they crashed out in the first round to Real Salt Lake, losing 3-2 on aggregate.

The 2009 season saw another good performance on the field for the club, finishing fourth out of the eight clubs now competing in the Western Conference. They finished a respectable sixth in the overall standings that season as well. It meant they qualified for the MLS play-offs through the wild card route, and in the first round they met city rivals LA Galaxy. But in true Chivas style, the club failed to get past this round once again, losing 3-2 on aggregate.

It was in November 2009 that the club went through another managerial change, hiring Martin Vasquez. It proved be a disastrous season for the Goats, and they finished bottom of the Western Conference, winning eight games, drawing four and losing 18. It was the start of the end for the club, as things started to unravel on and off the pitch.

On 29 August 2012, Vergara and his wife took full ownership of the club, buying out all other shareholders. The club went through a further six coaches, with none of them able to impress Vergara nor the fans. First Martin Vasquez was replaced after just one season by Robin Fraser who was hired on 4 January 2011. Fraser didn't improve things on the field for the club and they finished eighth out of the nine clubs competing in the Western Conference in 2011. The 2012 season was even worse, with the club finishing bottom of the Western Conference, and second to last in the overall rankings, 18th out of 19 clubs, only finishing above Canadian side, Toronto FC.

Mexican Jose Luis Real was hired to take his place for the 2013 season. The managerial change did little to affect the performance on the field, with the club once again finishing bottom of the Western Conference, and second from bottom of the overall league. Vergara was getting impatient with his managers at this point, and it was no surprise when Real was fired. He was replaced by Colombian, Wilmer Cabrera. The 2014 season would be a defining one for the club, but for all the wrong reasons.

While Chivas made a small improvement on the pitch, finishing seventh in the Western Conference and 16th in the overall league, it was off the field where most of the drama was unfolding. On 20 February 2014, the MLS announced it had purchased Chivas USA from Vergara and his wife and had planned to look for suitable investors to make sure the club stayed located in the Los Angeles region, while still competing in the MLS 2015. Various news stories came out during this time about who those potential investors were going to be. Names like Vincent Tan, the owner of Cardiff City, were mentioned in a $100 million takeover, but issues surrounding where he would relocate the club meant the deal never went through. In the end, Chivas USA ceased operations as a senior soccer club on 27 October 2014. Their development academy continued to run until June 2015.

44.

British Club (Mexico)

BRITISH FOOTBALL Club Ciudad de Mexico was founded in 1902 by an English immigrant, Percy Clifford. His dream of becoming one of the best players in Mexico had become an obsession. He had previously been a member of the sports club, Club Reforma, but had decided to create his own football club, with the financial backing from Club Britanico, a sports club from Mexico City that had been founded in 1899. Clifford was given a pitch to play on, which was situated in Mexico City, in front of the Club Britanico headquarters. He was given equipment and kits for his team too. The club would wear a dark maroon shirt, with white shorts and black socks. They were known to be well kitted-out as well, always looking their best before a match as the club's ethos, and probably Clifford's, was that sport and eloquence should coincide with each other. In my research, there was an indication that this was done to show the other football clubs and locals that they were better than them, but that can never be proven. However, there was one British stereotype that did in fact happen while British Club played their matches, or when they took their half-time break. The players could be seen spending their half-time drinking tea at tables, surrounded by beautiful women.

Back to the football: the club played in the Primera Fuerza, which was considered the national league in Mexico at the time (although there were other regional leagues). The league had been founded in 1902, by five clubs. Clifford's British Club was one of them, alongside his former team Reforma AC, Pachuca AC, Orizabi AC and Mexico Cricket Club. Orizabi were to win the first title in 1902, with British Club finishing third. The 1903 season saw the club finish third again, but a new champion was crowned, Mexico Cricket Club. The 1904/05 season heralded some changes. In a weird turn of events, the first two champions of the Primera Fuerza, Orizabi and Mexico Cricket Club, both dissolved and dropped out. They were replaced by Puebla AC and San Pedro Golf Club, who acquired most of Mexico Cricket Club's players. That season Pachuca won their first title, with British Club finishing second and only losing out to Pachuca on goal difference.

The 1905/06 season saw San Pedro Golf Club change their name to Mexican Country Club. Reforma went on to win their first title that season, while British Club finished fourth. The 1906/07 edition was once again won by Reforma, with British Club finishing runners-up.

It wasn't until 1907/08 that British Club won their first title, albeit after one of the clubs in the league, Puebla AC, had pulled out midway as they could not afford the travel expenses. They subsequently dissolved and never returned. Mexico City FC joined that season as Mexico Country Club had a split, meaning they too dropped out of the league. The British Club side that won it that year consisted of only British men, with Percy being one of them. John Hogg, whose brother Horace also played for the club, finished top scorer for the club that year, with four goals in eight games. Percy himself would finish top goal scorer in two other seasons, which would indicate he was a striker or a forward of some sorts back then, when positions on the field had not been established.

The 1908/09 edition was somewhat anticlimactic, with only three clubs participating after Mexico City FC dissolved after only one season. Reforma were crowned champions and the league was expanded to four clubs the following season when Popo Park FC joined. Once again, Reforma AC were crowned champions, but it was off the field where things were changing for British Club. It was decided that going into the next season, British Club and Popo Park FC would merge and compete as one football club, as they saw this as the best chance of competing with Reforma. The plan didn't work, and Reforma won the championship again, while the merger split and left Popo Park FC dissolved in the process. In the meantime, another club had joined, Club Mexico.

The 1911/12 season would prove to be British Club's last, as they finished bottom of the four-club league. In fact, they didn't even finish off the season and withdrew midway. Percy Clifford's dream of becoming one of the best players in Mexican football was probably never achieved, but he is one of the men who is accredited as being a pioneer of Mexican football, and I would suggest that may have meant more to him.

45.

Palermo FC (Italy)

THERE ARE two versions of events surrounding the founding of Palermo FC. One says the club was founded in 1898, by an Englishman named Joseph Whittaker, but the more commonly known story is that the club was founded in 1900, by a colleague of Whittaker, Ignazio Majo Pagano.

The club was first known as the Anglo Palermitan Athletic and Football Club. Pagano had discovered the game of football while attending college in London. The original colours of the club were red and blue and they played their first game against an English amateur side on 30 December 1900, losing 5-0. Their first official game, however, was a 3-2 win against Messina Football Club.

In 1907 the club changed its name to Palermo Foot-Ball Club, with the club colours changed to their current ones of pink and black. Up until the First World War, Palermo took part in a competition known as the Lipton Challenge Cup, which had been set up by Scottish businessman Thomas Lipton. It was generally contested by two sides, Palermo and Naples FBC (now known as SSC Napoli). The first final took place in 1909, and Napoli won it 4-2. Palermo got their revenge the following season when they beat Napoli 4-1. The 1911 final was once again won by Napoli, 2-1, while Palermo took the title back in 1912, winning 6-0. The 1913 edition saw Palermo win it again, but this time they beat the now defunct US Internazionale Napoli 5-0.

311

In fact, Palermo won the last three editions of the trophy, winning the 1914 and 1915 titles, beating Naples FBC 2-1 on both occasions.

Things were put on hold while the war was taking place. It wasn't until 1919 that the club started up again, but this time under the name of Unione Sportiva Palermo. Founded by a group of students, the club competed in the Campionato Lega Sud in the 1920s, a competition set up for southern Italian clubs, while the northern teams had their own competition. But the club hit hard times and dissolved for the first time in 1927. They reformed only a year later when they merged with another Sicilian club, Vigor Palermo. The new club's name was Palermo Football Club and they entered the Primera Divisione, the equivalent of the modern-day Serie C. It only took them a couple of years to gain promotion to Serie B, with another promotion secured in 1932 to Serie A. They won the league with 50 points, three clear of second-placed Padova and nine points ahead of third-placed Hellas Verona.

In their first season in Serie A, the club finished 12th out of the 18 clubs competing, while Juventus won the title. The next season saw the club finish 15th, one place above the relegation zone, two points ahead of Padova in 16th place. Their survival was hugely down to the goalscoring of Aldo Borel, who netted 12 goals that season. The 1934/35 season saw Palermo finish ninth in a league that had been cut down from 18 clubs to 16. It would be the 1935/36 season when the club would have their first relegation from Serie A, finishing 15th.

They didn't bounce back straight away, finishing seventh in their return to Serie B. The next season the club finished seventh again. They would finish in that place for a third consecutive season, with no signs of progressing or getting relegated either. During this time, the club were forced to change their pink and black colours to red and yellow because of the fascist regime. The club once again fell into financial difficulties and were expelled from the league. But not to disappear forever, as they merged with Union Sportiva Juventina Palermo, to create the club known as Unione-Sportiva Palermo-Juventina and took their place in Serie C in 1941, and then entered Serie B in 1942.

With World War Two commencing, the club had to halt their participation in football, but did revert to their pink and black colours. In 1947/48 they gained promotion to Serie A, after winning Group C by one point over runners-up, Pisa. Their return to Serie A saw the club finish 11th out of the 20 clubs. Torino won the league that year, their sixth league title. The 1949/50 season saw the club finish 13th, with the title staying in Turin, going to the black and white side this time, Juventus, who collected their eighth title. It was tenth place for Palermo in the 1950/51 season, followed by 11th as the club became a well-established Serie A outfit. That was how it seemed, until the 1951/52 season when they finished 16th, one place above the relegation zone, three points above Como. It was only a stay of execution, as the following season the club were relegated once again.

It wasn't until 1956 that the club returned to Serie A, but the next few years proved to be somewhat unpredictable, with relegation and promotions. The 1961/62 season saw the club finish eighth in Serie A, and things were looking good for them. But in true Palermo style, just when things looked like they were progressing on the field, they were relegated in 1963 and didn't return to Serie A until 1968. The club were then relegated again two years later, in 1970, and they remained in Serie B for most of the 70s. But that wouldn't be the whole story of Palermo at this stage of their existence.

In the 1970s, while still playing in Serie B, the club reached two Coppa Italia finals. The first was in 1974, when they lost to Bologna in a penalty shoot-out. The next final saw the Sicilian club lose in extra time to giants Juventus. The club then had a fall from grace, being relegated all the way to Serie C1. After surviving another relegation in 1985, the club were expelled from the league once again. For one year there was no professional football for Palermo, and once again the club reformed and took their place in Serie C2. They won that in their first season. The following seasons saw the club have mixed fortunes, with promotions, relegations and cup runs all being a part of their story in the 90s. Then, 2001 saw the club pip Sicilian rivals Messina to promotion to Serie B. Their first season back saw the club finish mid-table, and plans were put in place to try and reach Serie A in the next five years.

Maurizio Zamparini was the driving force behind these plans when he bought the club for €15 million. The 2003/04 season saw the club finally reach Serie A again when they won Serie B on goal difference, beating Cagliari by seven goals. This was the start of the golden years for Palermo. The club finished sixth in 2006/07, qualifying for the UEFA Cup first round, where they met Cypriot side Anorthosis Famagusta, beating them 6-1 on aggregate. They continued on to the group stages, playing in Group B, a difficult section consisting of Espanyol, Lokomotiv Moscow, Brondby and Maccabi Petah Tikva. The Italian club finished top of the group, setting up a knockout stage clash with Slavia Prague, which Palermo won on the away goals rule after drawing 2-2 on aggregate. The round of 16 saw the club take on German side, Schalke 04. But this was as far as they would go, losing 3-1 on aggregate.

The club finished in eighth place in Serie A in the 2005/06 season and were supposed to play in the UEFA

Cup once again in 2006/07 but were not allowed to enter due to the big scandal that was rocking Italian football at the time. They did qualify for the UEFA Cup first round after finishing fifth in the 2006/07 league season. But unlike their first European adventure, they didn't get past the first round, losing to Czech Republic side Mlada Boleslav on penalties, after drawing 1-1 on aggregate. But the following seasons were still to produce some form of success on the field.

The 2010/11 season was a great one for the club, with the Sicilian side gaining qualification to the UEFA Europe League and reaching their third Coppa Italia Final. It wasn't to be third time lucky, however, as they lost 3-1 to Inter Milan. With the club about to undertake another European adventure, spirits were high. That was until the club were dumped out in the first round by Swiss minnows, FC Thun.

Another managerial change occurred, and while their European form was almost non-existent, their domestic form surprised a few, and under the highly inexperienced Devis Mangia, the club finished fifth, just outside the Champions League places. But his time at Palermo only lasted one more season, as the club finished 16th in the league the following campaign, and another managerial change was on the horizon.

The 2012/13 season proved to be disastrous and saw the club relegated to Serie B. The club went for inexperience once again, and hired Gennaro Gattuso, but he was sacked shortly after with a poor run of results. They replaced him with Giuseppe Iachini and gained promotion with a record total points tally of 86. They had finally returned to Serie A for the 2014/15 season and it was a successful campaign, with the club finishing comfortably in 11th position. It was also the season that saw the emergence of Argentinian striker, Paulo Dybala, who scored 14 goals in the league.

His contribution to Palermo would be short-lived, as he was bought by Juventus the following season. It was a chaotic season for Palermo, with no less than seven managerial changes made, resulting in the club just avoiding relegation on the final day, with a 3-2 win over Hellas Verona, securing 16th spot.

The 2016/17 season was much the same, with manager Davide Ballardini leaving his position after only two games and being replaced by Roberto De Zerbi. He didn't last long either, and was replaced mid-season by Eugenio Corini. The club were a bit of a circus off the field, with long-time owner Zamparini deciding to sell to an Italian American, Paul Baccaglini. Many saw this as a positive move and felt the club would finally become a stable one on and off the field. That isn't how it worked out, and that season saw Palermo relegated when they finished 19th and so another season in Serie B beckoned. With this, the original sale of the club also fell through, with Zamparini not accepting the final offer from Baccaglini, and so Zamparini remained the owner. Bruno Tedino was appointed as the new head coach, tasked with gaining immediate promotion back to Serie A.

All looked well, with the club on target for promotion, sitting top of the league halfway through the season, but their fortunes took a downward spiral and results on the pitch saw them fall down the table. It also brought about another managerial change with Tedino sacked and Roberto Stellone now the man in charge. Amid all the chaos, they did finish fourth and reached the promotion play-off, where they faced off against Frosinone in the final, after beating Venezia in the semi-finals, 2-1 on aggregate. But it wasn't to be this time, and they fell to a 3-2 aggregate defeat meaning another season in Serie B awaited them.

The 2018/19 season was known more for its off-field antics than on-field performances. Once again, it looked as though Zamparini was going to sell the club, this time to a London-based investment company, led by English businessman Clive Richardson. It seemed to be all going according to plan until January 2019, when the club failed to make a single signing in the winter transfer window. It then became apparent that they were in huge financial trouble, and as a result the takeover broke down, with Richardson citing that the group were not given full disclosure of how bad things were financially within the club. Surprisingly, the club were sold a few days later to Daniela De Angel and Rino Foschi. This ownership didn't last long, as they sold the club on in May of that year to hotel and tourism company, Arkus Network.

On the field, the club finished third in Serie B in the 2018/19 season but missed out on the promotion play-off as they were given a 20-point deduction, due to financial irregularities. It meant they finished the season in 11th place. This was after the Italian Football Federation had initially placed them bottom of Serie B, and effectively relegated them to Serie C. The club appealed and won, meaning they would play the 2019/20 season in Serie B. That was until they submitted the wrong paperwork to the FIGC [financial regulator] in regards their application for the new season, failing to include any insurance policy. Because of this, the FIGC had no other option but to exclude the club from not only Serie B, but all professional Italian football competitions.

However, not to be deterred, a number of people and groups showed an interest in starting a phoenix club, all the way down in Serie D. On 24 July 2019, the Mayor of Palermo, Leoluca Orlando, announced a group named Hera Hora SRL were to be the chosen ones to bring Palermo back into the footballing world. Their first season in Serie D ended in winning the title and saw promotion to Serie C.

With the next season cancelled due to the Covid-19 pandemic, it wouldn't be until 2021/22 that Palermo would get the chance to gain promotion back to the second tier of Italian football, just three years after they had been excluded. And that is exactly what they did, finishing third, behind Bari and Catanzaro in Group C (South). Entering the promotion play-offs in the third round, they defeated Triestina 3-2 on aggregate. They then beat Virtus Entella 4-3 on aggregate in the quarter-finals to make it to the last four. There, they eased their way past Feralpisalo 4-0 on aggregate and met Padova in the final. Winning both legs, 1-0, the *Rosanero* gained promotion to Serie B for the 2022/23 season.

46.

Chester FC (England)

FOUNDED IN 1885 when two clubs, Chester Rovers and Old King's Scholars FC merged, Chester FC originally played their home games at Faulkner Street. In their early years, they only played friendlies, with no competitive league to play in until 1890, when they entered the Combination League (the second one created, which consisted of mainly north-west English and Welsh clubs). Twelve clubs were in the competition, including Chester's biggest rivals, Wrexham. Other clubs included Denton, Burton Swifts, Northwich Victoria and Hyde. The only club to have competed in this competition and to still be in the Football League today are Macclesfield.

Chester moved to the Old Showground but only lasted a year there due to the ground being redeveloped into houses. The club disbanded for the year 1900, only to come back in 1901 when they played their home matches at Whipcord Lane. But that only lasted until 1906, when they moved out to go to their new stadium, Sealand Road. This would become known to the fans as the Stadium and became their first long-term home. It was here that the club tasted their first success, winning the Combination League in 1909. In 1910 the club moved to the Lancashire Combination League. They played there until after the First World War. They then became founding members of the Cheshire County League.

In 1931 the club joined the Football League for the first time, under the guidance of former Liverpool, Spurs and Crystal Palace player, Charlie Hewitt. They took the place of Nelson FC. During their early years, in the 1930s, Chester FC were as stable as it got, finishing in the top ten of Division Three North. Their main successes came in the FA Cup where they recorded their biggest ever FA Cup win, a 5-0 victory over Fulham in 1933. That was also the year they beat bitter rivals, Wrexham, in the Welsh Cup, to lift the trophy for the second time in their history. In 1936 they recorded their highest league victory (this might be an enjoyable fact for Chester FC fans today, considering their rivalry in the league nowadays), a 12-0 win against York City. A few other cup victories in the Football League Division Three North Cup and another Welsh Cup triumph were about as good as it got for Chester FC with poor league finishes, coupled with the splitting of the team during the Second World War creating a downward turn in the club's fortunes.

It wasn't until the 1960s that the club started to give their loyal fans something to shout about. The arrival of manager Peter Hauser gave them a lift in 1963. The 1964/65 season saw them just missing out on promotion by one solidary point and it wasn't for the lack of goals either. Out of the 119 goals the club scored that season, five strikers managed to score 20 each. But it was to be a short uplift as the club didn't make any impression in the league until the 1974/75 season when they finally gained their first promotion since joining the Football League in 1931. And it was by the slimmest of margins as they just beat Lincoln City to fourth place by virtue of having a better goals-per-game average. This was due to having the best defence in the league, only conceding 38 goals in 46 games (23 wins, 11 draws, 12 losses). Ken Roberts was the manager to write his name in the club's history books by becoming the first to lead the club to a promotion. That season also saw the club go on a cup run in the Football League Cup. They reached the semi-finals, beating the then Football League champions Leeds United 3-0. The club were finally beaten by the eventual winners of the competition, Aston Villa, in a thrilling 5-4 loss.

Chester stabilised themselves in the old Third Division until the leagues were re-organised. In 1977 the club lifted their first English National Trophy, beating Port Vale 4-3 on aggregate. They started to gain a reputation as giant-killers in cup competitions. After the Leeds win, they also beat a First Division club, Coventry City, in the League Cup in 1978/79 and knocked out Newcastle United in the FA Cup in 1979/80 when they were top of the Second Division. As it happens, a certain Ian Rush scored in that game, before he made the £300,000 move to Liverpool that summer. Rush, arguably one of the best Welsh strikers of all time, played for Chester FC between 1978 and 1980, playing 34 games and scoring 14 times. However, the club did not emulate the success of their former striker and ended up bottom of the whole Football League in 1984, having to be re-elected. (In 1983 the club had added the 'City' to their name to become Chester City FC.)

In 1986 the club returned to the old Third Division under the guidance of manager Harry McNally. They stayed there, flirting with relegation at times. In 1990 the club had to move out of their Sealand Road home and take residence in Macclesfield's Moss Rose ground for two years, finally settling in their new ground in the city, the Deva Stadium. The special thing about this ground is that it lies directly on the Wales–England border. The pitch itself is in Wales, but the entrance to the stadium is in England.

The club had mixed fortunes in the 1990s, getting relegated from Division Two, only to gain promotion the year after as Division Three runners-up. In 1995 they were again relegated back to Division Three. They came close to gaining promotion in 1997 but lost out in a play-off semi-final to Swansea City. It didn't get much better for the Blues, as they went into administration in October 1998. Despite being bought by American Terry Smith, the club's fortunes on the pitch did not improve and they were relegated out of the Football League for the first time in 69 years in 2000. For the next ten years the club would struggle with off-field problems and financial instability.

However, they did make a return to the Football League in the 2003/04 season, after going the whole season only losing four games and eventually lifting the Conference trophy. It was the club's first national title. But their return to the Football League was overshadowed by the sudden resignation of their manager, Mark Wright, who left a day before the start of the season. Chester City struggled that season, but the return to the club of Ian Rush as manager helped them survive relegation. This wasn't enough for some as Rush was heavily criticised for his team's style of play and so he left in April 2005. From then on it was a case of a managerial merry-go-round with Wright returning not once but twice in a four-year period. But even he could not save them from dropping out of the Football League for the second time in their history and they were relegated into non-league football at the end of the 2008/09 season.

The club were placed into administration again that summer with £7 million worth of debts and a 25-point deduction looming. They were given a lifeline and were allowed to play in the Conference up until January 2010 when things spiralled out of control and saw games for the club being suspended due to unpaid players' wages and the club struggling to stay afloat. In the end, the Football Conference expelled the club from the competition, leaving them in limbo. Eventually the club were wound up on 9 March 2010, despite attempts to join the Welsh Premier League. And so, 125 years of Chester City FC had ended. But the fans were not to give up. The next chapter of this club was just beginning.

In May of that year the club's supporters got together to create a newly formed club, fan-owned Chester FC. They joined the Northern Premier League Division One North. They gained three successive promotions to return to the Conference, the league they had been expelled from. However, the club hit hard times on the pitch and have suffered a few relegations since, leaving the current club in the sixth tier of English football, the National League North, from 2019.

One man who knows all about following the current Chester FC is Danny McNally and it's safe to say he epitomises what the current club and its model is all about. On his Twitter account it says it all: Chester Owner, Volunteer and Season Ticket Holder. So, no surprise that he gave me a brilliant insight into what the club is like these days. His favourite moment obviously came in those first three fantastic seasons of back-to-back promotions.

Cheers for taking the time out to answer questions on Chester FC. Firstly, what is your favourite memory from supporting Chester FC?

Danny McNally: The first three seasons after reformation were incredible; winning three titles in a row to steamroll straight back into the Conference, where the old Chester City ended. If I was to pick a favourite moment in those three years, it would probably have to be Matty McGinn smashing in a late equaliser to win the league in front of a sell-out 5,000-plus crowd at home to Northwich Victoria in the Evo-Stik Premier, 2011/12 season.

What is your favourite away day and stadium to visit?
Danny: There are some really good local away days for us Chester fans; going to the likes of Stockport and their famous Edgeley Park home, or Prenton Park when Tranmere tumbled into non-league. Telford is always an easy train journey down the border to a decent ground, away concourse and terrace to make some atmosphere – and fortunately our fans always travel in good numbers. I'd probably have to choose Kidderminster as my favourite away day: tidy ground, always an open, attacking match and the best pie you'll have at a football match.

I've done quite a bit of research on Chester City as they were previously known, but in your own words, what is it like to support the current Chester FC?
Danny: It's been more than a decade since Chester FC were formed, so fans are perhaps starting to learn the patience required. As is always said, we own our club, we're in control of its destiny. Okay, we might not have a rich private owner to sell us a Championship dream, but where did that get us in the past? Liquidation. After the most incredible first three years I could have ever wished for, we hit a ceiling at Conference level. Were we not prepared? Quite possibly, after the speed at which we returned. After five years of struggle, the 2017/18 season saw Chester relegated, back to the Conference North. After a 'transition' season with mass changes both on and off the field, we settled in the National League North. We may be at least two leagues below where we want to be, but to be in control of our own future is something we cannot take for granted; now we must strive towards the original aim set out in 2010 –

to return Chester to the Football League. We certainly appear more prepared off the pitch, with a settled board making good progress commercially and a helping hand by local businessman Stuart Murphy. Exciting times ahead for Chester FC.

Who is the best player you have seen put on the Chester jersey and who was your favourite player ever to put the Chester jersey on? It can be the same player if you like.

Danny: We've been blessed with some really talented players since reforming. Antoni Sarcevic scored 28 goals in 80 appearances for us from midfield ... he was a class above, demonstrated in winning Conference North Player of the Year in our title-winning, 100-points, 100-goals 2012/13 season. He left after that season, for Football League Fleetwood Town for a then club-record, six-figure fee. We've been blessed with a number of incredible loanees too. We gave Oli McBurnie his platform to explode on to the scene, coming in from Bradford City in 2015 and scoring his first senior goals, before he went to play for Sheffield United in the Premier League. Going back a year further, Matty Taylor was in the mood for goals in his short spell at the Deva, bagging six in seven before firing Bristol Rovers into the Football League. If we're going to talk pure passion for Chester FC and football, George Horan epitomises everything you want from a captain. An absolute rock at the heart of defence who led us from nothing to Conference football once again. 'We all dream of a team of George Horans' was still sung long after he left in 2014!

I know the club was resurrected by the fans, so I'm sure there are plenty of people behind the scenes that deserve a thank you. Do you have any special mentions for anybody at Chester FC?

Danny: They say you don't know what you have until it's gone, and this may perhaps be the case with David Harrington-Wright, who was chairman of City Fans United, who own Chester FC, from April 2018 to 2020. It's an incredibly demanding role, and entirely voluntary. Our chairmen rarely last 12 months which just shows how tough it is. David faced some really tricky situations; at one point the ground was flooded, with tens of thousands of pounds worth of damage and unable to host any games! Despite running three businesses, David navigated the club out of this situation and into the most strong and stable position in years.

Finally, is there anything you would like to add?
Danny: As is always said – we own our club, we're in control of its destiny.

47.

Finnpa (Finland)

FOUNDED IN 1965 by the staff of Finnish national airline, Aero, and originally named Aeron Pallo, the club's name changed to Finnairin Palloilijat or FinnPa (which translates as 'Ball Players of Finnair') when the airline changed its name to Finnair. The club wore an all-blue strip for their home colours and an all-white strip for their away colours. In their first season, Aeron Pallo competed in Tier 5 of their district league, the Piirinsarja, which is in Helsinki. They got promoted and played the 1967 season in Tier 4, the Aluesarja in the Group 2 Helsinki section. This league was effectively the fourth tier of Finnish football and was run by the Finnish FA. The club won their section and so earned back-to-back promotions.

The 1968 season saw the club compete in the third tier of Finnish football, the Maakuntasarja. They were placed in Group 1 which consisted of clubs from Helsinki and Uusimaa. The club finished sixth, halting their early progress. The 1969 season was much the same, finishing fifth in their group, meaning they would stay put in the Third Division. In 1970 the league was renamed III Divisioona. The club placed seventh that season. The 1971 campaign saw them falter a bit and they were relegated to IV Divisioona for 1972, after placing 11th in their group. They failed to gain promotion at the first time of asking, placing third, but it wasn't too long before they did get promoted back to the Third Division, winning their group in the 1974 season. Once again, they continued their momentum and completed back-to-back promotions, winning the III Divisioona title in 1975. They even went one further this time and completed a hat-trick of promotions, as they became II Divisioona East Group champions and stepped up to the I Divisioona for the first time. But the 1977 season proved to be the limit of their quality at the time and they found themselves being relegated after just one season, placing tenth.

FinnPa would spend another three seasons in the II Divisioona, East Group, finishing fourth in the 1978 season and seventh in 1979, until in the 1980 season they finally won promotion once again to the I Divisioona, coming first in the West Group this time around. This time the club lasted much longer in what was then the country's second tier, competing in eight seasons in a row in I Divisioona, with mixed results. The format had changed slightly, which gave FinnPa a chance. They finished 11th in 1981, but that didn't relegate them. Instead, they were placed into a relegation group in which they finished fourth, avoiding the drop. The 1982 season saw a big improvement, with the club finishing fourth and qualifying for the promotion group. Unfortunately, promotion was a step too far for FinnPa that season and they finished eighth in their group, miles away from reaching the top league in Finland. However, the dream remained alive, although in 1983 the club finished ninth and had to compete in the relegation group once again where they finished third, to remain in I Divisioona for another year. In fact, they would play another five seasons in that division, finishing eighth in 1984 and seventh in 1985, 1986 and 1987. The 1988 season proved to be too much for the club and they finished 11th, dropping down to the third tier once again. They then just missed out on promotion, finishing in fourth place, but the start of the 1990s proved to be a good era for the club. In the 1990 season they came first in the East Group and gained promotion once again to the second tier of Finnish football.

This time the club were looking to go one further and gain promotion to the Veikkausliiga, Finnish football's top tier. They didn't waste any time in trying and in their first season back in the second tier, the club finished second, qualifying for the promotion play-off. They didn't win it and remained in the I Divisioona for another year. But that is all it took for FinnPa to reach the promised land and the club rectified their loss in the promotion play-off in 1991 by winning it in 1992, after once again coming second in the league.

They didn't disappoint in their first season in the top flight, qualifying for the Championship group, and finishing fifth overall, winning 13 games, drawing seven and losing nine. With another change in format in 1994, the league would be played without a Championship and relegation group split at the end of each season. It was 14 clubs competing over 26 games in a full league format. FinnPa Helsinki finished tenth out of those 14 clubs in 1994, winning eight, drawing nine and losing nine. Another solid season followed with the club finishing mid-table in eighth, winning nine, drawing five and losing 12 games. The 1996 season saw the return of the split league format and FinnPa qualified for the Championship group, finishing fourth in the regular season. They were to finish fourth in the Championship group as well, just missing out on an Intertoto Cup place by two points.

It was the 1997 season that was arguably the most successful one in the club's history. After just missing out on European qualification the season before, the club made a huge push and achieved their goal by finishing third and qualifying for the UEFA Cup. It was a huge achievement in what was another changed format in the Finnish top division. There were now only ten clubs competing but that didn't matter to FinnPa as they looked forward to playing in Europe for the first time in their history.

The 1998/99 UEFA Cup draw took place and FinnPa were drawn to play Israeli club Hapoel Tel Aviv in the first qualifying round. It was to be the furthest they would get in European competition as they lost both home and away legs 3-1, losing on aggregate 6-2.

The following season, 1998, was FinnPa's final one. They finished ninth out of the ten teams in the Veikkausliiga, winning five games, losing 11 and drawing 11, which saw them play a relegation play-off against Tampereen Pallo-Veikot. They lost and it sent them back to the second tier. But Finnair then announced they would not be supporting the football club financially anymore, meaning the club folded.

48.

FC Malcantone Agno (Switzerland)

FOUNDED ON 1 July 1955, the club adopted the colours red and white, giving them the nickname *'Die Rot-Weissen'* (the Red and Whites). Playing most of their football in the Swiss fourth tier, they didn't really rise up the ladder until the 1998/99 season, when they were promoted to the Swiss 1. Liga. Malcantone were immediately one of the top sides in the division. The division itself was split into three different groups, based on geographical location. FC Malcantone were playing in Group 3 and won it in the 2001/02 season. This set up a promotion play-off against SC Young Fellows Juventus, a club that had only been created in 1992. Unfortunately, Malcantone were beaten 4-2 on aggregate and had another season in the Swiss 1. Liga to look forward to.

The 2002/03 season was just as successful on the pitch for the Red and Whites, as they once again won their group, Group C. This time, they would be facing FC La Chaux-de-Fonds in a promotion play-off match. Malcantone beat FCC, a club who were founded back in 1894, 3-2 on aggregate, meaning they gained promotion to the Nationalliga B. At the same time, the club moved stadium to play at the Stadio Cornaredo. Things were looking positive for the Swiss club, and after years of just dwelling in the lower leagues, they felt it was time to show Swiss football that they were around and not just making up the numbers.

The 2003/04 season saw the rebranding and reformatting of the Swiss league. The league that Malcantone were now playing in was known as the Swiss Challenge League and was the second tier of Swiss football. If they could manage the unthinkable and gain promotion, they would be playing in the Swiss Super League, against some of the country's top clubs. While that didn't happen, the club had a super season on the field, finishing fourth in the league, six points behind Vaduz, who had occupied the second promotion spot. The league that year was won by FC Schaffhausen. It was still regarded as a great achievement by the club, and something they could build on for the next season.

But that was to be it from FC Malcantone. The 2003/04 season was their last as a club, as they merged with the already defunct FC Lugano. It was a strange move, as Lugano had already been expelled from the Swiss Football League, but they were re-admitted into the Swiss Challenge League in FC Malcantone's place and have been able to re-build the club ever since. Morotti Joseph, who was the president of FC Malcantone at the time, was given leadership of this newly formed club.

At the time of writing, FC Lugano were playing in the Swiss Premier League, after winning the Swiss Challenge League in 2014/15 and gaining promotion. They finished fourth in the 2021/12 season and benefitted from some considerable investment over the last few years.

49.

Karlstad BK (Sweden)

FOUNDED ON 19 October 1923, Karlstad BK mostly played in the second and third tiers of Swedish football. Their club colours were blue, white and red, while they played their games at the Vaxnas IP and Tingvalla IP. The city itself is the 20th-largest city in Sweden and has a population of just under 100,000 people.

In their first three years of existence, the club played in the Allinnsserien Division, in the Varmland section. In the 1928/29 season they began playing in tier three of Swedish football, in Division Three, in the Nordvastra section. They finished fifth in their first season, playing 18 matches, winning nine, drawing two and losing seven. The next season was much the same, with the club improving by one place, finishing fourth in the Nordvastra that year. It would be a further six seasons of finishing mid-table in that section before they finally made a breakthrough in the 1935/36 season. They finished top of their group, beating runners-up, Mariehofs IF, by just one point to gain promotion to the second tier of Swedish football for the first time.

The club only lasted two seasons at that level before being relegated in the 1937/38 season, when they finished bottom of their group, winning just two games all season. After a third-place finish in the 1938/39 season and a fourth-place finish in 1939/40, they finally gained promotion again, winning their group in the 1940/41 season. They won it by a single point, just pipping IFK Bofors, for a chance of promotion via the play-offs. They won their play-off match and once again found themselves in the second tier.

This time, their relegation was confirmed after just one season, when they finished ninth out of ten clubs competing in the Division Two Vastra. It was disappointing for the club, but in true Karlstad fashion, it didn't take long for them to gain promotion once again. In fact, it took them only two seasons: finishing third in 1942/43 only spurred them on to win the Nordvastra in the 1943/44 season. This time the club would spend a total of nine seasons in the second tier, narrowly missing out on promotion on two occasions, when they finished runners-up in 1947/48 and again in the 1951/52 season. However, in the 1952/53 season the club were relegated again.

The 1953/54 season saw them immediately reinstate themselves as a Division Two side when they won their group by three points ahead of Billingfors IK. Four seasons in Division Two followed, with the club never really challenging for promotion, finishing seventh, third and fourth and then eventually tenth and being relegated again in 1962. But it was becoming a common theme that the club would be relegated, then find themselves winning the Third Division group the next year. It was almost like they were stuck in limbo. Too good for the Third Division but not good enough for the Second Division. This is how it seemed throughout their history as they yo-yoed between the two tiers. That was until the 1971/72 season, when they were relegated once again from the second tier, finishing 12th in their group.

The club, who most thought would bounce back up nearly straight away like they usually did, found themselves in the third tier for eight seasons in a row. They failed to gain promotion through the play-off system in 1975/76, after winning their group. Eventually, in 1978/79, they climbed out of the third tier and began life in the second tier once again.

Reformatting of the Swedish league system was now being put forward, and so the tiers and divisions would be different. What didn't change were the promotions and relegations of Karlstad from tier two to tier three and up again. Up until 1990 they were in tier three, Division Two, but saw themselves relegated once again, to the lowest level they had been since they were created. They won tier four with ease and went back into tier three, but that was the most progress they would make in eight seasons, as the club were relegated once again in 1999, and went back down to tier four. It got even worse for the club in 2000 when they fell further down the ladder and found themselves in tier five. Six seasons later and the club had hit an all-time low. They finished eighth in their group in 2005 and were now destined to play in the sixth tier of Swedish football, due to a reconstruction of the Swedish football pyramid which saw each tier fall one level. The club spent two seasons at this level before winning it in 2007.

After two seasons in tier four, they were once again promoted in 2009, coming second in their group. Back-to-back promotions occurred when the club secured second place in their group, the Vastra Gotaland in 2010, meaning for the first time in over a decade they were back in tier three. It lasted three seasons, with a seventh-, eighth- and then a poor 14th-place finish seeing them drop back down to tier four.

Five seasons later, they arrived back in tier three, winning the Norra Gotaland and securing their promotion once again. But 2019 was to be the last season the club would play in the Swedish footballing pyramid, and after a fifth-place finish in the Norra, only six points behind second-placed Umea FC, the club did not continue for the next season. Instead, they merged with Carlstad United to form IF Karlstad Football. In 2022 they were playing in the third tier, in the Ettan division. Notably, at the time of writing, former England manager, Sven-Goran Eriksson had joined up with them in an advisory role.

50.

Thurles Town FC
(Republic of Ireland)

THURLES TOWN AFC were founded in 1950 and played in the North Tipperary District League. Their home ground is the Thurles Greyhound Stadium, a stone's throw away from Semple Stadium. Nicknamed 'the Town', Thurles Town AFC decided to merge with Kilkenny side Peake Villa and consequently became known as Thurles Town FC. The merger happened so they could enter the League of Ireland in 1977. But their stay in Ireland's top league was short-lived and they only played five seasons, with their highest finish being ninth in the 1979/80 campaign.

Their first season in 1977/78 ended with only one solitary win to their name and they finished 16th (last place), drawing eight and losing 21 times. The 1978/79 season saw an improvement in their form and league position as they finished 12th, winning a total of eight games, drawing five and losing 17. As previously said, the 1979/80 season was the Town's best one in the League of Ireland, as they finished ninth, above the likes of St Patrick's Athletic, Shelbourne FC and Drogheda United among others. This was largely down to the goalscoring efforts of their top scorer Neville Steadman who bagged a total of 17 goals for the club, making him the third-highest scorer in the league that year behind Alan Campbell of Shamrock Rovers (22) and Tony Morris of Limerick United (19). (As it would happen, Neville Steadman would go on to write a bit of history for another club in the League of Ireland, Shamrock Rovers, as he was the last man to score at Milltown, in a Reserve Cup game back in 1987. He also won the League of Ireland with Shamrock Rovers in 1983/84, in a side that also featured Liam Buckley and prolific goalscorer Alan Campbell.)

That was the end of the progress for Thurles Town, who ended the next season, 1980/81, 16th (last) after winning seven games, drawing four and losing 19. The club had one more season in the League of Ireland in 1981/82 but once again they finished bottom of the pile (16th) winning only three games, drawing five and losing 22.

It proved to be the end of their five-year spell in the top flight and they went back to playing in the North Tipperary District League while Peake Villa continued playing in the Kilkenny League and the Tipperary Southern and District League. You may think that it was all doom and gloom for this club, never winning anything and just basically making up the numbers. Even in their own District League they failed to win a title for 56 years and you would have forgiven them for giving up and just joining in with the rest of the town in supporting the GAA sports.

However, the people connected to the club tell a very different story and persistence paid off when in 2016 the club won their first ever North Tipperary District League title with a little help from their captain, Barry 'Birdie' Ryan. The former Kilkenny City player managed to score 40 goals in the 2016/17 season and was named Tipperary player of the year. Barry told me about that season and what it meant to him and his family.

'As a junior club they had never won the league in their 40-year existence; at the end of my career in 2016 I signed with them and captained them to their first league. I went back, with a few local lads that had been away with other clubs and we played for two seasons and won two leagues.

'It was a huge celebration for the club to finally win a Tipp Premier League. Kevin Kilbane came down to present the medals at an award ceremony. I scored 40 goals so was lucky enough to get the club player of the year and the Tipperary player of the year so it was a special year for me, and my father was also at the awards so it was a bit of family history too, having both played with them.'

As Barry said, his family had already had a connection to the club with his dad Martin 'Birdie' Ryan playing for Thurles Town FC and Kilkenny City in the League of Ireland.

'We both played League of Ireland for Kilkenny City … My dad was a centre-forward, he played with EMFA, which was what Kilkenny City were known as, and he won an Oscar Traynor Trophy with them. According to the Peake Villa website he trialled for the Irish under-21 team with Frank Stapleton. He also spent 18 months in England with Reading FC.'

I asked Barry what he knew about his dad's playing days for Thurles Town FC when they were a League of Ireland side and the story he produced is one of folklore down here.

'I was only born in 1980 so I missed out on all of that. Neville [Steadman] stayed in our house a few years back, he was down for some reunion and I was told all about how he was a Rovers legend. My father played with Thurles Town in the League of Ireland. Incidentally, he scored against Peter Shilton when they played Stoke in a friendly. The Stoke friendly is still talked about in Thurles because Garth Crooks and Peter Shilton both played, it finished 8-1 but Birdie Ryan nutmegged Shilton so it became a bit of local folklore! I'd say it was the highlight of his whole career.'

I'm sure it was a magical moment and one that made me smile, thinking of the local Thurles man making a fool out of one of the best goalkeepers to play the game. (To make things look a little better I did a bit of research on that game and in the record books it is down as a 7-2 win for Stoke.) As I always do, I asked Barry if he knew why the club dropped out of the League of Ireland and would we ever see them back again. His answer was quite like that of the Kilkenny City fans.

'There were hardly any local players on the Thurles team which is why it failed. No, Thurles Town won't be back in the LOI but I'd like to see them become a sustainable and successful junior club. It's difficult in a GAA town, but I do think 100 per cent eventually we will see a Tipperary team play in the League of Ireland.'

When asked which League of Ireland club he currently follows, his reply was no surprise and may have been influenced by a certain connection to Neville Steadman.

'I'm a big admirer of Shamrock Rovers under Steven Bradley, I like the football they play and so many technical players like Greg Bolger, Ronan Finn and of course [Jack] Byrne.'

Epilogue

THROUGHOUT MY journey, while writing this book, I have encountered so many fascinating characters, who know more about football than their interviews probably show. With some, I chatted away on the phone for hours about football, the leagues they were interested in and how they came to form a love of the sport that so many share. When I first started this project, I was under the illusion that I would know most of the facts and things that I would be told when I did my research. How wrong was I! The world of football keeps on popping up amazing facts and stats that I would never have come across if I hadn't written this book – the major fact being every country in the world has a 'Forgotten Club'.

There is just no hiding away, and in this day and age, when football and football clubs are becoming ever more reliant on money, not just for success but to survive, I think we are going to see a lot more football clubs disappear from our world. While the so-called bigger clubs get richer, other clubs are having to start taking risks to even compete at the level they are at, which means financial mismanagement is even more likely. I found that once a club gets itself into trouble, there is usually no way to turn it around, despite the club's efforts. Some clubs turn to drastic measures and sign a superstar to try to get the attendances up and collect the extra gate money, but this rarely works as the gate money is usually given out to the said superstar, and he only usually plays a handful of games for the club.

While every country has had a 'Forgotten Club', some countries surprised me with the number they have had. When we think of countries like England, Germany, France, Italy and even Poland, we think of them as football fanatic nations, that always fill their stadia when games are being played, and yet, they are the nations that have the highest number of clubs that have either gone defunct, merged together or have just disappeared. In England, more than 600 clubs have vanished in approximately 120 years. Now, most of these occurred in the early days of Association Football, and let's remember, England were one of the first to have football clubs. However, that number seems to be high. The fact that even the oldest football club in the world, Sheffield FC, are no longer around, except when they play their annual exhibition matches, says a lot. Even here in Ireland, St James Gate FC, the first club to win the League of Ireland, in 1922, and the first club to win the FAI Cup, both in the same season, have ceased to exist just recently. There was barely even a mention about it in the media. How can this happen? In contrast, in England, Bury FC, another one of football's oldest clubs, went bust as well, but that was much publicised. It still happened though, and the club and their fans are having to rebuild.

In Germany, it seemed as though a lot of clubs just couldn't compete with each other for sustainable fan bases and therefore a lot of them ended up merging together. We saw this in the story of ESV Ingolstadt, while I could have picked another hundred examples of this. But Germany itself has gone through a lot of political upheaval in its history, and it was probably no surprise to see it as one of the highest contributors to the list of defunct football clubs.

Italy, however, was a bit of a different story, and huge clubs seem to fall in that nation. Is it down to corruption? I don't know that for sure, but what I do know is big clubs have fallen, and in this book I could only tell the story of two of them, Cesena FC and Palermo FC, but I would have loved to feature other giants who have gone by the wayside like Parma and more recently Chievo Verona. Again, it just seems as though the bigger clubs are sucking up all of the resources while the other clubs, middle-sized and smaller, are having to feed off the scraps.

France was a funny nation to visit, as the two clubs I wrote about had limited success, but Calais did have that big underdog story. I didn't get an interview from anybody for these French clubs and that was simply because nobody wanted to talk to me. Why? I don't know. Maybe it is a French thing to forget bad times and just move on. That is certainly how it felt, even when I was doing my research on both of those clubs. It felt as though they had served their purpose and that was that. No need for nostalgia here. I wonder if a club like Marseille, Lyon or even PSG were to fold, would there be the same reaction and response? I highly doubt it, but I also highly doubt we will see that circumstance arise in the near future, as those clubs seem to be secure with their finances, for now.

Spain only had one club feature, and it was a club I really enjoyed covering, as there seemed to be a real passion behind them. There was also a feeling of ill-will with fans and the Spanish FA, which is understandable given that it was the Spanish FA's decision to expel CF Reus in the end. But in Spain, generally, there weren't a lot of clubs to choose from and certainly not from modern times, which probably says a lot about Spanish football now. I do say this while fully in the knowledge that at the time of writing, FC Barcelona, one of the biggest clubs in Spain, and possibly the world, is in a financial crisis, however, I don't believe they will ever go defunct. They can't. It wouldn't be allowed to happen. Although, if you were to ask Spanish football fans, and especially those from the Catalonian region, they would be a little bit more pessimistic. If it did happen, it would prove that no club is untouchable, and it could happen to any club in the world.

Other countries that I covered like the USA seemed like they had a surprisingly small number of defunct clubs, but that was a bit of a false fact, as the USA has a lot of defunct leagues. To its credit, America has progressed rapidly over the past decade in regards making soccer a popular sport in their country, and against the odds, with huge sports already established over there. Chivas USA, who went bust nearly a decade ago, are the last professional club to do so, and that shows that the MLS has got its house in order.

I think a strong MLS is good for world football, as it gives the European leagues something to think about when trying to attract players, especially from South America. The MLS is growing, with new clubs joining the league every season, and becoming instant successes as well. LAFC are just an example of this, having only been founded in 2018 and just recently winning the MLS Cup (2022). They have also managed to attract star names like Gareth Bale to the club. Probably before all of this, you could look at American soccer and say, 'Yes, they are in trouble,' because that is when a lot of their clubs were going defunct. Atlanta Chiefs were the club that featured in this book, but I could have chosen a lot of clubs from the National American Soccer League days (NASL). The LA Aztecs are one that stand out, and are probably the most high-profile club to have bowed out of the American soccer pyramid. A club that just paid over the odds for superstars like George Best to try and attract the masses: it is a story we have seen all too often and one that seldom works out.

South America was a tricky one, as there were a lot of clubs that just disappeared and there was no information available about some of them at all. Brazil and Argentina were the front-runners for the number of defunct clubs that South America produced, and there was a slightly different reason for clubs disappearing in these countries than their European counterparts. In my research, I found the South American leagues to be quite confusing, long-winded and very hard for a club to gain promotion from, especially the lower leagues. It just seemed to me that clubs were putting in such an effort and many of them were getting nothing out it. For example, in one of the lower leagues in Brazil, for one particular season, there were 104 clubs competing for two promotion spots. It just seemed unfair to me, that clubs were asked to put money and effort into what was basically a lottery. The size of these countries did not help, although there were and are many regional leagues for clubs to try and survive in; however, the prize money and gate receipts are not exactly going to be able to pay huge wages to attract star players.

To Africa, and more specifically, South Africa, as that was the only country I visited on that continent. I did do a bit of research on some clubs from different countries like Egypt, Ghana and Tunisia, but none of them gave me enough information to make it worthwhile for me to feature a club from those countries in this book. South Africa was intriguing because it brought up the racial divide that may have resulted in a lot of clubs folding. It was not something I saw happen much around the rest of the world, and so the Dangerous Darkies had to feature. A country that is well known for its racial problems, is one that seems to be doing fine now, but it is only since the 1970s that progress has been made in this regard.

Other countries like Japan, China and Australia all featured, and while I only picked a handful from these nations, I did investigate other clubs from there. Japan seemed to be quite mysterious in the way its clubs just disappeared. There was barely any information on any of them, even the bigger ones, while China has plenty of clubs to choose from – the Jiangsu story just couldn't be left out. A club who had been around since the 50s, finally won the league and then went bust – that is something I didn't believe until I read about it myself. Australia also has a host of football clubs that have disappeared, but again that is mainly due to the reformatting of its league over the last few years, and trying to get it right while it battles for fans against the more popular sports like cricket, rugby and Australian Rules football.

All in all, my journey around the world was wonderful, and I have learned so many things, not just about football but about different cultures. One thing is for certain though, I will never run out of football clubs to research and write about. There will always be another 'Forgotten Club'.

Thank you

I WANT to thank the following people, because without their support this book would never have been written. My mother and dad, my brother Marc, and my two sisters Hayley and Rachel. Thank you for putting up with me, it means a lot. To my aunties, Threase, Mairead and Catherine who were always there for me growing up. To my Forgotten Clubs team, Bence Horvath, Jeff Webb, Ross Kilvington, Michael Brownless and Graham Farrell: all of you believed in what we were doing when I asked you to put time and effort into producing top quality content for Forgotten Clubs.

To Jane and the team at Pitch Publishing for giving me this opportunity. To Mark Leavy, who always provided me with opportunities and a place to work. To John Quinn, for instilling that work ethic in me when I was younger. To my friends: Paddy Lane, who advised me and kept me motivated to get this done, even when it felt at times that I could not breathe. My friend Twanda, who always believed this would happen, keeping me positive and always being there when I needed him.

To my housemate, Adam Madden, for not only motivating me mentally, but making sure I took care of myself physically, keeping me on my toes and not letting me get lazy. To Colly O Brien, who told me to go write a book one day. To John O Donoghue, for still being my friend even when it seemed we had lost touch. To Bren Turley, for always looking out for me. To Dan Burke, who sat beside me when I was struggling and in a hospital bed and told me that I could do whatever I put my mind too. To David Reilly, for always remembering my birthday and to Joey Reilly for not beating me up when we hung around as kids, even when I did annoy him.

To Keith Martin, Mark Flynn, Graeme Walsh, Shane Gaffney, Ian O Carolan, Rob Kennedy, Gareth Dunne, David Daly, Sean McBride, Luke Kelly, Jack Connolly, Niall Creevy, Eamonn Connolly and Aaron O Neil who took care of me when I couldn't take care of myself. To Andrew King, I don't need to say any more.

This book is to everyone who believed in me, everyone who also inspired me to go and write it. I cannot thank you enough.

Finally, I want to dedicate this book to my Nana. Hopefully I have done you proud. Never Forgotten.

#staycheeky

Credits

This book would not have been written had it not been for the following people who contributed to it by either participating in interviews, helping me source facts or just giving me advice along the way.

Chris Lee, Clint Jones, Charlotte Patterson, Paul McGarraghy, Maroun Mahfoud, Bence Horvath, Matt McGinn, Marc Boal, John Leonidou, The Belgian Podcast, The Other Bundesliga, Ryan Hubbard, Jenn Ramczyk, Alex McGuinness, The Estonian Football Podcast, Emin Urcan, Luka (Georgian footy), Danny McNally, Xiaouu, Hugo (African Insider), Tim (Aldershot), Stijn Kluskens, Rich Nelson, Andy Wilson, Stephen Brandt, Martijn Schwillens, Barry Ryan, Nicole Hack and Phil Harrison.

References

Online/Books

Another kicking for southern Italy's football, Financial Times. http://www.90minut.pl/skarb.php?id_klub=2529

Austria's GAK agree to leave top flight. FIFA. 11 April 2005. Archived from the original on 18 September 2007. Retrieved 15 May 2006

Aldershot Town: Relegated club goes into administration. BBC Sport. Retrieved 10 November 2014.

Bouc, František, *Dukla Returns*. The Prague Post (6 December 2006). Archived from the original on 15 June 2013. Retrieved 14 June 2013.

Club aims to build strong community. www.independent.ie. 13 February 2008. Retrieved 17 December 2016.

Canadian Soccer History – Great Teams, Galt FC 1904

Chester City: A Brief History. chester-city.co.uk.

French Federation profile. Archived from the original on 6 May 2017. Retrieved 5 September 2014.

Grüne, Hardy, Karn, Christian, *The big book of German football clubs*. AGON Sportverlag, Kassel 2009, ISBN 978-3-89784-362-2, p. 66.

Grüne, Hardy, *Encyclopedia of German League Football*. Volume 2: Bundesliga & Co. 1963 to today. 1st League, 2nd League, DDR Oberliga. Numbers, pictures, stories. AGON Sportverlag, Kassel 1997, ISBN 3-89609-113-1, p. 81.

HFC Haarlem gaat fuseren met HFC Kennemerland (in Dutch). Sportweek.nl

Harkimo: Katsoimme viisaaksi keskittyä yhteen lajiin (in Finnish). MTV3. 2004-03-05. Retrieved 2008-10-23.

Historia y Fútbol Argentino – 1931

Hummer, Steve, *Remembering Soccer's Chiefs, 50 years after they won it all.* The Atlanta Journal-Constitution, (March 9, 2018). Cox Enterprises. Archived from the original on 3 May 2021. Retrieved 21 November 2019

Jongbloed, Jan, *Soccervoice.* Retrieved 11 May 2020.

Sezon 1976/77 – II liga (gr. północna) – tabela rozgrywek – Historia Polskiej Piłki Nożnej – HPPN.PL

Leonidou, John, *Underdogs APOP clinch Cypriot Cup.* UEFA. (16 May 2009). Archived from the original on 8 May 2022. Retrieved 8 May 2022.

Liquidation du Calais Racing Union Football Club: Clap de Fin Pour Une Étoile Filante di Football.

Karlstad BK

Kayseri Spor Kulübü Ana Tüzüğüdür (PDF). Kayserispor. org.tr. Kayseri Spor Kulübü. Archived from the original (PDF) on 8 January 2016. Retrieved 27 February 2016.

Kariyushi FC dissolution "Painful decision" next month's operation fee cannot be drawn, 12 December 2009, Ryukyu Shimpo

Renzo Barbera (in Italian). PalermoCalcio.it. Archived from the original on 23 April 2011. Retrieved 4 May 2011.

Historia del futbol en México. Femexfut.

HULIQ, *Bob Bradley Named Interim U.S. Men's Soccer National Team Head Coach* (December 9, 2006)

Kicker Almanach 1980 (in German), publisher: Kicker, published: 1979, page: 266, accessed: 12 November 2008

Kontaktuppgifter och tävlingar – Juventus IF – Svenskfotboll.se.

Newsham, Gail J., *In a League of Their Own! the Dick, Kerr Ladies, 1917-1965* (9 February 2018) (Special Centenary ed.). [Great Britain]. p. 246.

Numerous articles regarding Mr. Gonzalez's advocacy in defence of Bolivian high-altitude football/soccer

The Football Association announces that Jiangsu Sainty has changed its name to Jiangsu Suning 100% transfer (in Chinese). China FA. 4 January 2016. Archived from the original on 31 October 2016. Retrieved 6 June 2016.

Labdarúgás: majd' 10 év után ismét felnőttcsapat a BVSC-ben. Nemzeti Sport. 18 July 2012.

Troche, José María, *La Gira de Corrales*

L'A.J. Andranik contre la Renaissance. L'Orient. 26 February 1939. Retrieved 3 February 2021.

Newsnight Investigation. BBC. 27 June 2006. Retrieved 7 May 2010.

Official website of KA Akureyri

Organigramma | CDA A.S.D. RC CESENA (in Italian). A.S.D. Romagna Centro Cesena. Retrieved 14 October 2018.

Reus, la avellana mecánica, reta al Atlético (in Spanish). Sportyou. 25 November 2015. Retrieved 28 June 2016.

Russian Premier League. Retrieved 20 December 2013.

Partizan will not play in Premier League, pressball.by, retrieved 2012-01-31

*Partizan Minsk – the DIY Football Club from
   Belarus*. Futbolgrad. 13 August 2013.

Persoglia, Tony, *History of Canberra Cosmos*. OzFootball
   Archives. Retrieved 16 September 2007.

Regrets still linger over Sporting Fingal's sad demise.
   www.irishtimes.com. 9 March 2013. Retrieved 14
   December 2016.

South Africa 1992. rsssf.com. Retrieved 3 May 2010.

Sandvik, Trond, *Skal tjene penger på millionsatsing*. Bergens
   Tidende (11 November 2002) (in Norwegian). p. 17.

Spirit lives on in Soccer NSW youth competition. Soccer
   NSW. 12 March 2004. Archived from the original on
   14 July 2014. Retrieved 9 July 2014.

The Swansway Chester Stadium. Chester FC.
   Archived from the original on 21 December 2014.
   Retrieved 16 April 2015.

Viana, Eduardo. *Implementation of Professional
   football in the State of Rio de Janeiro*. Rio de Janeiro:
   Editora Cátedra
   https://web.archive.org/web/20171216040902/
   http://www.fshf.org/garat/components/club.
   php?club_id=10828

Weiner, Rebecca, *The Virtual Jewish History Tour South
   Africa*. Jewish Virtual Library. Retrieved 2009-06-03.

www.thurlestownfc.ie

www.rsssf.com

Sensi-Zamparini: affare fatto (in Italian). RAI Sport.
   21 July 2002.